PRELUDE TO REVOLUTION

RICHARD BAUM

Prelude to Revolution

MAO, THE PARTY, AND THE PEASANT QUESTION 1962–66

COLUMBIA UNIVERSITY PRESS · NEW YORK AND LONDON

1975

LIBRARY OF CONGRESS
CATALOGING IN PUBLICATION DATA
Baum, Richard, 1940–
   Prelude to revolution.
   "Outgrowth of a doctoral dissertation in-
itiated in Taiwan and Hong Kong in
1967–68."
   Includes bibliographical references and
index.
   1. China—Politics and
government—1949–
I. Title.
DS777.55.B348   320.9'51'05   74–23894
ISBN 0–231–03900–X

320.951
B 347 P

To My Parents—
For Bearing Forbearance

ACKNOWLEDGMENTS

THIS BOOK IS THE OUTGROWTH OF a doctoral dissertation initiated in Taiwan and Hong Kong in 1967–68. A primary debt of gratitude is owed to Frederick Teiwes, whose close collaboration provided a constant source of fresh ideas and critical insights during the formative stages of research. Without him, this book would never have been written. Special thanks are also due the scholars and staff of the Universities Service Centre, Hong Kong, and the Institute of International Relations, Taipei, for their assistance in the collection of documentary materials.

My research assistants, Wong Yuk-lam, Teng Hua, Wong Chai-sang (Hai Feng), and Louise Bennett, provided invaluable service in the collection and analysis of data used in this study. Gordon Bennett and Ezra Vogel were extremely generous in sharing with me their refugee interview materials. Ting Wang provided a great deal of first-hand information about the Socialist Education Movement as well as sharing with me his unique newspaper clipping files. David Denny, Frederic Surls, Janet Salaff and Parris Chang were a constant source of intellectual stimulation throughout my sojourn in Taiwan and Hong Kong. John S. Service expertly edited many of the documentary translations utilized in this study.

For financial assistance I would like to thank the Foreign Area Fellowship Program, whose grant made this research possible, and the Center for Chinese Studies and the Institute for International Studies of the University of California, Berkeley. I am particularly indebted to Robert A. Scalapino and Chalmers Johnson for patiently encouraging and supporting my research efforts.

The following institutions have given me permission to reprint material:

1. The RAND Corporation, for permission to quote from "The Cultural Revolution in the Countryside: Anatomy of a Limited Rebellion," in Thomas W. Robinson, ed., *The Cultural Revolution in China* (Berkeley and Los Angeles: University of California Press, 1971), pp. 367–476.

2. The Far Eastern Economic Review, Ltd., for permission to quote from "Peach Garden Pestilence," *Far Eastern Economic Review*, 58, no. 7 (November 16, 1967): 323–26.

3. The Regents of the University of California, for permission to quote from *Ssu-Ch'ing: The Socialist Education Movement of 1962–1966* (University of California, Center for Chinese Studies Research Monographs, 1968).

4. The Regents of the University of California, for permission to quote from "Liu Shao-ch'i and the Cadre Question," *Asian Survey*, 8, no. 4 (April 1968): 323–5.

5. The Contemporary China Institute, School of Oriental and African Studies, for permission to quote from "Revolution and Reaction in the Chinese Countryside: The Socialist Education Movement in Cultural Revolutionary Perspective," *The China Quarterly*, no. 38 (April–June 1969): 92–119.

6. The United States Information Agency, for permission to quote from "Ideology Redivivus," *Problems of Communism*, 16, no. 3 (May–June 1967), pp. 1–11.

And finally, to my wife, Carolyn, and our children, Matthew and Kristen, I owe more than I can possibly acknowledge in this space.

RICHARD BAUM

CONTENTS

LIST OF ABBREVIATIONS

CB: Current Background
CKCN: Chung-kuo Ch'ing-nien
CNP: Chung-kuo Ch'ing-nien Pao
JMJP: Jen-min Jih-pao
JPRS: Joint Publications Research Service
NCNA: New China News Agency
NFJP: Nan-fang Jih-pao
SCMM: Selections from China Mainland Magazines
SCMP: Survey of the China Mainland Press
URS: Union Research Service

INTRODUCTION

In the autumn of 1962, Chinese Communist Party (CCP) Chairman Mao Tse-tung personally initiated a nationwide campaign of politico-ideological indoctrination and Party rectification designed to rekindle the sputtering flame of China's socialist revolution and to immunize the Chinese people against the pernicious influence of Nikita Khrushchev's apostate "modern revisionism." At first limited in scope and moderate in tempo, Mao's campaign—known as the Socialist Education Movement—gradually gathered force and momentum until, in the latter half of 1966, the entire Chinese nation was caught up in a political storm of unprecedented magnitude and intensity—the Great Proletarian Cultural Revolution.

This book examines in depth some of the underlying causes and consequences of Mao's oft-expressed anxiety over the future of Chinese socialism; it is specifically concerned with the Chairman's seemingly obsessive preoccupation in the early 1960s with the possible threat of a "capitalist restoration" in China, his prescriptions for dealing with that threat, and the mass campaign—the Socialist Education Movement—he initiated in an attempt to raise the class-consciousness of the Chinese people and thereby inoculate them against the devious machinations of putative class enemies both at home and abroad. A second, closely related goal of this study is to shed new light on a series of profound intra-Party conflicts and cleavages that originated during the Socialist Education Movement and that subsequently erupted into China's tumultuous Cultural Revolution.

Through detailed analysis of a rich body of hitherto largely unexplored data on the subject of the origins, aims, instrumentalities, and outcomes of the Socialist Education Movement, we are provided with a rare opportunity to gain insight into the dynamics of the political process in contemporary China. By focusing on a single mass campaign, we are able as well to explore such important— but elusive—problem areas as ideological goal selection, political and administrative decision-making, intra-elite conflict and conflict management, techniques of mass political mobilization, and bureaucratic processes and behavior in a communist system.

The Socialist Education Movement was initially launched in response to Mao Tse-tung's impassioned plea to the CCP Central Committee's Tenth Plenum in September 1962: "Never forget class struggle!" From the outset, the movement was aimed primarily at rectifying a number of adverse—and potentially critical—political, economic, and organizational problems, which had arisen at the time of the collapse of China's Great Leap Forward in 1960–61. Throughout the early 1960s Mao watched with growing discomfort as his grandiose vision of an imminent transition to communism turned into a nightmare of emergency retreats and liberal economic reforms. In the rural heartland of China, the massive people's communes—cornerstones of the Maoist vision—were disaggregated and administratively decentralized in 1961–62 in an effort to maximize local economic initiative in the wake of three successive years of crop failure; private agricultural plots and rural free markets, abolished during the initial euphoric upsurge of the Great Leap, were reinstituted in 1961; in the following year, millions of peasants were unofficially permitted to "go it alone" in agricultural production, marketing, and land reclamation; and such ideologically regressive measures as piece-rate systems of labor remuneration and individual material incentives (e.g., the adoption of household quota systems in farm production, with individual bonuses for overfulfillment) were introduced in order to raise the "productive enthusiasm" of China's crisis-bound workers and peasants.

A second major source of concern to Mao Tse-tung in the early 1960s was the growing trend toward bureaucratization within the CCP itself. This concern was clearly expressed in the party's ideological journal, *Red Flag*, which reported that a number of administrative cadres had developed tendencies to "indulge in idleness and hate work, eat too much and own too much, strive for status, act like officials, put on bureaucratic airs, pay no heed to the plight of the people, and care nothing about the interests of the state." [1] In addition, many Party cadres had assertedly become "divorced from the masses"—i.e., they had become immersed in paperwork and formalistic office routines and had neglected their duties as pacesetters and propagandists among the masses. Finally, it was reported that many Party officials and administrative cadres had been guilty of "departmentalism," a catchall term of derogation referring to such deviant behavior as the establishment of protective interpersonal relationships among mutually dependent and mutually vulnerable officials, and the promotion of narrow, particularistic ("vested") interests in disregard of the broad, long-term interests of the state or of the masses.

What disturbed Mao Tse-tung even more than the aforementioned economic, organizational, and political problems, however, was the apparent indifference of a great many administrative cadres and higher-level Party officials to the potentially destructive long-term ideological ramifications of such problems. In the Chairman's view, one of the most dangerous byproducts, or second-order consequences, of economic liberalization and Party bureaucratization was the gradual emergence of an administrative ethos he pejoratively labeled "production in command." Epitomized in the controversial aphorism "Black cats, white cats, what does it matter? So long as they can catch rats, they are good cats!" this ethos stressed the purely instrumental calculus of economic planning and administrative decision-making, without regard for political or ideological considerations or consequences. [2] In opposing this tendency toward amoral instrumentalism, Mao expressed the fear that such an expediential, opportunistic approach to planning and management would facilitate the further growth and development of harmful "spontaneous capitalist tendencies" in the economy.

It was hardly accidental that Mao's growing concern over the effects of liberalism, bureaucratism, and instrumentalism at home coincided with the intensification of his verbal attacks against "modern revisionism" abroad—particularly in the Soviet Union. In Mao's view, bureaucratism and instrumentalism were the very wellsprings of revisionism, and revisionism was the first step on the road to a possible capitalist restoration. It was against this background of adverse developments and the Chairman's progressively increasing anxiety that the Socialist Education Movement took shape in the autumn of 1962.

Mao launched the Socialist Education Movement with the aim of reversing the extreme permissive tendencies of the post-Great Leap era and regaining the lost momentum of China's socialist revolution. The Movement lasted until 1966, when it was unceremoniously terminated and supplanted by the more spectacular Cultural Revolution. In that four-year period, China's rural political institutions underwent the most thorough and intensive purge in the history of the People's Republic, a purge that directly touched the lives of almost two million Party officials and administrative cadres in the countryside. Even more significant, in this period were sown the seeds of intra-Party discord that ultimately gave rise to the Cultural Revolution.

When the Socialist Education Movement began, there were few indications in the public media that it would be anything more than a routine consciousness-raising campaign. Indeed, most of the operational measures employed in the movement were well-worn, time-tested CCP organizational and mobilizational techniques. Prominent among these was the rectification campaign (*cheng-feng*), wherein basic-level Party and administrative cadres engaged in intensive study of Party doctrines and policies and underwent vigorous "criticism and self-criticism" to improve their understanding of the current situation and tasks and to expose and correct flaws in their work methods (*tso-fa*) and work styles (*tso-feng*).

Second, systems for regulating and regularizing cadre participation in physical productive labor were introduced in order to overcome growing tendencies toward bureaucratism and "commandism" on the part of those leading cadres at the commune and production brigade levels who were normally "divorced from production" *(t'o-li sheng-ch'an)*—i.e., who spent most of their time in their offices rather than in the fields. The requirement that all cadres spend a certain portion of their time working alongside the peasants as ordinary laborers was held to be the strongest guarantee that the Party's mass line would be implemented correctly in the countryside.

Third, compilation and publication of individual, family, village, and commune historical records (the so-called "four histories"), and public recollection and discussion by older peasants of the suffering and exploitation endured at the hands of class enemies in the "old" society, were advocated. The four histories were seen as effective means to arouse class hatred and direct it toward an identifiable local enemy—the so-called "four category elements": former landlords, rich peasants, counterrevolutionaries, and other assorted "bad elements."

Fourth, "poor and lower-middle peasants' associations" *(p'in, hsia-chung nung hsieh-hui)* were organized under the watchful eye of rural Party organs to oversee the financial and administrative work of management committees in the communes and to supervise the reform of local "four category elements." The peasants' associations were generally organized around core groups of proven peasant "activists" *(chi-chi fen-tzu)*, and their status was similar to that of functional auxiliaries of the CCP in various other sectors of society, such as trade unions in industry or students' associations in educational institutions.

Finally, the technique of dispatching to the rural areas large numbers of investigative "work teams" *(kung-tso tui)*—made up of leading cadres and ordinary working personnel from higher-level Party, military, state administrative, and educational institutions—was adopted as a basic approach to the problem of exposing and rectifying deviant behavior of basic-level cadres. The work teams, by "striking roots" *(cha ken)* among the peasants in the villages and gaining the confidence of the local populace, were expected to gather reliable information on the deeds and misdeeds of local officials. When corruption or administrative mismanagement was uncovered, the work teams were responsible for initiating criticism and mobilizing the masses to participate in the process of cadre rectification.

During the subsequent Cultural Revolution, Mao Tse-tung's supporters made a number of serious accusations concerning the existence of a conspiracy to undermine and subvert the Socialist Education Movement. Primary targets of these accusations were China's Chief of State and erstwhile Maoist heir-apparent, Liu Shao-ch'i, and his reputed partner in crime, CCP Secretary-General Teng Hsiao-p'ing. The charges revolved around the central assertion that Liu Shao-ch'i and Teng Hsiao-p'ing were "hidden counter-revolutionary elements" and "bourgeois power holders" who

. . . madly sabotaged the socialist revolution in the countryside and came out against the masses of poor and lower-middle peasants. [They] pursued an out-and-out counterrevolutionary revisionist line, a line which represented a vain attempt to restore capitalism in the rural areas, a line which would, in fact, have allowed the landlords, rich peasants, counterrevolutionaries, bad elements and Rightists to make a comeback.[3]

The Maoist catalogue of grievances against Liu and Teng for their respective roles in the alleged subversion of the Socialist Education Movement was compiled retrospectively during the Cultural Revolution. According to documents and articles published by the Maoists in 1967, the Socialist Education Movement got off to a good start in the first half of 1963 with the promulgation of the so-called "First Ten Points"—a document reportedly drafted under Mao Tse-tung's personal supervision. Following this, however, the correct orientation of the movement was allegedly distorted with the appearance of a "monstrous poisonous weed" in the form of the "Second Ten Points"—a document drafted and promulgated in the autumn of 1963 by Teng Hsiao-p'ing and his close associate, Peking Party boss P'eng Chen.

According to the Maoists, the Second Ten Points in effect "negated the essential content of the struggle between two roads [i.e., between the proletariat and the bourgeoisie] and completely discarded the line, principles and policies . . . which Chairman Mao had explicitly formulated in the First Ten Points." [4]

The ill wind that ostensibly began to blow in the Chinese countryside as a result of Teng Hsiao-p'ing's subterfuge was allegedly given substantial further impetus a year later, when Liu Shao-ch'i—China's "number one bourgeois powerholder"—personally revised the Second Ten Points in September 1964.

Based on the controversial "T'aoyüan Experience" of Liu's wife, Wang Kuang-mei, the Revised Second Ten Points laid down a policy line for the Socialist Education Movement that was later characterized by the Maoists as " 'left' in form but right in essence" (*hsing "tso," shih yu*). More specifically, Liu was charged with having used the Revised Second Ten Points to underwrite the practice of launching excessive and indiscriminate political struggles against lower-level cadres in the countryside, in opposition to Mao's mild policy for reforming aberrant officials.

During the Cultural Revolution, Liu's subversion of Maoist cadre policy was referred to as "attacking the many in order to protect the few" (*ta-chi i ta-p'ien, pao-hu i hsiao-ts'o*), since it allegedly sprang from Liu's desire to "divert the spearhead" of the Socialist Education Movement away from a small number of inveterate anti-Party, anti-socialist "bourgeois powerholders" within the Party, and direct the movement instead against the vast majority of "good and comparatively good" cadres at the basic levels.[5]

Official CCP history now holds that Liu Shao-ch'i's erroneous policy line concerning the cadre question was immediately and overwhelmingly rejected by the broad masses of revolutionary peasants and cadres—most prominently by the cadres and peasants of the famous Tachai production brigade in Shansi Province, scene of an extensive cadre purge in the autumn of 1964. And Chairman Mao himself, upon perceiving the counterrevolutionary essence of Liu's line, reportedly stepped into the breach to remedy the situation by personally "reversing the verdict" in the case of Tachai's cadres and issuing his celebrated "Twenty-Three Points" in January 1965.

In pointing out, for the first time, that the central objective of the Socialist Education Movement was to rectify high-level bourgeois powerholders within the Party, the Twenty-Three Points purportedly "signalled the bankruptcy of the bourgeois reactionary line," dealt a "telling blow" to counterrevolutionary forces in the countryside, and thrust up a new Maoist hero—Tachai brigade Party branch secretary Ch'en Yung-kuei. The promulgation of the Twenty-Three Points has thus been acclaimed as a decisive turning point in the putative "struggle between two roads"—an event that paved the way for the purge of Liu Shao-ch'i and Teng Hsiao-p'ing during the Cultural Revolution.[6]

Whether or not such extreme claims and allegations are warranted by the facts (one purpose of the present study is to arrive at such a determination), there can be little doubt that Mao Tse-tung's firm belief in the existence of a high-level counterrevolutionary conspiracy played a major role in his decision to terminate the Socialist Education Movement and launch the Cultural Revolution, and to single out Liu Shao-ch'i and Teng Hsiao-p'ing (along with such supporting actors as P'eng Chen and Wang Kuang-mei) as primary targets of an intensive mass campaign of repudiation and vilification.

Apart from questions of alleged sabotage and counterrevolutionary conspiracy, another aspect of the Socialist Education Movement, bureaucratic obstructionism, is of particular interest to social scientists. Throughout the movement, sizeable numbers of campaign-weary, stability-seeking Party officials at all levels of the CCP hierarchy sought to routinize the movement and minimize the disruptive effects of the rectification campaign. The phenomena of bureaucratic footdragging and evasion of responsibility were well-documented in a number of provinces, and the existence of significant numbers of entrenched Party officials who were reluctant to conscientiously implement Mao's instructions concerning the Socialist Education Movement was undoubtedly instrumental in the Chairman's decision to launch the Cultural Revolution.

As a result of experiences gained during the Socialist Education Movement, Mao apparently concluded in 1966 that Party rectification was too important a task to be left to an increasingly bureaucratized and unresponsive Party establishment. Therefore he turned to the youth (Red Guards), the Army, and the worker-peasant masses ("revolutionary rebels") of China to carry out the struggle against bourgeois powerholders within the Party. In thus abandoning traditional methods of Party rectification, Mao sought to discover a new answer to the age-old question, *Quis custodiet ipsos custodes?*: "Who guards the guardians themselves?"

1 THE SOCIALIST EDUCATION MOVEMENT: ORIGINS AND EARLY DEVELOPMENT

THE IMMEDIATE ORIGINS of the Socialist Education Movement can be traced to the CCP Central Committee's Tenth Plenum of September 1962, which was convened in an atmosphere of high tension, both domestic and international. In the latter part of 1962 the Sino-Soviet dispute was on the verge of moving from the stage of latency to that of open polemics, and China's internal political and economic situation was just beginning to improve following three years of severe crop failures and a series of emergency administrative retrenchments made necessary by the collapse of the Great Leap Forward.[1]

The official press communiqué of the Tenth Plenum was quite frank in its assessment of the current situation. "It should be pointed out," it stated, "that some of our work is not well done. For instance, because of the incompetence of leading personnel, some production teams, factories, and commercial enterprises have either produced less or become unwelcome to the masses. We should endeavor to change this state of affairs . . . without delay." [2]

The communiqué also gave renewed stress to the Maoist thesis concerning the "continued existence of classes and class struggle throughout the entire period of transition from capitalism to communism"—a barb aimed not only at "modern revisionists" in the Soviet Union, but also at Party bureaucrats within China who had manifested "various opportunistic ideological tendencies." [3]

In an unpublished speech presented to the Plenum, Chairman Mao repeatedly stressed the importance of heightening Party members' ideological vigilance.[4] "We must recognize," he said, "the possibility of the restoration of the reactionary classes. It is necessary to heighten our vigilance as well as to educate the youth, the masses, the middle-level and basic-level cadres, and even the veteran cadres. Otherwise, a country like ours may head in the [wrong] direction. . . . From this moment on, we must talk about this every year, every month, every day; at conferences, at Party congresses, at plenary sessions, and at each and every meeting." [5]

Clearly, China's aging leader was deeply concerned about the course of economic, political, and ideological developments in his country. That there was indeed a great deal for him to be concerned about has been confirmed in a unique set of official CCP documents captured by the Chinese Nationalists during a 1964 commando raid on the Party headquarters of Lienchiang county, Fukien province.[6]

The Lienchiang documents constituted a lengthy and detailed catalogue of political and socioeconomic developments in the people's communes of a single rural county during the six-month period from October 1962 to March 1963. A great deal of space in these documents was devoted to the question of certain "unhealthy tendencies" that had arisen among commune members and basic-level cadres in the county during the "three hard years" of 1959–61, when the retreat from the Great Leap Forward had been accompanied by a general relaxation of the Party's radical collectivist agricultural policies. Such unhealthy tendencies fell into five categories: (1) "spontaneous capitalist tendencies" on the part of the better-off peasants, many of whom preferred to "go it alone" by relying for income primarily on their private plots and family sideline occupations rather than on less profitable collective undertakings; (2) the resurgence of such "feudal" customs and practices as religious festivals, money marriages, spiritualism and witchcraft; (3) a general decline in cadre morale, as evidenced by the ever-increasing number of rural cadres who found the rewards and perquisites of officialdom incommensurate with the burdens and tensions, and thus expressed a desire to resign from their posts; (4) the rise of corrupt practices among the rural cadres, centering around the misappropriation of public funds for private purposes; and (5) the increasing boldness and self-confidence of the so-called "four category elements"—former landlords, rich peasants, counterrevolutionaries, and "bad elements"—many of whom had taken advantage of the temporary difficulties of 1959–61 to sabotage the collective economy, thereby eroding the enthusiasm of the peasantry for socialism, and paving the way for a counterrevolutionary restoration in the countryside.

By far the most serious problem revealed in the Lienchiang documents was the prevalence of economic corruption and political impurity among rural cadres. As one commune member reportedly complained, "On the surface cadres are moral and virtuous, but in their hearts they are devious." Another complaint dealt with the cadres' tendency to monopolize all power in the communes: "The handle of the sword is always in the hands of cadres. We are powerless." [7]

Cadres' control over the allocation of collective funds, materials, land, and labor were frequently reported to have resulted in corruption. One report told of a production brigade leader who abused his position by inviting people to a banquet and then demanding that they make "donations" to help him finance the building of his house. Other reports cited numerous examples of the cadres' misappropriation of public funds, their use of collective materials and labor to build private houses, and their preferential treatment in such matters as applications for state loans. On the whole, this situation was regarded as extremely serious, since "cadres whose revolutionary will is weak . . . drift with the current."

These were not just isolated instances of aberrant behavior, as the following statistical summary of cadre malpractices in a single production brigade (or village) indicates: "On the basis of incomplete statistics, among the cadres there were two who had engaged in peddling, forty who had committed graft and misappropriation, ten who had gambled, five who had privately slaughtered hogs, three who had arranged marriages-by-sale, one who had engaged in superstitious practices, three who had given extravagant parties, and 36 who had been unwilling to serve as cadres."

The last-mentioned aberration—the desire to resign from official duty—was surprisingly widespread. The Lienchiang documents provided ample evidence that many cadres considered the burdens and tensions of office to outweigh the advantages. Many apparently felt that being a cadre involved suffering a loss, and they reportedly said: "I am not going to do it; get someone else." [8] According to statistics presented in the Lienchiang documents, this attitude was held by 1,188 cadres—roughly eight percent of all production brigade and team-level cadres in the county.

Some of the reasons for this demoralization were made clear in the documents. One factor was the high standard of thought and behavior demanded of cadres, which restricted their participation in private economic activities.[9] Tensions with the peasant masses were another major source of the decline in cadre morale. Some peasants reportedly felt that the general reduction in individual income in the crisis years following the Great Leap Forward was the fault of the cadres, and thus became "quite angry with them." The cadres, in turn, felt that the commune members were ungrateful and difficult to lead, thus resulting in "some bad feelings between the cadres and masses." [10] One concrete example of such tensions concerned the weighing of fertilizer. Peasants in one production brigade apparently tried to pass off watered-down fertilizer on the cadre in charge of weighing, and when he registered his disapproval they "gave him a hard time, abused him, and even cursed him." [11]

Apart from questions of cadre morale and malpractice, a major difficulty frequently cited in the Lienchiang documents concerned the rampant growth of private economic activity, and the bad effect this was having on the socialist enthusiasm of the peasants. According to the documents, over 2,500 peasants in the county had quit agriculture to go into business (*ch'i-nung chiu-shang*), and over 25 percent of the production teams in the county were permitting peasants to "go it alone" (*tan-kan*) in grain production and land reclamation. In one production brigade, it was reported that more than one-third of the 224 persons investigated had been guilty of such transgressions as abandoning farming for commercial activities, excessive private reclamation of land, theft, unlawful emigration to the cities, and slandering the government.[12]

The adverse situation in Lienchiang county was summarized in a candid discussion of "principal problems that still exist":

(1) Individual commune members keep good fertilizer for themselves and hand over to the brigade fertilizer containing water. . . .

(2) Some do not go out to work after their quotas have been set, but surreptitiously attend to their own "small freedoms" and open up uncultivated land. . . .

(3) Some work only because discipline requires them to do so, but the efficiency of their work is not high. . . . They skimp on their work and waste time. . . .

(4) Some rely on state support and do not strive to stand on their own feet. They have delayed in repaying state assistance loans, have even gone so far as not to repay them, and have distributed state funds among the commune members. . . .

(5) The spirit of individual enterprise continues. . . . Individual production teams . . . have discovered that even a small area of land given over to household contract production has bad effects; but they persist in household contract production. . . .

(6) The felling of [collective] trees has continued, . . . harming collective wealth and destroying collective forests.

(7) Some have abandoned farming for peddling and industry. Some persons engage in speculation. . . . Some who abandon farming for subsidiary industries let flocks of ducks and geese damage crops. Work of the labor force has been reduced through emigration.

(8) Some steal valuables such as farm tools, fertilizer, and materials that belong to the collective. . . .

(9) We still have not suppressed the evil tendencies of capitalism, feudalism, and extravagance; as a result, we cannot manage collective production effectively.[13]

The political situation in the Chinese countryside in the winter of 1962–63, as portrayed in the Lienchiang documents, was thus rather precarious. But the prospects for reversing the potentially dangerous trends of this period were nevertheless held to be favorable. The instrument for this reversal was to be the Socialist Education Movement.

The concept of "socialist education" was by no means novel in the winter of 1962–63. Dating back to the CCP's first major Party rectification movement in the hills of Yenan in the early 1940s, socialist education had by 1962 become a more-or-less routine approach to the problems of ideological backsliding and lack of political sophistication among Party members and cadres. But this time it was to be socialist education with.a difference. As the Lienchiang County Party Committee First Secretary put it in February of 1963, "This cannot be an ordinary movement. We must let our banners fly and sound our battle drums. We must arouse the masses. We must understand clearly that if we do not conduct the movement on a large scale, we can neither suppress the evil tendencies of capitalism and feudalism nor elevate the [class] consciousness of the masses and cadres." [14]

As for the content of the new Socialist Education Movement, Premier Chou En-lai, speaking in Shanghai before an East China Advanced Collective Producers' Representatives' Conference, identified eight broad propaganda themes which were to serve as focal points for socialist education work in the rural communes:

"(1) *First the collective, then the individual.* This refers to systems of ownership and problems in agricultural production.

(2) *First the nation, then the individual.* This refers to problems in production work.

(3) *First ask of oneself, then ask of others.* This also refers to problems in work and production.

(4) *First reprimand oneself, then reprimand others.* This refers to the problem of interrelationships between people in both work [*kung-tso*] and labor [*lao-tung*].

(5) *First give one's concern to the public interest, then to private interests.* This refers to the problem of income distribution.

(6) *First work for the public interest, then for private interests.* These are problems in the political and ideological spheres.

(7) *I work for all the people; all the people work for me.* "All the people" means the whole body of laboring people who are establishing the socialist road under the leadership of the working class.

(8) *I work for the world; the world works for me.* This refers principally to internationalism." [15]

Shortly after Premier Chou En-lai's Shanghai speech, Chairman Mao delivered an important address on the subject of socialist education to a Central Committee working conference in February 1963. Commenting favorably on a series of situation reports prepared for presentation at the meeting by the Hunan and Hopei provincial Party committees, Mao revealed the extraordinary political significance he attached to the new movement:

"How can we achieve socialist construction when there is peaceful coexistence in politics, the attitude of muddling through in organization, and the attitude of superficiality in economics? . . . Once we grasp class struggle, miracles are possible [*chieh-chi toucheng i-chua, chiu-ling*]." [16]

According to a number of official media reports from various provinces, the main obstacle in the way of firmly grasping class struggle in the rural communes in this early period of the Socialist Education Movement was the lack of politically reliable or effective cadre leadership at the basic levels of the production brigade and production team. To remedy this, in January 1963 leading cadres in the countryside were instructed by the Party center to take appropriate steps to raise the ideological, political, and managerial levels of local cadres.[17] While the reasons for the weakness of leadership at the basic levels were held to be numerous and complex, the most frequently cited factor was the alleged impurity (*pu ch'un*) of the cadres' work styles. According to an editorial which appeared in early January in the authoritative *People's Daily*,

. . . a number of production teams are not well run. . . . The work styles of the cadres in these teams are not pure. . . . The cadres themselves lack socialist consciousness, and they even manifest spontaneous capitalist tendencies. . . . Such cadres lack all awareness of serving the people. . . . They do not actively participate in labor, and they are always thinking about eating more and owning more. They not only fail to listen to the opinions of the masses, but they also force their demands upon the masses. . . . Such phenomena are relatively few in number when looked at on a nationwide scale, but we must treat them conscientiously and resolve them effectively. . . . If we don't have a cadre corps which possesses a high level of socialist consciousness, it will be impossible to smoothly achieve the great historical tasks . . . of consolidating the collective economy and constructing a new socialist countryside. . . .[18]

The problem of impure cadre leadership in the communes was linked to the question of class line in the countryside with the injunction, "When selecting and promoting cadres, comrades with backgrounds as poor and lower-middle peasants [*p'in, hsia-chung nung*] should be given priority. This is because their class status and economic status enable them not to be too stubborn about preserving the system of small-scale private ownership of the means of production, and it enables them to accept socialism more readily." On the other hand, people of middle peasant and upper-middle peasant (*chung, shang-chung nung*) origins were not to be automatically excluded from appointment or promotion as basic-level cadres, since "some of them have proved themselves . . . to have a higher level of socialist consciousness." [19]

As for the policy to be adopted toward those veteran cadres who had committed errors of one sort or another or who had demonstrated shortcomings in the course of carrying out their official duties, it was stated that:

"Aside from those extremely few elements who persist in taking the capitalist road, . . . and who ought to be given necessary punishment or necessary removal from their posts, with respect to the vast majority of cadres who have shortcomings it is a question of education; it is a question of using the method of criticism and self-criticism to reform their work styles." [20]

In accordance with the above dictum, a policy of "severe in ideological criticism and lenient in organizational treatment" was officially prescribed as a means of solving ideological problems among the cadres, with the stated objectives being "to take warning from the past in order to be more careful in the future," and "to treat the illness in order to save the patient." [21]

The existence of a potentially critical leadership gap at the basic levels in the winter of 1962–63 also led to a renewed emphasis by the Party center on the policy of *hsia-fang* (lit: "downward transfer"). Because of an urgent need to "strengthen the work of Party organizations in the countryside," it was decided to "send a number of outstanding Party members, cadres, and working personnel who are loyal to the revolutionary cause, . . . who are capable workers, and who are well versed in the mass-line work method, to work in the countryside over a long duration." [22] By the end of February 1963, in Kwangtung Province alone, some 30,000 cadres from provincial, special district, county, and commune offices were reported to have entered basic-level units in the countryside. Curiously enough, however, the major tasks of these outside personnel were defined not in terms of carrying out class struggle, but rather in terms of "helping the production team cadres with production leadership work in . . . spring farming." [23]

Outside (*hsia-fang*) personnel were grouped into "work teams" (*kung-tso tui*), with responsible Party cadres taking the lead. Upon entering the production brigades and teams, they were expected to eat, live, and labor together with the basic-level cadres and ordinary commune members (hence, the so-called "three togethers"), thereby setting a personal example in carrying out the Party's mass-line style of production leadership work. They were also expected to mobilize the production team members to launch emulation campaigns designed to "study, compare, and catch up with" advanced rural production units, and render assistance to those units which were economically backward. [24] This practice of sending higher level cadres down to the basic levels of production was referred to as "penetrating a point" (*shen-ju tao i-ke tien*). [25]

Despite the considerable sound and fury that accompanied the initiation of the Socialist Education Movement in the winter of 1962–63, there is substantial evidence to indicate that Party functionaries at the intermediate and lower levels dragged their feet in implementing the new campaign. [26] Whether the revolutionary nature and significance of the movement was insufficiently understood, or whether pragmatic and conservative officials deliberately evaded the issue—or more likely because of a combination of these factors—the class struggle never really got off provincial drawing boards in this early period. Indeed, the prevailing notion among many Party officials at the provincial and subprovincial levels was seemingly that the new campaign was to be a mere carbon copy of the relatively mild, more-or-less routinized rural *cheng-she* (commune rectification) movements conducted annually in the countryside since 1959, which had centered around questions of economic and administrative reform rather than class struggle.[27]

Thus, precisely when Chairman Mao was calling for an all-out intensification of political and ideological struggles on all fronts in Chinese society, Party bureaucrats in many areas continued to stress not politics but production, not ideology but economics, not class struggle but technical reform.[28] On the whole, it appeared to be largely a case of business as usual in the countryside. The sound and the fury, it seemed, were signifying nothing.

There can be little doubt that Mao Tse-tung, as he viewed these developments in the first few months of 1963, became progressively more disturbed over the increasing tendencies toward routinization and goal-displacement in the implementation of the Socialist Education Movement. Thus, for example, in early May he stated that "Although the [Socialist Education] Movement has been launched, class struggle is still imperfectly grasped." [29] And he went on to score leading Party officials in the provinces for not taking the movement seriously enough:

> After the Tenth Plenum, only [Liu] Tzu-hou [of Hopei] and [Wang] Yen-ch'un [of Hunan] talked clearly and consistently about socialist education, while the others did not speak. For five months, Honan failed to grasp class struggle. . . . After the February meeting . . . there was a change, but it was not an all-encompassing one. There were some regional Party committee secretaries who . . . did not have a thorough understanding.[30]

Because they lacked a thorough understanding of class struggle, regional and provincial Party leaders were either unable or unwilling to conscientiously implement the Socialist Education Movement. Mao viewed the superficiality of their efforts with particular alarm. "There are some people," he charged, "who cannot penetrate the superficial. . . . [They] are boldly subjective in hypothesizing, but cautiously subjective in seeking evidence." [31]

The Chairman's growing displeasure with the course of the rectification movement in the countryside was clearly manifested toward the end of May 1963 when the Central Committee, acting under Mao's personal supervision, promulgated a "Draft Directive on Some Problems in Current Rural Work." [32] Known in Maoist parlance as the "First Ten Points," this directive served notice to Party officials throughout the country that their superficial, perfunctory, and lackadaisical attitudes toward class struggle would no longer be tolerated.

The First Ten Points

During the Cultural Revolution, the Maoists repeatedly charged a "handful of Party persons in authority taking the capitalist road" with attempting to negate the primary class-struggle orientation of the Socialist Education Movement. Mao's rising concern over the reluctance of large numbers of Party officials to take the question of continued class struggle seriously was clearly reflected in Article IV of the First Ten Points:

> Not all of our comrades have paid attention to the various phenomena of class struggle. . . . Many have failed to observe these phenomena and have not given them the serious thought required. Instead, they adopt an attitude of indifference, thereby letting the phenomena continue to develop. . . . The Central Committee believes that among our cadres and Party members, efforts should be made through socialist education to rectify the standpoint of the proletariat and overcome the mistakes that cause betrayal of the proletarian standpoint, so that our cadres and Party members can provide correct leadership. . . .[33]

The "various phenomena of class struggle" alluded to in this passage were further spelled out in the text of the First Ten Points in language strongly reminiscent of the earlier Lienchiang documents. Altogether, nine such adverse phenomena were cited. The most important of these were the proliferation of counterrevolutionary propaganda in the rural areas and the creation of counter-revolutionary organizations by former landlords and rich peasants; the attempt by various rural "bad elements" to corrupt the basic-level cadres, to the point where it was acknowledged that "in some communes and brigades, leadership power has actually fallen into the hands [of the overthrown landlords and rich peasants]"; a resurgence of commercial speculation and profiteering by "new bourgeois elements" in the countryside (activities said to have reached serious proportions); a marked increase in the frequency of such acts as exploiting rural hired labor, contracting short-term, high-interest loans, and speculative buying and selling of land; a rise in the number of sabotage activities by rural reactionary forces, including the wanton destruction of public properties, the collection of intelligence by counterrevolutionary elements, murder, and arson; and the emergence of a group of corrupt elements—thieves, speculators and degenerates—"who have ganged up with landlords and rich peasants to commit evil deeds." [34]

The necessity to overcome these dangerous tendencies had been clearly stated by Mao Tse-tung a few weeks before the promulgation of the First Ten Points, in his "Note on the Seven Well-Written Documents of the Chekiang Provincial Committee Concerning Cadre Participation in Physical Labor," dated May 9, 1963: [35]

Class struggle, production struggle, and scientific experimentation are three great revolutionary movements . . . that are a guarantee for Communists to do away with bureaucratism and avoid revisionism and dogmatism. . . . Without them, landlords, rich peasants, counterrevolutionaries, bad elements and ogres of every kind would crawl out; our comrades would do nothing about it; and many people would resort to collaboration with the enemy and become corrupted and demoralized. . . . If our cadres were thus dragged into the enemy camp, . . . many of our workers, peasants, and intellectuals would then fall easy prey to both the hard and soft tactics of the enemy. If things were allowed to go on this way the day would not be far off—perhaps only several years or a decade, or several decades at most—before a counterrevolutionary restoration on a nationwide scale would inevitably occur. . . . The whole of China would then change color. . . . Isn't that a most dangerous prospect? . . .

In the eyes of the Maoists, then, the basic question posed by the steady rise of corruption, sabotage, and spontaneous capitalism in the Chinese countryside was, "Who will win in the struggle between socialism and capitalism, . . . between Marxism-Leninism and revisionism?" [36]

The Socialist Education Movement, as we have seen, had been initiated by Mao to immunize the Chinese people—in particular the Communist Party members and cadres—against the twin viruses of renascent capitalism and Soviet-style revisionism. The First Ten Points, in turn, constituted the first tentative Maoist attempt to provide a concrete formula for an effective and long-lasting anticapitalist, antirevisionist vaccine.

In common with earlier official policy pronouncements, the First Ten Points identified poor cadre leadership as the major obstacle to grasping class struggle in the rural villages. Mao himself had declared, in early May, that widespread corruption among basic-level cadres constituted a major obstacle to the correct implementation of the Socialist Education Movement. "Looking at our cadres today," he stated, "the majority are imbued with the idea of eating more and enjoying more benefits [and are] tainted with extravagance and waste." [37] And he went on to declare that "The more corruption is exposed, the happier I will be." [38]

Although Mao did not regard petty corruption among cadres as a manifestation of class struggle, he did view it as a serious problem which had to be rectified before class struggle could be firmly grasped. Thus the First Ten Points stated that all basic-level cadres would be required to "wash their hands and bodies" and become "clean of hand and foot"—i.e., put their own houses in order—as a precondition to launching the struggle against class enemies in the countryside. [39]

For this purpose, the First Ten Points decreed that a "Four Cleanups" (ssu-ch'ing) movement should be launched among all the cadres in the rural areas, to expose and rectify cadre corruption and mismanagement in the areas of economic accounting, allocation and use of state and collective properties, management of collective granaries and warehouses, and assessment of remunerative workpoints (kung-fen) in the communes and production brigades. According to the Maoists, "the Four Cleanups is like a magic mirror. Whether one is a just or false official becomes immediately clear. . . . Cadres who have been guilty of all kinds of shortcomings and errors undergo criticism and can review their mistakes and shed their burdens. Thus, with a clear conscience they can speedily and happily 'take a warm bath' and receive 'inoculation' against future errors." [40]

Because the First Ten Points held that cadre corruption in the areas of accounts, properties, granaries, and work-points was the most prevalent source of peasant dissatisfaction with the existing rural leadership, conscientious implementation of the Four Cleanups was viewed as essential for the overall success of the Socialist Education Movement. The major guarantee for insuring such conscientious implementation was to be the active participation of the rural peasant masses in the "cleansing" process. Indeed, the call for mass participation in the rectification of rural cadres constituted the very core of the First Ten Points.

"The first thing to be done," it was stated, "is to set the masses in motion to conduct an all-out, thorough check of accounts, granaries, properties, and work-points. . . . This will be a large-scale mass movement." [41] To insure proper leadership and coordination of the mass movement, the First Ten Points called for the revitalization of long-dormant poor and lower-middle peasants' organizations in the countryside. [42] The poor and lower-middle peasants, who reportedly constituted some 65 to 70 percent of China's total rural population, and who, by virtue of their relative poverty, have traditionally been regarded by the Maoists as the most reliable class ally of the proletariat, were now instructed to form a "class army" to do battle against the forces of corruption and reaction in the countryside:

> To assure this movement of strong leadership, we must rely on organizations of the poor and lower-middle peasants; we must do a good job of investigation and research among the masses; and we must set the masses in motion. Decisions for and disposition of all important problems must be made only after full discussion with the masses. During the course of the movement, the masses must be given every opportunity to fully air their views, make criticism of errors and shortcomings, and expose evil people and evil deeds. [43]

In addition to the task of participating in the exposure and rectification of the rural cadres' "four uncleans," the newly refurbished peasants' organizations were also empowered in the First

Ten Points to assume a supervisory role in the day-to-day administrative work of commune and production brigade management committees. "All important commune and brigade affairs," it was stated, "should be discussed with [the peasants' organizations]. . . . Attempts to exclude them are not permissible." [44]

Although the manifold problems of cadre corruption, spontaneous capitalism, and sabotage by rural four category elements were held to be relatively serious, the First Ten Points indicated, in orthodox Maoist fashion, that the primary remedy for such problems lay in education and persuasion, rather than coercion and punishment. In the area of cleansing the cadres, it was held that

> Evil deeds exposed as a result of the [Four Cleanups] movement should be carefully analyzed. They should be dealt with individually on the basis of their different conditions. . . . The principal objective is education rather than punishment. . . . For those comrades who have committed minor errors . . . sincere assistance should be extended to help them "wash their hands and bodies" and redeem themselves. . . . Nevertheless, all money taken illegally through corruption or theft, and all other property that should be retrieved, must be returned [by the cadres] and accounted for. As long as the matter has been straightened out in this manner, the masses naturally will not make excessive demands. . . . Efforts must be made to prevent compulsory confessions; physical punishment of any kind should be strictly prohibited. Those criticized must be given the chance to defend themselves. [45]

In general, cadre mistakes and shortcomings were to be treated as "contradictions among the people"—i.e., nonantagonistic contradictions that could be handled on the basis of the conciliatory Maoist formula for conflict resolution, "unity-criticism-unity." Mao's personal approval of lenient treatment for aberrant cadres had been stated in early May, when he directed that corrupt basic-level officials could redeem themselves "simply by going out and returning their booty; having done that, they will no longer be considered corrupt elements. Their names will not be publicized." [46]

Even in those (relatively few) cases where cadre corruption or thievery was regarded as serious, the more severe and humiliating method of convening mass struggle meetings was deemed inappropriate; instead, such cases were to be handled and disposed of "through legal channels." By thus calling for a general policy of leniency and restraint in the rectification of cadres, the Maoists' major premise—one long a hallmark of Mao's cadre policy—was that "over 95 percent of the cadres are good or basically good and can be united in the struggle against class enemies." [47]

In contrast to the lengthy and detailed statements concerning the aims and instrumentalities of the cadre-oriented Four Cleanups, little was said in the First Ten Points about the methods of conducting class struggle against four category elements in the countryside. Instead, and in line with the predominant inoculative orientation of the Socialist Education Movement, major stress was placed on "vaccinating" the peasants against the serious diseases of spontaneous capitalism and sabotage of the collective economy by class enemies.

Immunization against these ostensibly contagious diseases was to be achieved chiefly through intensive, didactic propaganda and indoctrination work among the rural masses. In passing favorable judgment on a situation report issued in February 1963 by the Honan provincial Party committee, the First Ten Points identified a number of "keypoints" and "correct methods" to be stressed in conducting socialist education among the peasantry:

> In Honan province . . . the work of socialist education has been carried out with good results. In Honan, they have made good use of combining the history of the revolutionary struggles of their own communes and brigades, the history of agrarian reform, and the history of collectivization to remind the older generation of the suffering they sustained under the oppression of the exploiting classes, . . . thereby arousing their class sentiments. With this method, they have also made the younger generation realize the fact that the fruits of revolutionary struggle did not come easily. The youngsters were made to pore over the "family record" of the proletariat. Thus the class consciousness of the poor and lower-middle peasants has been heightened . . . and as they become resolutely determined to break with capitalism and feudalism, it has become possible to swiftly organize a class army. [48]

In discussing the general work methods of the Socialist Education Movement, the First Ten Points stressed the need for leading cadres to undertake on-the-spot investigations and experiments at selected "squatting points" (*tun-tien*) in the countryside. Only in this way could Party leaders collect information that was not superficial or one-sided, detect problems as they arose, and sum up experiences to improve future work. The Maoists regarded the lack of such careful, on-the-spot investigatory and preparatory work by leading cadres as a major reason for the Socialist Education Movement's poor start in the winter of 1962–63:

> The responsible comrades of some Party organs . . . talked about investigation and research, but they lacked enthusiasm and the determination to train their eyes on the lower levels. . . . Therefore, they were unable to successfully carry out investigation and research. . . . It is still necessary to shout loudly at certain comrades on this point. At present, we still have some comrades in leading positions, and many in general work, who do not understand . . . the scientific and revolutionary epistemology of Marxism.[49]

To overcome such epistemological problems, and to ensure that Party officials (particularly the increasingly bureaucratized middle-level cadres) would not become "divorced from the masses," the First Ten Points decreed that henceforth all Party committeemen at the four levels of county, commune, production brigade, and production team would be required to participate actively in collective production labor in the countryside on a rotating basis.[50]

Turning to the question of operating procedures, the First Ten Points stated that the Socialist Education Movement in a given rural locality should be conducted in three stages: "First, devote some 20 days to the training of a group of cadres; second, [use these cadres] to train additional cadres and activists from among the poor and lower-middle peasants; third, start the all-around effort. When taking these steps, 'spot testing' [shih-tien] is a necessary process. . . . This method of carrying out the work by dividing it into stages and subjecting it to spot testing is correct."[51]

Despite the solemn declaration that class struggle in the Chinese countryside was acute and complex, and would persist over a considerable historical period, the First Ten Points concluded optimistically that "facts prove that many [of the aforementioned] problems are not only easy to discover, but are also easy to solve. What is important is whether or not our comrades can get close to the masses, . . . discover problems in good time, and summarize experiences." Along with this characteristic Maoist expression of faith in the potential efficacy of the new movement came a prediction that "When this educational movement is concluded, there will appear throughout the nation a new climate for progress into greater prosperity." And it was confidently asserted that the basic objectives of the Socialist Education Movement could be totally accomplished within three years.[52]

Trial and Error: Summer 1963

In line with the call of the First Ten Points for further spot-testing and experimentation, in the summer of 1963 an extensive search was made for appropriate methods and techniques for conducting socialist education work among rural cadres and peasants.[53] Although the new Socialist Education Movement qua mass movement received little systematic publicity in the mass media in this period, considerable coverage was given, on an individual ad hoc basis, to four of the dominant themes of socialist education stressed in the First Ten Points: the need for the universal establishment of poor and lower-middle peasants' organizations; the demand for cadres' increased participation in productive labor; the call for a campaign to audit and clean up rural accounts, properties, granaries, and work-points; and the initiation of a peasant-oriented ideological education campaign focusing on the history of class struggles in the countryside.

With respect to the question of peasants' organizations, the First Ten Points had remained conspicuously silent on such important points as the scope and limitation of the official powers and duties of these organizations, the nature of their relationship to basic-level Party organs in the countryside, and the criteria for admission to membership. Hence, shortly after the promulgation of the First Ten Points, provincial Party organs throughout the country began to map out experimental plans for spot-testing various approaches to the problem of organizing poor and lower-middle peasants in the rural areas.

In the south China province of Kwangtung, for example, an editorial published in the major regional newspaper, *Southern Daily*, in late May signalled the initiation of a drive to set up "poor peasants' representatives' groups" *(p'in-nung tai-piao hsiao-tsu)* at the basic lev-els. The functions and responsibilities of these new groups were defined in the following terms:

> . . . to act as the assistant to the management committee of the produc-tion team; under the leadership of the Party, to conduct class education and education in Party policy among the poor and lower-middle peasants as well as the broad masses of commune members; to raise the ideological consciousness of the poor and lower-middle peasants; to consolidate the collective economy; and to take the lead in accomplishing various produc-tion tasks.[54]

Significantly—and this is a point to which we shall have occasion to return later—the above editorial made no mention of the role of peasants' organizations in exposing and cleaning-up the corruption of basic-level cadres. Nor, for that matter, was there any mention of the supervisory functions of the poor peasants' representatives' groups vis-à-vis Party organs or management committees at the basic levels—a noteworthy deletion in view of the high priority ac-corded this function in the First Ten Points.

While thus downgrading (by omission) the investigatory and su-pervisory roles of the peasants' organizations, Kwangtung Party of-ficials did concede the need to strengthen the consultative role of the poor and lower-middle peasants in the planning and manage-ment of production team affairs. This role was deemed crucial because "in those production teams where leadership is grasped by upper-middle peasants, spontaneous capitalist tendencies will emerge . . . and leadership is likely to be usurped by the landlords and rich peasants."[55]

As for the relationship between the newly established poor peas-ants' representatives' groups and Party branches in the production brigades, it was implied that the peasants' organizations owed their existence to—and should therefore respond unquestioningly to the leadership of—local Party organs.[56] On the other hand, however, rural Party branches were admonished to "rely on the poor peas-ants' organizations, listen to what they have to say, win their assis-tance, and organize the poor and lower-middle peasants through them."[57]

The main problem to be overcome in the drive to put the newly

refurbished peasants' organizations on a sound footing in the countryside was the general lack of enthusiasm for the new policy on
the part of rural Party members and cadres, many of whom were
apparently reluctant to share power with—and submit to supervision by—the "crude and backward" poor and lower-middle peasants. As revealed in the following investigation report from a production brigade in Polo county, Kwangtung, rural Party members
and cadres simply did not take the task of organizing the peasants
seriously:

Ten production teams of Haohsia brigade recently set up poor peasants'
representatives' groups. However, at the time these groups were formed,
Party members and cadres lacked sufficient understanding of the important
nature of this work. . . . As a result, many problems arose. The election
of representatives was not guided by careful consideration, and a number
of people with low class consciousness and a poor sense of responsibility
were admitted to the poor peasants' representatives' groups, thereby lowering the political quality of these groups. Some commune members who
were elected as representatives to these groups had insufficient understanding of the nature and role of the groups. Accordingly, they were not
sufficiently enthusiastic about their work. Although ten representatives'
groups were set up, not one of them drew up any clearly defined systems
of work or undertook any meaningful activities. . . .

Why have these problems arisen? According to our findings, the main
reason is that Party members and cadres in many production teams lack
sufficient understanding of the vital purpose to be served in establishing
these groups. When the groups were set up, [the cadres] failed to carry out
ideological work in a penetrative manner and failed to set the commune
members in motion. Nor did they solicit the views of the masses. When
they picked representatives [*sic!*] they did so perfunctorily, without going
through serious pre-election discussion with the poor and lower-middle
peasants. . . . The selections were made by a few cadres, and the results
were not made known to the commune members until some time later.
Acting thusly, [the cadres] considered their job finished.[58]

The above passage tends to confirm the observation made by
Professor Ezra Vogel, in his study of Kwangtung provincial politics in the early 1960s, that the Maoist policy of forming strong
watchdog organizations composed of the most class-conscious and
politically active peasants was generally unpopular with rural
cadres and provincial-level officials alike.[59] Not only had the rural
cadres in Kwangtung lacked sufficient understanding of the impor-

tant purpose of establishing peasants' organizations, but they had also attempted to manipulate these organizations by controlling the selection process whereby peasant activists were recruited as group representatives. Not only had provincial officials failed to stress, in the mass media, the investigatory and supervisory roles of the peasants' organizations, but they had also given primary emphasis to the absolute subordination of the peasants' associations to local Party organs. Nowhere were class struggle or the rectification of administrative malpractices cited as primary objectives in the formation of peasants' groups.

If preliminary experimentation with the establishment of poor and lower-middle peasants' associations produced less-than-spectacular results in the summer of 1963, the initial drive to augment and systematize cadre participation in productive labor was apparently somewhat more fruitful—at least to judge by the large amount of space the mass media devoted to the latter campaign.

Immediately following the promulgation of the First Ten Points in the latter part of May, a series of "Talks on Cadre Participation in Collective Productive Labor" was published in the authoritative *People's Daily*. These "Talks" reiterated the view of the First Ten Points that regular participation in physical labor by cadres at all levels was necessary both to guarantee sound direction to agricultural production and to reduce the alienation of cadres from the peasant masses.[60]

In order to resolve the contradiction between "labor" (*lao-tung:* direct participation in productive activity) and "work" (*kung-tso:* the performance of official administrative and leadership duties), and in order to free the cadres from their offices for increased involvement in the former, Party committees at all levels were instructed in the early summer of 1963 to hold fewer meetings and conferences, reduce the frequency and length of their written reports, and spend less time compiling superfluous or meaningless statistical charts and tables. Complaints from Party officials, who claimed (not without justification) that they were overburdened with a myriad of administrative chores, were met with the demand that the officials improve their work methods so as to cut down on the amount of time spent in their offices.[61]

In July 1963, an entire double issue of the ideological journal *Red Flag* was devoted to a discussion of the policy of cadres participating in labor and to a review of experiences gained in various rural localities in the course of experimentation with this policy.[62] Not only was cadre participation in labor held to be the best method for raising the labor enthusiasm of the masses and for helping the cadres to rectify their bureaucratic work styles, but it was also advocated as a means of "smashing and rooting out all kinds of reactionary forces which are trying vainly to erode and undermine the revolutionary dictatorship of the proletariat . . . in our country." [63]

To encourage cadres to spend more time on the front lines of production and less time in their offices, the number of "subsidized work-points" *(pu-t'ieh kung-fen)* normally awarded to administrative personnel for the fulfillment of non-production-related tasks (i.e., "work") was generally reduced to a maximum of two percent of the total annual work-points of the production brigade or team.[64] Since it had previously been a common practice among administrative cadres who were "divorced from production" or "semi-divorced from production" *(pan t'o-li sheng-ch'an)* to claim four percent (or, in some extreme cases, as much as ten percent) of the total annual work-points of a brigade or team as their fixed subsidy, this new restriction meant that many cadres would now have to spend more time in the fields, earning work-points as ordinary laborers, in order to maintain their previous income levels.

If this measure was not sufficiently compelling, a second system was adopted on an experimental basis in many areas, whereby a minimum annual quota of labor days was fixed for cadres at each level, from the county down to the production brigade. Such quotas varied from place to place, but a common practice was to fix the number of mandatory labor days for county-level cadres at 60 man/days per year, commune-level cadres at 120 man/days, and brigade-level cadres at 180 man/days.[65] The twin systems of fixing minimum labor-day quotas and maximum limits on the amount of subsidized work-points for cadres together constituted the essence of the policy of "three fixes" *(san ting)*, which was later universally adopted throughout the Chinese countryside.[66]

As might be expected, many cadres in county-, commune-, and brigade-level Party and administrative organs resisted the idea of leaving the relative comfort and security of their offices for extended tours of duty as common farm laborers. Such resistance was generally manifested indirectly, however, and in ways that strongly suggest the relevance of Parkinson's Law:

> T'an Tsu-ping, Secretary of the Party committee of Ma-an commune [in Luchai County, Kwangsi], said that recently he was required to spend over 20 days away from the commune at cadre meetings and conferences. . . . In the 24 days following his return to the commune, . . . he prepared reports as required by the district Party committee, and spent seven whole days attending various meetings. Before the submission of his reports, he made the rounds of various production teams to check and ascertain conditions. This, coupled with taking his turn on guard duty and handling routine notifications and telephone calls, took five additional days. During this 24-day period, he . . . reported overall production statistics once every three days, covering a total of 64 items in each report. . . . All he could manage during the entire [44-day] period was six man-days of labor.[67]

Such reports of ostensibly overburdened rural administrators declaring their inability to meet their labor-day quotas were rather common in the summer of 1963; and in many cases, the buck of responsibility for this state of affairs was passed upward to Party committees at the county, district, and commune levels. For example, the above report concluded that brigade Party branch secretary T'an Tsu-ping had been unable to fulfill his quota because of the excessive number of "irrational demands" made on his time by the county Party committee.[68]

As mentioned earlier, the Party center's response to increasing bureaucratism on the part of middle-level cadres was to admonish Party committees at all levels to hold fewer meetings, simplify their administrative procedures, and reduce the number of situation reports and statistical summaries required of subordinate-level personnel. In this campaign to simplify rural administration, and thereby free office personnel for additional assignments in productive labor, the technique of the emulation campaign was widely used. For example, Party branch secretary Ch'en Yung-kuei, of the (soon-to-be-famous) Tachai brigade in Shansi province, was raised to the status of a national model cadre in the summer of 1963 because of his "outstanding record of participation in collective productive labor" over a period of several years:

Various communes and brigades [in Hsiyang County, location of the Tachai brigade] have adopted the method of publicizing "pace-setters" . . . in performing labor and leading production. . . . They have also summed up the labor performance experiences of their own cadres. . . . The county Party committee put down Ch'en Yung-kuei's experiences in a book for use at Party training classes. It issued copies of this book to basic-level Party branches throughout the entire county for study and discussion. . . . At meetings called by the county and by the communes, the experiences of Ch'en Yung-kuei are always recommended to the audience. . . . Everyone reviews himself with Ch'en Yung-kuei's "mirror" as his standard. Those cadres who used to avoid or neglect labor are able to "take a warm bath" in this way.[69]

A substantial number of rural cadres received favorable public commendation for their outstanding achievements in participating in collective labor in the summer of 1963. Equally significant, however, was the Party's admission that in many areas the campaign to increase cadre labor participation was not having the anticipated salutary effect upon the attitudes and work styles of rural officials. In an investigation report published in the *People's Daily* in mid-August, for example, it was acknowledged that "Facts drawn from many localities demonstrate that many cadres still do not understand—or do not understand clearly—the great revolutionary significance of cadre participation in collective productive labor." [70] The main reason for this failure, it was argued, was that the mere mouthing of slogans, or even the establishment of concrete "systems" (i.e., rules and regulations) governing cadre participation in labor, could never take the place of penetrative and repetitive ideological education among the cadres.

Apparently, many cadres regarded the labor participation campaign as a "one-shot" affair, to be endured today and forgotten tomorrow. The *People's Daily*, in exposing this state of affairs, heavily scored the prevalent attitude of perfunctoriness on the part of leading cadres at the county and commune levels, many of whom had allegedly attempted to "thoroughly resolve the question of . . . cadre participation in labor at a single meeting." Such superficiality in the conduct of the campaign was severely criticized, and Party organs at all levels (particularly the county level) were warned that the labor participation campaign was to be a continuing one, lasting not for a single meeting, but rather for several years.[71]

If systematic, regular participation in labor by cadres was regarded as the surest guarantee against the twin evils of bureaucratism and alienation from the masses, then the campaign to "clean-up" (*ch'ing-li*) rural accounts, work-points, granaries, and properties was regarded as an essential guarantee of cadre-peasant harmony. As we have seen, the First Ten Points had indicated that peasant dissatisfaction with the administrative practices (or malpractices) of rural cadres in the management of these matters was the source of considerable tension in many production brigades and teams.

Nevertheless, and despite the high priority attached to the task of conducting the Four Cleanups in the First Ten Points, it appears that official inertia or deliberate obstruction prevented the Four Cleanups from getting off the ground in the summer of 1963. Not only was the campaign given minimal publicity in this period (which, other things being equal, might well be accounted for by the Party leaders' reluctance to wash the dirty linen of rural cadres in public), but the publicity that was released indicated that the primary objective of the campaign (i.e., the "shedding of burdens" and "washing of hands and bodies" by aberrant, unclean basic-level cadres) had been distorted somewhere along the transmission belt between the Central Committee and local Party organs in the countryside.

Instead of focusing upon the exposure and rectification of cadre corruption in the areas of accounts, work-points, granaries, and properties, the Four Cleanups campaign was apparently confined, in this early period of spot-testing, to the rationalization of existing economic accounting procedures in the rural areas. As revealed in the following report from a production team in Honan Province, for example, the task of cleaning-up work-points was being treated as a simple matter of administrative readjustment, aimed not at rectifying cadre corruption but at reducing existing inequities in the area of remuneration for peasant labor:

When the team's work-points for the previous stage were audited, many commune members proposed various ways of improving the system. Some said "Work points are food. They must not be muddled up." Others said ". . . the accountants simply jot down what each individual tells them. . . . Mistakes are inevitable." Still others said "It is unreasonable for cadres to allot work-points for cowherds collecting dung on the same basis as for those who collect middle-grade manure."

The production team's management committee took these opinions seriously and, together with the commune members, looked into ways of improving matters. All decided to adopt the method of having both individual commune members and team accountants maintain [separate] account books, with each publishing their respective work-point totals once a month [thereby exposing discrepancies or inequities]. . . .

The enthusiasm of the peasants in [this] production team for taking part in collective production has been greatly heightened as a result of such measures.[72]

In a similar report from Hunan Province, the job of cleaning up accounts and work-points was expressly linked to the question of "making good preparations . . . for production work in the cultivation of the early and middle rice crops."[73] Nowhere were the launching of political struggles or the rectification of "four unclean" cadres mentioned as primary objectives of the campaign; on the contrary, the results of the campaign were to be gauged solely in terms of "raising the peasants' enthusiasm for collective production." Significantly, although there was some stress placed on the need to "launch the poor and lower-middle peasants to make proper arrangements for work-point allocation," such mass participation was to be confined primarily to the area of "self-assessment"—i.e., putting the peasants' own work-point accounts in order.[74]

Clearly, the phenomenon of goal displacement had occurred in the Four Cleanups campaign. Such goal displacement can best be understood as a function of the desire on the part of leading rural Party officials to shift the focal point of the campaign away from themselves or their subordinates.[75] The general lack of enthusiasm with which Party officials greeted the May 1963 call for the initiation of an intensive anticorruption drive is also indicated by the fact that, in contrast to the highly publicized, widespread campaigns to organize a "class army" of poor and lower-middle peasants and systematize cadre participation in productive labor, spot-testing in the Four Cleanups was apparently conducted in only a very few rural districts in the summer of 1963.

In interviews conducted by the author with 11 former brigade- and team-level cadres and 23 peasants from various rural districts in Kwangtung Province—all of whom had some knowledge of the parallel drives to organize the poor and lower-middle peasants and promote cadre participation in labor in the summer of 1963 (such knowledge could have been gained at first-hand or via a well-established informal grapevine of interpersonal communications known as *hsiao kuang-po*, or "little broadcasts")—only one of the respondents claimed to have heard of the term "Four Cleanups" in this early period. Apparently, Party officials at the provincial and subprovincial levels, for reasons discussed earlier, simply tabled the Central Committee's demand for a mass cleanup of cadre corruption in the countryside.[76]

The fourth and final major arena of rural socialist education spot-testing in the summer of 1963 lay in the initiation of a youth-oriented mass campaign to "recall the history of class struggles" in the countryside. Known variously as the "four histories" (i.e., the revolutionary history of individual peasants, villages, collective farms, and communes) or the "recall and compare" movement (i.e., recall the bitter past and compare it with the sweet present), this campaign was designed primarily to provide didactic class education and "education in socialism" for those rural youths who were born or had reached maturity in the period after China's liberation in 1949, and who therefore lacked first-hand experience with class exploitation and oppression in the "old" society.[77]

Under the leadership of local branches of the Young Communist League (YCL) in the countryside, the campaign to "recall and compare" involved sending groups of rural youths out to interview old, poor peasants in their own or neighboring villages. The purpose of these interviews was to elicit from the older peasants personal recollections of misery and abuse suffered at the hands of the evil landlords and rich peasants in preliberation society. Armed with these interviews, the youngsters were then organized to set up village- and countywide class-struggle exhibitions, write "big character posters" (*ta-tzu pao*) for public display, and give public lectures on the history of class struggles in the local area. In many cases, the recollections of the old peasants were compiled and published in book form, for widespread distribution to YCL members and other rural youths.[78]

One obvious reason why the "recall and compare" movement was able to get off to a relatively fast and effective start in the summer of 1963 was that rural Party officials by and large had no significant vested interest in undermining or retarding the development of the campaign, the focus of which was on class struggle in the remote past rather than in the present.[79]

On the other hand, however, many young people in rural China were apparently not particularly impressed with the movement to "recall and compare." The point was reached where it was officially admitted that many youngsters were beginning to express disbelief in their elders' stories of class exploitation and oppression. In a certain commune in suburban Peking, for example, it was reported that a number of local youths, "after having listened a few times to stories about the miserable old days, got tired of them and would not listen any more. Some were even skeptical as to the veracity of the stories." [80]

The main reason for such skepticism on the part of rural youths was acknowledged to be the existence of a sizeable generation gap between the older peasants and their hothouse-nurtured offspring:

Youths of this generation have grown up in a socialist society. Many of them do not know the evils of the old society, have not personally experienced the brutality of class struggle, and do not understand that the fruits of revolutionary victory cannot be secured without difficulty. Some of them do not even understand what landlords and capitalists are, what exploitation and class struggle are all about. After hearing the miseries disclosed by old poor peasants, some youths naively ask such childish questions as: "Did we [peasants] really have nothing in the past?" "Why did you not appeal to the law courts?" "Why did you not attempt to reason with the landlords?" Many other youths hold the belief that in a socialist society everyone will have good food and good clothes and can go to school in the cities; thus, they are not prepared ideologically for the class struggle between the proletariat and the bourgeoisie, between capitalism and socialism.[81]

Routinization and the Search for Stability

Michel Oksenberg, in his excellent analysis of the institutionalization of the CCP before the Cultural Revolution, has argued
that "the incessant demands which the government made upon
their lives led many Chinese to place a high premium upon security
and quietude. To enjoy the warmth of the hearth, to escape the un-
pleasant political pressures exerted by the CCP, to enjoy those limited pleasures which entailed low risk of criticism—these became
the main goals of many Chinese." [82] We may go one step further
and hypothesize that this same search for security and quietude
was (and most likely still is) a key element in the motivation and
behavior of many leading officials and ordinary cadres within the
CCP itself. [83]

This argument, if valid, would help to explain the general lack of
enthusiasm with which Party officials at the provincial and subprovincial levels apparently greeted the Maoist call for a "great revolutionary movement" of intensified class struggle in the spring of
1963. Having become increasingly bureaucratized and routinized in
the 13 years since the CCP came to power in 1949, middle- and
lower-level Party cadres generally sought to divert the new Socialist Education Movement away from the potentially highly un-
settling path of mass political mobilization and cadre rectification to
the less treacherous (and hence less anxiety-provoking) path of routine ideological education and propaganda work, aimed not at the
intensification of class struggles, but rather at the preservation of
their own tranquility. In many cases, these officials simply went
through the motions of implementing the movement without any
visible enthusiasm or effect. [84]

The result of all this, as mentioned in our earlier discussion of
socialist education spot-testing in the summer of 1963, was effectively to shift the orientation of the Socialist Education Movement.
A good indication of the subtle nature of this shift is provided in
the following "Ten Principles on How to Successfully Run a Production Brigade," adopted and popularized in Kiangsi Province in
the late summer of 1963:

"(1) Love and care for the collective

(2) Obey the Party

(3) Have a firm class standpoint

(4) Think of the public interest

(5) Go along the road of the masses

(6) Take the lead in labor

(7) Run the brigade democratically

(8) Be brave, persevering, loyal, and honest

(9) Persist in scientific research

(10) Persist in study" [85]

On the surface these are, of course, admirable leadership qualities for communist cadres to possess. But where is the mention of the necessity for rural cadres to firmly grasp class struggle? Where is the reference to the need for reliance upon class organizations of poor and lower-middle peasants? Where is the demand for cadres to be "four clean" with respect to their work-points, accounts, granaries, and properties? Far from constituting a call for systematic, serious class struggle or cadre rectification, these Ten Principles read like a passage from the Boy Scout Oath—a definition of moral rectitude, totally devoid of concrete behavioral norms or operational standards. Given the widespread publicity attached to the Maoists' May 1963 call for the initiation of an intensive struggle against class enemies, the extreme blandness and lack of class-struggle orientation of these Ten Principles can hardly be attributed merely to official oversight.

Finally, there is a considerable amount of evidence indicating that many middle-level Party cadres, in their attempts to blunt the spearhead of the Socialist Education Movement in 1963, gave primary stress to the economic functions of the movement, thereby diverting it from a *class* struggle to a *production* struggle. During the summer of 1963, and in line with the call of the First Ten Points for on-the-spot rural investigations by leading Party cadres, provincial media throughout China gave considerable publicity to the rural "squatting-point" experiences of provincial, special district, and county-level officials. In almost every case, however, such basic-level squatting investigations were linked only to the question of facilitating the solution of immediate problems in current rural production work—problems such as improving the quality of field management (i.e., the application of fertilizers and the elimination of insect pests), mobilizing the local labor force to undertake emergency preparations against impending drought, and overcoming the "lax and languid tendencies" of peasants and basic-level cadres so as to ensure that the sowing and harvesting of crops would be completed on schedule. Nowhere in these squatting investigation reports was there mention of the need for relying on class organizations of poor and lower-middle peasants in the effort to secure a good harvest; nowhere was there mention of the *political* objectives of grass-roots investigative work undertaken by higher-level officials; nowhere, in short, was there any indication of the primacy of class struggle.[86]

A good illustration of the tendency for leading Party cadres to stress economic rather than political priorities in their basic-level rural investigations is provided in the following report of the squatting experience of the First Secretary of the East China Party Bureau, K'o Ch'ing-shih, at a commune near Chian municipality, Kiangsi:

> Secretary K'o went out in the heat of summer to see how the early rice was growing. When he came to the No. 1 production team of Hsinfeng brigade, he asked . . . about the state of the team's production and the peasants' livelihood. . . . [When informed that] a serious drought had destroyed most of the early rice crop last year, . . . and that the state had provided 12,000 catties of relief rice, Secretary K'o said, "Good! The peasants' livelihood must be well provided for." When told that a bumper early rice harvest was anticipated this year, Secretary K'o expressed satisfaction. . . . When he left, K'o congratulated the commune on the good growth of early rice and instructed the peasants to "grip grain production in the second half of the year and fight for a bumper harvest of early and late rice."[87]

Clearly, the initial spot-testing phase of the Socialist Education Movement had not produced the desired upsurge of mass political mobilization in China's rural communes. For various reasons (including bureaucratic inertia and official obstructionism), the movement had become bogged down or diverted from its intended path all along the line. It was against this background of bureaucratic inertia and official obstructionism that a second major socialist education directive was promulgated by the Party Central Committee in September 1963.

2 SUMMING UP THE EXPERIMENT: THE "SECOND TEN POINTS"

As WE HAVE SEEN, the summer of 1963 was a period of experimentation. By September, there had been four months of preliminary spot-testing since the promulgation of the First Ten Points. Now the Central Committee issued a new directive—again in the form of ten points—designed to provide more detailed policy guidelines for the implementation of the movement, and to identify and provide corrective measures for the numerous problems and misconceptions that had come to light in the course of spot-testing during the previous period. Entitled "Some Concrete Policy Formulations of the Central Committee of the CCP in the Rural Socialist Education Movement," the September 1963 directive has since come to be known in Peking's lexicon as the "Second Ten Points." [1]

It is now known that the Second Ten Points were drafted on the basis of a report submitted to Mao Tse-tung by Peking Party boss P'eng Chen. Following the spirit of that report, CCP Secretary General Teng Hsiao-p'ing—a man subsequently purged as a "bourgeois powerholder" during the Cultural Revolution—supervised the actual drafting of the Second Ten Points. [2]

Because of Teng's close connection with the Second Ten Points, some Western observers (following the Maoists' lead) have retrospectively interpreted this document as highly revisionist.[3] However, such interpretations appear to be based in part upon *ad hominem* arguments; and for this reason it is necessary to undertake a rigorous and detailed textual analysis of the Second Ten Points before passing judgment on the document's pro- or anti-Maoist qualities.

The Second Ten Points

As the preface to the September 1963 directive states, the major purpose of the Second Ten Points was to "greatly supplement the contents of the rural Socialist Education Movement." In line with its supplementary function, the new directive was ostensibly intended to clarify and reinforce, rather than supersede, the various policy formulations that had been incorporated into the First Ten Points. Such clarification and reinforcement were deemed necessary because "a number of problems concerning concrete policies have arisen in the course of spot-testing in various places." [4]

Foremost among these newly discovered problems was the alleged failure of many leading Party officials at the provincial, special district, and county levels to provide conscientious political leadership in their spot-testing experiments. The Second Ten Points took an extremely critical view of these officials' "impure thoughts and work styles" and "lack of a firm class standpoint." "Some of the leading cadres," it was stated, "are unclean of hand and foot, and the masses have lost respect for them. When such cadres ask their subordinates to carry out the Four Cleanups, they cannot possibly expect good results." [5]

Specifically, leading cadres at the provincial, special district, and county levels were scored in the Second Ten Points for their errors and shortcomings in four important areas of work. First, it was acknowledged that many leading cadres had been content merely to issue commands to their subordinates without "getting off their horses" (*chu ma*) to undertake direct, personal investigations and research at the basic levels.[6] Second, it was claimed that an attitude of leniency and perfunctoriness had prevailed among many leading cadres with respect to the question of conscientiously exposing and criticizing "four unclean" rural cadres. This attitude was said to stem from the tendency of higher level officials to "ignore the seriousness of problems among the basic-level cadres." [7] Third, the existence of a widespread tendency for leading cadres to "shirk and look down upon labor" was alleged. This erroneous tendency was linked to the admission that many Party officials "still do not understand the great revolutionary significance of participation in collective productive labor." [8] Finally, it was acknowledged that many officials, in the course of their spot-testing experiments, had failed to do a conscientious job of organizing poor and lower-middle peasants' associations; and the majority of those peasants' associations which had been organized were said to have been "set up overnight . . . [and] either exist in name only or are critically impure." [9]

In order to help resolve these various leadership problems, and to further clarify the aims and instrumentalities of the Socialist Education Movement, the Second Ten Points set forth a number of specific policy guidelines for the implementation of the movement. Broadly speaking, these guidelines fell into two categories: procedural and substantive.

On the procedural side, concrete measures were prescribed in the September 1963 directive for the cleansing of all leading cadres involved in the Socialist Education Movement:

> Cadres in leading organizations at the provincial, special district, and county levels must . . . lead the "handwashing" and "bathing. . . ." They must first correct their own class standpoint and improve their own thinking and work styles before they can lead . . . the Socialist Education Movement. . . . Therefore, all cadres at [these] levels should first participate in the Five-Anti Movement. . . . About ten days should be spent on the convocation of three-level cadre meetings, in order to assist cadres at the level of department or bureau chief and above to "wash their hands," discard their "burdens," and "go to the front lines unencumbered." [10]

The great significance attached to this demand for prior "handwashing and bathing" by leading cadres was clearly revealed in the assertion that the performance quality of higher-level leadership was "the key to the question of whether the Socialist Education Movement can be carried out smoothly." [11]

With leading cadres compelled to undergo mandatory self-cleans-

ing (through the time-tested Maoist methods of repetitive ideological study and "criticism and self-criticism") before undertaking the
work of socialist education spot-testing, the next procedural step
outlined in the Second Ten Points was a call to strengthen the system of basic-level investigations and research. Because of the hap-
hazard and superficial manner in which many leading cadres had
conducted their rural squatting-point experiments in the previous
period, it was now ordained that all leading Party organs, from the
provincial to the county level, should organize and train work
teams made up of capable Party cadres who had "made serious confessions and self-examinations" in the previous period. These work
teams were to be dispatched to carry out investigatory work for a
period of three months in a limited number of rural "points" (*tien*)
which had been preselected by Party committees at various levels
for concentrated spot-testing.[12]

Although the duties of the work teams were not spelled out in
any detail, it is clear from the language of the Second Ten Points
that these outside personnel were expected to play a major role in
guiding and overseeing the Socialist Education Movement in their
rural squatting points. There was, however, considerable am-
bivalence in the document's prescription for the maintenance of
harmonious relationships between work teams and members of the
local rural establishment:

> In the Socialist Education Movement, it would obviously be wrong for
> the work teams merely to circulate among the basic-level cadres . . .
> without striking roots and linking up with . . . the poor and lower-middle
> peasant masses. However, it would be equally wrong for them to shunt
> aside basic-level organizations and existing cadres, instead of carrying out
> work by relying upon them. This method of doing things would create an-
> tagonisms between the basic-level cadres on the one hand, and the work
> teams and poor and lower-middle peasant masses on the other, thereby un-
> dermining the smooth development of the movement.[13]

The warning to the work teams implied here—that they must
not undermine the authority of the existing power structure in the
countryside—was further reflected in the description of the division of authority between outside personnel and local cadres. The
work teams were to serve as "staff advisors" (*ts'an-mou*) to local

cadres and were to strictly avoid monopolizing the leadership functions of the latter. Yet at the same time, they were given an explicit
mandate to "make suggestions, carry out guidance and assistance,
and enlighten the basic-level cadres in the analysis of problems and
the determination of policies and methods." [14] These somewhat
ambivalent and contradictory imperatives, together with the previously noted demand that the work teams "strike roots and link
up" (cha-ken ch'ung-lien) with the poor and lower-middle peasants,
were to be the source of considerable friction between work teams
and local cadres in many communes and brigades during subsequent stages of the Four Cleanups campaign. (See chapters 3 and
4.)

In addition to the aforementioned provisions for self-cleansing by
leading cadres at the county level and above, and for the organization, training, and dispatch of Party-led work teams to the rural
areas, two other procedural measures were recommended in the
Second Ten Points as effective means of ensuring sound leadership
over the Socialist Education Movement. The first of these concerned methods to be adopted for rectifying Party personnel in
basic-level rural organs; the second pertained to the rectification of
"ordinary" (i.e., non-Party) cadres in the communes, production
brigades, and teams.[15]

A "closed door" method was prescribed for the rectification of
rural Party members, wherein class education, criticism, and self-
criticism were to be conducted at specially convened meetings of
the local Party committee, branch, or small group (corresponding
to the levels of commune, brigade, and production team, respectively)—away from the inquiring eyes and ears of the local peasantry.[16] For non-Party cadres (who generally occupied positions of
secondary importance in the local power structure), on the other
hand, an "open door" method of rectification was prescribed. This
method consisted of the convocation of mass meetings of poor and
lower-middle peasants at the commune, brigade, and team levels
for the purpose of publicly exposing and criticizing the "four unclean" mistakes of ordinary cadres—with the added stipulation that
those cadres who were judged by the masses to be seriously unclean in their economic and administrative behavior would be

required to pay financial indemnities to compensate for all misappropriated grain, work-points, funds, or properties.[17]

On the substantive side, the Second Ten Points went far beyond the First Ten Points in specifying the major policy priorities of the Socialist Education Movement. Broadly speaking, these priorities were grouped into four categories: (1) the "struggle between two roads"; (2) Party reform; (3) organizing the poor and lower-middle peasants; and (4) the Four Cleanups.[18]

"STRUGGLE BETWEEN TWO ROADS"

Under the rubric of "struggle between two roads" were grouped such important policy problems as how to expose and suppress the counterrevolutionary activities of the "four category elements," and how to subject these elements to mass supervision and dictatorship by the poor and lower-middle peasants; where to draw the line between the legitimate (small-scale) private commercial undertakings of individual peasants and illegal speculation and profiteering by peasants with serious spontaneous capitalist tendencies; and how to classify, analyze, and deal with erroneous tendencies on the part of members of various class strata in the countryside.

On the question of how to deal with rural "four category elements," the Second Ten Points called for the initiation of an all-out struggle against capitalist and feudal forces in the countryside. In issuing this call, however, the September 1963 directive was somewhat equivocal on the question of how such struggles were to be conducted:

> In dealing with the four category elements engaged in [counterrevolutionary] restorationist activities, . . . we should mobilize the masses to carry out education and struggle in order to suppress them. After the struggle, these elements are to be put under the supervision of the masses and . . . subjected to dictatorial treatment, with a view to remaking the great majority of them into "new men." Those among them who have committed vengeful acts of violence, such as murder, robbery, arson or poisoning, and have thereby aroused great indignation among the people, should be immediately arrested and punished according to law. Other four category elements engaged in destructive activities should be dealt with by adopting the basic principle of "killing none and arresting few (less than five percent)" [sic]. . . . The arrest of an offender should be strictly car-

ried out under two conditions: first, that the crime is serious, the evidence is clear, and the offender indicates no repentance; and second, that the majority of the masses demand the arrest.[19]

The official rationale for this policy of leniency toward class enemies lay in the claim that the vast majority of four category elements could, given proper handling by the enlightened masses, be reformed to become "good elements." Moreover, despite their status as class enemies, the four category elements were held to be "part of society's productive labor force," and therefore constituted a potentially important physical input into China's labor-intensive rural economy. Finally, it was claimed that excessively harsh treatment of four category elements would be disadvantageous to their sons and daughters, and would tend to alienate the latter from the peasant masses.[20]

On the question of where to draw the line between the supplementary private economic activities of individual peasants and the more serious spontaneous capitalist tendencies of a minority of relatively affluent rural dwellers, the Second Ten Points once again came down strongly on the liberal side. The distinction between illegal speculation and profiteering on the one hand and legal vending and peddling on the other was drawn in such a way that all but the most flagrant acts of commercial sabotage were placed in the category of "legitimate marketing and trading activities." [21] In addition, it was asserted that the private plots and privately reclaimed wastelands held by individual peasants were to be considered inviolable—even in those cases where the amount of such "self-retained lands" (*tzu-liu ti*) exceeded legal limits.[22] Similarly, the "proper family sideline occupations" of individual peasants were not to be limited or impaired except in cases where such private endeavors "adversely affect the collective economy." [23]

The stated objective of such relatively lenient economic policies was to "unite and consolidate over 95 percent of the peasant masses." In order to secure such unity and consolidation, it was held that a clear distinction should be drawn between "class enemies planning to stage a comeback," and "those backward peasants who have allowed themselves to be utilized by the enemy out of temporary foolishness." Acts of petty theft, "superstitious frauds," and small-scale loans and property transactions among friends and relatives were uniformly viewed as "contradictions among the people" and were to be handled "with an attitude of practicality"—i.e., tolerance. Only in the most serious cases of unlawful activity— such as extortion, blackmail, high-interest lending, black-marketeering, and the like—were more stringent disciplinary measures called for. But even in these relatively serious cases, it was held that "the prescription for persuasive education should still be strictly observed." [24]

For the majority of minor economic offenses committed by non-four category elements in the rural areas, sincere, voluntary public repentence and financial restitution by the offender were regarded as sufficient punishment. Mass struggle rallies, third-degree interrogations, arbitrary arrests, and corporal punishment were all strictly prohibited in such cases. [25]

In sum, the policy line set forth in the Second Ten Points for dealing with spontaneous capitalist tendencies in the countryside was a remarkably lenient and tolerant one: [26]

In the Socialist Education Movement, we have only to adopt the above-mentioned prescriptions and measures to be confident of consolidating over 95 percent of the peasant masses to wage a common struggle against the enemy. As for the remaining less than five percent, we should not indiscriminately consider them as targets for our blows. They have committed serious mistakes, some of which even fall into the category of contradictions between the enemy and ourselves. Yet, they are all originally working people, and most of them are somewhat different from the ["four category elements"]. So we must do our best to win them over. Among them, those who really deserve our blows are the very few who are determined to be enemies of the people. [27]

The final policy problem discussed under the general heading of "struggle between two roads" in the Second Ten Points was the so-called middle-peasant question—how to classify, analyze, and "consolidate" members of the pivotal intermediate rural class stratum. [28] The most important problem to be solved in dealing with the middle peasant question was held to be the adoption of a correct attitude toward the upper-middle peasants (*shang-chung nung*): "Improper handling of the upper-middle peasants often affects the relationship with other middle peasants. In this light, the question of whether the upper-middle peasants are correctly handled is the most important question in determining whether over 95 percent of the peasant masses can be consolidated during the Socialist Education Movement." [29]

In order to secure such consolidation, and to ensure that the middle peasants would not be "pushed over to the side of the landlords and rich peasants" in the course of the Socialist Education Movement, the Second Ten Points held that economic contradictions between the upper-middle peasants and the poor and lower-middle peasants should be regarded as nonantagonistic "contradictions among the people." The relatively serious spontaneous capitalist tendencies alleged to exist among the upper-middle peasants were not to be dealt with by harsh methods of struggle, but rather by persuasive criticism and education: "In opposing a few upper-middle peasants for their spontaneous capitalist tendencies, we should only adopt the methods of criticism and education, and should not use the methods of struggle which we employ against our enemies. We should not deprive them of their rights as commune members, label . . . them as capitalists, or encroach upon the legal profits which they earn by . . . laboring." [30]

Finally, a stern warning was issued to Party cadres and work teams against indiscriminately reclassifying people as upper-middle peasants simply because they had improved their economic fortunes or manifested ideological backwardness since the collectivization period (1955–56). Neither wealth alone (i.e., the possession of relatively more "means of production") nor political attitude (the level of class-consciousness) were regarded in the Second Ten Points as appropriate criteria for determining upper-middle peasant status. Wealth, if adopted as a criterion, would allegedly be "wholly disadvantageous to the work of encouraging the peasants' activism in collective production," while political attitude was assertedly "unscientific . . . lacking in uniformity, . . . and is difficult to control." Instead, the main standard by which upper-middle peasant status was to be judged was whether or not "minor exploitation" (e.g., high-interest lending, market speculation, or profiteering) had occurred: "What we oppose is only the capitalist line of harming the public sector to benefit the private, harming others to benefit oneself, and enriching a few by contributing to the impoverishment or bankruptcy of the majority." [31]

PARTY REFORM

Under the heading of Party reform, the Second Ten Points called for all basic-level Party organs in the countryside to undertake an internal housecleaning under the guidance of locally deployed work teams.[32] The urgency of the need for such a housecleaning was revealed in the acknowledgment that "in places where intra-Party problems are serious, relations between the Party and the masses have become strained and class enemies are active. Without rectifying Party organizations, the Socialist Education Movement cannot be carried out smoothly." [33]

The contents of the new Party reform movement were spelled out in some detail in the Second Ten Points. Altogether, seven specific rectification measures were proposed:

"(1) All Party members must go through intensive class education and socialist education. They must measure themselves against the required standards of Party membership and undergo criticism and self-criticism.

(2) Problems within Party organs must be thoroughly exposed. An examination of each member's social standpoint, class standpoint, political background, ideological attitude, and work performance should be carried out.

(3) Degenerate elements and landlords, rich peasants, counterrevolutionaries, and bad elements who have sneaked into our Party should be thoroughly purged.

(4) Party members who have committed serious or relatively serious mistakes, and who fail to repent after repeated persuasion, should be properly dealt with.

(5) Party members and cadres, especially Party branch secretaries, should be educated to serve as examples by their active participation in collective labor.

(6) The leading nuclei of the Party's basic-level organs should be reinforced and strengthened.

(7) Routine work and the organizational life of the Party's basic-level organs should be clarified and strengthened." [34]

Work teams and higher-level officials responsible for guiding the Party rectification movement at the basic levels were cautioned that "The disciplining of [wayward] Party members should be in strict accordance with the Party Constitution. The accused should be allowed to explain and defend their actions, and all disciplinary measures should receive prior approval by higher-level organs." All such punitive measures were to be carried out in the "latter stages of the movement," and were primarily intended to serve educative rather than repressive functions. The operative principles were "to learn from past mistakes in order to take better precautions in the future," and "to treat the illness in order to save the patient." Strict observance of these Maoist principles was said to be the fundamental guarantee for realizing the twin goals of ideological purification and intra-Party unity. [35]

ORGANIZING THE POOR AND LOWER-MIDDLE PEASANTS

With respect to the question of peasants' organizations, the First Ten Points had provided only very broad and tentative policy guidelines. The Second Ten Points now dealt with this organizational question at somewhat greater length. Most important were new provisions concerning the criteria for membership in, and leadership of, the poor and lower-middle peasants' associations.

Contrary to the prevalent practice adopted in various spot-testing experiments during the previous summer (when peasants' groups in many areas had been organized on a small-scale, semi-exclusive and "representative" basis) the Second Ten Points clearly stipulated that organizations of poor and lower-middle peasants at the basic levels in the countryside were to be of a mass nature—i.e., inclusive of the great majority of poor and lower-middle peasants. The only people who were to be systematically barred from participating in these mass organizations were those (few) poor and lower-middle peasants "who have close connections with the four category elements, or who have committed serious mistakes and have been reluctant to repent despite repeated reprimands." [36]

Leadership roles in peasants' organizations at the basic levels were to be filled by politically reliable "backbone elements" drawn primarily from the ranks of the "old" poor peasants, with the addition of "a certain number of lower-middle peasants with higher class consciousness and pure backgrounds." In addition, a token number of leadership roles were to be reserved for proven activists among the younger peasants and women of the local area. [37]

The work of enrolling members and recruiting leaders for the poor and lower-middle peasants' organizations was to be undertaken by members of the local Party branch or locally resident work team by "paying visits to the poor and suffering and striking deep roots among the masses." Unless the peasant masses were thoroughly and penetratively mobilized in the early stages of the movement, it was warned, the peasants' organizations "would be established . . . solely by administrative order, would exist only nominally, and would not function well." Hence, mass mobilization was held to be the "basic item of work" in the drive to establish viable, politically active peasants' associations in the countryside. [38]

In contrast to these rather specific prescriptions for the mobilization and recruitment of poor and lower-middle peasants, the Second Ten Points were extremely vague on the subject of the rights, duties, and responsibilities of the peasants' associations, once formed:

> In addition to participating in political movements, such organizations should function in routine production and construction, in strengthening the collective economy, and in consolidating the proletarian dictatorship. In establishing systems of work, it should be guaranteed that these organizations will assist and supervise the work of communes, production brigades, and production teams, as well as the work of cadres at these three levels. Management committees, when discussing important questions, should invite representatives of the poor and lower-middle peasants to attend the meeting. [39]

The vagueness of the above prescriptions was clearly purposeful, since it was explicitly acknowledged that "where the organization of rural class ranks is concerned, . . . we have not yet obtained much experience." For this reason, it was held that more time was needed before concrete answers could be given to such important questions as the missions and powers of the poor and lower-middle peasants' organizations, and the proper relationship between the peasants' organizations and the local Party organs and management committees. These and other questions were to be solved after additional experimentation and summing-up; and it was suggested that those departments of the CCP Central Committee most directly concerned with rural work should, on the basis of such experimentation, "draw up concrete regulations in the first half of 1964 governing the rights and responsibilities of poor and lower-middle peasants' organizations." [40]

THE FOUR CLEANUPS

Under the slogan "Unite more than 95 percent of the rural cadres," the Second Ten Points asserted that "four unclean" practices by ordinary cadres at the basic levels were "mostly limited to such common mistakes as excessive eating, excessive acquisitiveness, and petty theft." On the other hand, however, it was also acknowledged that "in some cases, the mistakes are more serious. . . . A few landlords, rich peasants, counterrevolutionaries, and bad elements have sneaked into the cadre ranks." [41]

In light of this official distinction between the majority of "common" mistakes and a minority of "more serious" errors, the Second Ten Points called for painstaking investigation and analysis of the attitudes and behavior of individual basic-level cadres. As we have seen, such investigations were to be carried out by resident Four Cleanup work teams through such techniques as "striking roots and linking up" with the local peasants—i.e., gaining the peasants' confidence by practicing the "three togethers," so that they would talk freely and candidly to members of the work teams about the deeds and misdeeds of local cadres.

The work teams were explicitly cautioned against confusing the two categories of common and more serious cadre errors, and were sternly warned against the leftist deviation of "failing to distinguish between contradictions among the people and contradictions with the enemy, exaggerating the enemy's strength, forming a bad opinion of basic-level cadres, and even regarding them as major targets for our blows." [42]

The vast majority of basic-level cadres were held to be "good or comparatively good, capable of standing firm on the socialist path." Their shortcomings and errors were attributed not to counterrevolutionary motives but to insufficiently high class-consciousness. Accordingly, the methods prescribed for rectifying the "four uncleans" of these rural cadres were primarily those of "patient education and persausion" and "voluntary restitution," with organizational punishment being accorded only a secondary, supplementary role in those cases where aberrant cadres steadfastly refused to acknowledge or remedy their mistakes:

"The general principle is: employ education and supplement it with punishment; . . . be strict in criticism and the recovery of misappropriated money and valuables, and lenient in handling by the organization; be strict with those who resist and lenient with those who admit their errors." [43]

As for the five percent among the basic-level cadres whose mistakes were allegedly serious, it was held that careful analysis was necessary to distinguish between "degenerates beyond salvation, landlords, rich peasants, counterrevolutionaries, and bad elements who have sneaked into the cadre ranks," on the one hand, and "those who . . . have established ties with the class enemy . . . or have been won over by the landlords and bourgeoisie," on the other. The former category reportedly included "only slightly more than one percent" of the rural cadre force. Cadres in this category were to be treated as class enemies and "purged completely." The remaining "two, three, or four percent" of seriously unclean basic-level cadres were regarded as being "different from the class enemy." In dealing with them, methods of education, reform, and consolidation were deemed appropriate. [44]

In order to provide operational guidelines to assist work teams in the field and higher-level Party organs in the determination of appropriate disciplinary measures for wayward cadres, the Second Ten Points adopted a somewhat arbitrary rule of thumb whereby the total number of cadres targeted to receive organizational punishment (i.e., demotion, dismissal, or imprisonment) was tentatively "fixed at two percent, with the county as the unit." [45]

To ensure against excessive harshness in the handling of four unclean cadres, it was stipulated that "In those cases where it cannot be readily determined whether the [error in question] is a contradiction with the enemy or an internal contradiction among the people, the problem should first be handled as an internal contradiction among the people." Finally, to make certain that objectivity and reason would prevail in the determination of disciplinary measures, it was ruled that the disposition of individual cases would generally be put off "until the latter stages of the movement, when the leadership and the masses have cooled off somewhat." [46]

On the whole, the policy line of the Second Ten Points with respect to the conduct of the Four Cleanups campaign was relatively mild and tolerant. Although full financial compensation and restitution were called for in all cases of proven cadre corruption, the primary emphasis of the campaign was clearly educative rather than punitive, with the object being "to treat the illness in order to save the patient," and thereby "unify and consolidate over 95 percent of the cadres." In this respect, the Second Ten Points differed only marginally, if at all, from the First Ten Points. [47]

"Red" or "Revisionist"?

Let us return now to the question with which we began our discussion of the Second Ten Points—that of the document's alleged anti-Maoist nature. On the basis of the preceding textual analysis, it appears that Teng Hsiao-p'ing's September 1963 directive, although clearly liberal in many respects, was not nearly so blatantly counterrevolutionary as some of its critics—both within and without China—have suggested. [48]

The official charges against Teng Hsiao-p'ing have stressed that

The Second Ten Points . . . discarded the line, principles, and policies concerning the Socialist Education Movement which Chairman Mao had explicitly formulated in the First Ten Points. On the pretext of setting out clear-cut "criteria for implementing specific policies," it used a hundred and one devices to absolve the capitalist forces in the rural areas, bind the masses hand and foot, and in every way protect the agents of the bourgeoisie within the Party. On the pretext of conducting "socialist education," it directed the spearhead of struggle against the poor and lower-middle peasants. In producing this monstrous poisonous weed, that other top bourgeois powerholder [Teng Hsiao-p'ing] tried in vain to carry out the bourgeois reactionary line.[49]

In light of our analysis, it would appear that among these charges and allegations, those concerning the "absolution of rural capitalist forces" and the "binding of the masses hand and foot" are not without some ostensible justification. However, the remaining charges seem to be rather more spurious and unfounded.[50]

Whether or not Teng Hsiao-p'ing actually intended to "absolve the capitalist forces in the rural areas," the fact remains that the Second Ten Points did, on the whole, tend to blur rather than sharpen the distinction between "friends" and "enemies." In holding that the vast majority of four category elements could be reformed through proper methods of education and persuasion, the September 1963 directive served at least indirectly to blunt the spearhead of class struggle. And in holding that those relatively affluent peasants who pursued the path of individualism in the countryside should not be punished for their spontaneous capitalist tendencies except in extreme cases of blatant criminal behavior, the Second Ten Points did indeed, as Professor Vogel has pointed out, subtly depart from Mao's original intent as expressed in the First Ten Points.[51]

Most important, however, the Second Ten Points clearly embodied a spirit of legalism and circumspection that was in some respects tacitly detrimental to the Maoist goal of mass political mobilization in the countryside. The rural peasants, as we have seen, were prohibited by the Second Ten Points from conducting mass struggle meetings against four category elements; nor were they permitted to directly judge or determine punishments for four unclean cadres. Peasants' organizations were only allowed to participate on a nonvoting, consultative basis in the determination of local administrative policies. Party cadres were to be shielded from the masses by having their errors and shortcomings criticized and rectified behind closed doors; and all disciplinary measures against local class enemies and unclean cadres (both Party and non-Party) were to be delayed until the latter stages of the movement, when the masses had "cooled off." All verdicts in such cases needed the prior approval of higher-level Party committees before being carried out. Finally, there was the somewhat arbitrary (and distinctly lenient) provision for a two percent maximum quota for punishable offenses by class enemies and corrupt cadres.

All of the above substantive and procedural measures were ostensibly designed to prevent the occurrence of ultra-leftist excesses of political violence and arbitrary criminal denunciations in the course of the Socialist Education Movement; all of them, moreover, served as definite restraints against direct political action by the rural masses. In this sense, the Second Ten Points did serve at least indirectly to "bind the masses hand and foot." The important question, however, is whether in establishing such legalistic safeguards Teng Hsiao-p'ing was consciously seeking to obfuscate the main lines of the "struggle between two roads" and thereby promote the bourgeois reactionary line, as charged, or whether he was rather attempting to ensure that necessary caution and "due process" would be observed in the implementation of the Socialist Education Movement. My own inclination is strongly toward the latter point of view; yet it must be conceded that the pronounced overtones of legalism, liberalism, and political tolerance that permeated the Second Ten Points may have had the effect of tacitly undermining the spirit, if not the letter, of Mao's thesis on class struggle.[52]

3   FROM SPOT-TESTING TO KEYPOINTS: THE SMALL FOUR CLEANUPS

ALTHOUGH THE SECOND TEN POINTS would later be condemned as a "monstrous poisonous weed," there is no
record of such derogations having been made—or even intimated—
during the period immediately following the promulgation of the
document in September 1963. On the contrary, throughout the autumn of 1963 and 1964 official Party media uniformly stressed the
correctness of the various policy formulations that had been incorporated into the September 1963 directive. A few examples selected from the mass media of this period will serve to illustrate
this point.

One of the more controversial features of the Second Ten Points,
as we have seen, was the emphasis upon the need to distinguish
clearly between legitimate family sideline occupations (the small-
scale peddling activities and temporary transport and marketing
business undertaken by the majority of commune members) and
the more serious capitalist tendencies, speculations, and market-
disturbing activities of a few "bad elements." In December 1963,
the *Southern Daily* published an important editorial reaffirming the

liberal guidelines that had been set forth in the Second Ten Points. In restating the Party's class line of "relying upon the poor and lower-middle peasants, uniting with the middle peasants, and winning over all who can be won over (including the absolute majority of the upper-middle peasants)" [sic], this editorial stressed the need to refrain from using methods of struggle in all but "a very small number of serious cases" involving conscious and active attempts to undermine the interests of the state, the collective, and the peasant masses. The stated purpose of this injunction was "to prevent the alienation of the majority of upper-middle peasants who, though possessing rather more serious spontaneous capitalist tendencies, have demonstrated superior qualities as producers." [1]

Secondly, throughout the latter part of 1963 the mass media continued to stress that a major aim of the Socialist Education Movement was to promote agricultural production. Periodic reminders were issued to rural cadres and work teams that class struggles should not be allowed to detract from production struggles, and that socialist education work must be "strictly coordinated with production." [2]

A third controversial feature of the Second Ten Points was the explicit order that outside work teams refrain from shunting aside, monopolizing, or otherwise slighting or bypassing the leadership of local basic-level cadres. This injunction was repeated in a number of official media reports in the period following the promulgation of the September 1963 directive. For example, the authoritative *People's Daily*, in early October, published an investigation report written by the leader of a socialist education work team:

When at first our cadres went out to production teams to work, they did not pay any attention to giving play to the role of the production team cadres, and even concerned themselves with supervising details "as small as a sesame seed." As a result, . . . they fostered the idea of "depending on others" on the part of the team cadres. Later, this [erroneous] method of monopolizing work and taking over work from others was changed. [3]

The above examples all tend to point toward the conclusion that if the Second Ten Points was truly a "monstrous poisonous weed," as charged, it was most certainly not recognized or treated as such at the time. Nowhere in the official Party media of this period are there any indications of an attempt to significantly modify or repudiate the major policy formulations of the Second Ten Points.[4] More important, there is substantial, direct evidence that Mao Tse-tung had explicitly approved the dissemination of the Second Ten Points. For example, in March 1964 the Chairman personally directed that the "Double Ten Points" (i.e., the First and Second Ten Points, collectively) were thenceforth to be required reading material for all cadres and peasants throughout the countryside: "Recently we held a discussion to ratify two documents from members of the Central Committee. . . . These documents are being read to the masses. . . . I have recommended that whoever is not old and infirm, whoever is not illiterate, and whoever has prestige among the masses should take part in this reading." [5]

In a similar vein, in April 1964 Mao personally commended a plan by Public Security Minister Hsieh Fu-chih to popularize the Double Ten Points among all labor reform prisoners in China.[6] These facts strongly support the hypothesis that the Second Ten Points were not perceived as a revisionist-inspired "monstrous poisonous weed" until long after the fact of their promulgation.[7]

Whether or not there was a conscious conspiracy afoot to enervate Mao's radical thesis of class struggle, the net effect of both the Second Ten Points and the ensuing propaganda campaign in the mass media was to ensure that the Socialist Education Movement would be a relatively low-key affair. To be sure, a great deal of lip-service was paid in the autumn of 1963 to the need for intensifying mass vigilance against class enemies in the countryside,[8] but very few concrete programmatic measures were introduced to operationalize or institutionalize such vigilance. Political struggles were in effect subordinated to production struggles, and the Socialist Education Movement was largely didactic and normative in content, rather than negative and coercive. The metaphorical phrase "light breeze and gentle rain" was used frequently in this period to describe the nature of the movement.[9]

The first signs of an impending intensification of the rural Socialist Education Movement came in the winter of 1963–64, when the Maoist slogan "let politics take command" (*cheng-chih kua-shuai*) was raised to a position of prominence in the national Party media. In February 1964 the Chinese People's Liberation Army (PLA) was held up as a model of political and ideological virtue for the entire nation to emulate. At the same time, the call went out to "actively cultivate the revolutionary successor generation." It was also in this period that the campaign of vilification against Soviet "modern revisionism" began to reach near fever pitch in China. And it was in 1964 that the cult of Mao-study was first propagated among Party members and cadres on a nationwide scale.[10] As it was with these developments, so it was with the Socialist Education Movement, which left the experimental spot-testing stage in the winter of 1963–64 to enter the more intensive stage of "keypoint" implementation.

The traditional Maoist approach to conducting mass political movements in China has been to divide a given campaign into three successive stages: preliminary, eclectic spot-testing (*shih-tien*); intermediary, concentrated keypoint (*chung-tien*) work; and universal (*ch'uan-mien:* lit., "all around") extension. The purpose of the first, or experimental stage, is, as we have seen, to gather experience through trial-and-error by using various different approaches and methods. Following the summing-up of such experiments, and the selection of appropriate methods and techniques, the movement is then conducted intensively at a limited number of preselected geographical keypoints. Finally, these keypoint areas serve as cadre training grounds and demonstration centers in the ultimate drive to expand the movement outward to all surrounding areas. This "group-by-group and stage-by-stage" method is known generically as "from the 'point' to the 'plane,'" or "the 'point' leads the 'plane'" (*i tien tai mien*).[11]

The *People's Daily*, in its annual New Year "state of the nation" editorial of January 1, 1964, gave the first concrete indication of the coming shift from spot-testing to concentrated keypoint work in the Socialist Education Movement. After presenting a rather confident and optimistic assessment of the movement's initial accomplishments in 1963, the editorial went on to call for even more vigorous and penetrative promotion of the campaign in the coming year:

In the New Year, we must carry forward the Socialist Education Movement in even greater depth and breadth; we must carry it out group by group and stage by stage. Cadres at all levels throughout the country must participate in the movement in an organized and planned manner, on the one hand helping basic-level organs to carry out their work more effectively, and on the other hand receiving self-education along with the broad masses. . . . Working personnel [i.e., work teams] who take part in this movement must all conscientiously study the relevant Party documents [i.e., the First and Second Ten Points] and accurately grasp the policies and methods of the movement. In the countryside, they should do detailed, intensive work, mobilizing and relying upon the poor and lower-middle peasant masses and uniting with the entire peasantry. Moreover, they should do their utmost to eat, live, and labor together with the poor and lower-middle peasants.

Class education, and education in socialism, collectivism, patriotism, and internationalism should first be carried out among Party members and afterwards among the masses. . . . On the foundation of doing good work in ideological education, we must . . . improve the operations and management of the collective economy of the people's communes, . . . strengthen the system of cadre participation in collective productive labor, strengthen the Party's basic-level organizations, and strengthen the leading nucleus in the communes, brigades, and production teams. All these items of work must be closely coordinated with production work and should serve to promote production. . . .[12]

Despite the rather confident and optimistic tone of the *People's Daily* New Year editorial, and despite the fact that the economic situation in China was somewhat brighter at the beginning of 1964 than it had been a year earlier,[13] the decision to move from the preliminary spot-testing stage to the more intensive keypoint phase of the Socialist Education Movement was not made in an atmosphere of complacency or self-satisfaction. On the contrary, there were clear indications that Mao Tse-tung was not at all pleased with the progress of the movement.

Complaining in March 1964 that many provincial Party officials had conducted their spot-testing experiments with undue haste and superficiality, the Chairman sternly warned his comrades against trying to complete the movement too rapidly: "Some provinces want to finish socialist education this year. That's too fast. To speed it up or hurry it too much will not do. If you press it excessively, it will be done in a phoney manner." [14] Reflecting on the adverse consequences of such excessive haste, Mao concluded that "It is not strange that spot-testing has failed. We must pay attention to summing up the lessons of failure." [15]

Mao also expressed his displeasure in March 1964 with "some people" who advocated terminating the Four Cleanups and supplanting it with an emulation campaign to study the Tach'ing oilfield and the People's Liberation Army. In a blunt rebuke to such people, the Chairman stated that "This [idea] represents the faction which does not carry out class struggle." [16]

Despite the Chairman's obvious misgivings about the revolutionary dedication of some of his comrades, the mass media continued to paint a rosy picture of rural political conditions in the first half of 1964. Throughout this period, the Socialist Education Movement was publicly hailed as a campaign full of health and vitality. For example, in late February the First Secretary of the Central-South regional bureau of the Central Committee, T'ao Chu, claimed that

It is clear that excellent results have been achieved in those places where the Socialist Education Movement has been carried out: heavy blows have been dealt at the disruptive activities of the capitalist and remnant feudal forces; the class force of the poor and lower-middle peasants has been further strengthened; the mass of cadres have raised their level of revolutionary consciousness . . . ; thus the relations between cadres and masses have become closer. . . . An excellent situation has taken shape in the countryside. . . . The victorious development of this movement . . . will greatly consolidate the socialist position in the rural areas . . . and ensure that the clock will never be turned back in our country. With completion of this education movement, the nation will see a prosperous new situation.[17]

Such public displays of optimism and confidence by regional and provincial Party leaders stood in marked contrast to Mao Tsetung's mounting private sense of malaise. This contrast, born of the increasingly divergent political and institutional interests of the Chairman and his bureaucracy, was further exacerbated in the spring of 1964 as the Socialist Education Movement moved from experimental spot-testing to intensive keypoint investigations.

The Point and the Plane

The Second Ten Points had called for close coordination of socialist education work on the "point" and the "plane." Work at rural keypoints was to be conducted systematically and intensively for a period of three months. Work on the broad plane, on the other hand, was to be less concentrated and time-consuming, requiring "only about 20 days." [18] According to the September 1963 directive, the primary differences in the mode of implementation of the movement at the point and on the plane were three: (1) Party-led work teams would be dispatched only to keypoint rural areas and would not be employed on the broad plane; (2) the work of organizing poor and lower-middle peasants' associations was to be a major priority at keypoints but was not to be undertaken "in a hurry" on the broad plane; and (3) routine, didactic political and ideological education of peasants and cadres was to be stressed on the plane, while more concentrated efforts at mass mobilization, purification of class ranks, and systematic "cleansing" of basic-level cadres were to be emphasized at keypoints. [19]

On the plane, various time-tested methods of mass education and indoctrination were employed in the Socialist Education Movement in the spring of 1964. Among the most favored of these were the convocation of "recall-the-past" meetings, compilation of the "four histories," and a general campaign on the part of Party members, Youth League members, and local cadres to "talk about, demonstrate, discuss, record, and spread" the lessons of class education and education in socialism among the peasantry. In addition, the emulative movement to "compare, study, catch-up, and help" *(pi, hsüeh, kan, pang)* was stressed as a means of strengthening economic work in those production brigades and teams which had lagged behind. Systems of regulating cadre participation in labor were also normalized in this period with the universal adoption of the "three fixes" principle: fixed labor norms, fixed work-point subsidies, and fixed squatting points. Finally, socialist education work on the plane included the initiation of a mass propaganda campaign designed to promote the selection and public recognition of "five good" commune members and cadres at the basic levels.[20]

In contrast to the (continued) low-key conduct of socialist education work on the plane, the main content of which was limited to didactic, normative education and persuasion, the work of initiating concentrated keypoint investigations and demonstrations was conducted with significantly greater intensity in the spring of 1964. Unfortunately, the official mass media remained almost totally silent in this period on the subject of such intensive keypoint work; hence, we are forced to rely almost exclusively upon the oral testimony of refugees and the retrospective revelations made by Red Guards and other participants in the recent Cultural Revolution for information concerning the events of this period.[21]

In recruiting, training, and dispatching work teams to rural keypoint units, an "avoidance system" was used wherein no member of a work team was permitted to squat at a point in his native county. Thus, for example, Party members and cadres from county X would be sent to basic-level units in county Y to undertake their keypoint investigations. The purpose of this avoidance system (which, incidentally, is similar to the traditional Chinese imperial practice of prohibiting county magistrates from serving in their home districts) was to ensure a dispassionate, objective attitude on the part of work team personnel, and thereby reduce the likelihood that conflicts of interest would emerge.

Before their deployment to rural keypoint units, a number of politically reliable leading cadres were selected from Party organs at each level from the province to the commune to attend training classes, either at the provincial or county headquarters. The training period varied from several weeks to several months, and consisted of four stages: (1) repetitive study and group discussion of relevant Party documents; (2) conscientious criticism and self-criticism by each participant; (3) listening to, summing-up, and critically discussing detailed investigative reports delivered by various leading officials who had taken part in previous spot-testing experiments; and (4) intensive study of the local political and economic conditions and personnel files (*tang-an*) of individual cadres and peasants in the keypoint communes and production brigades to which the work teams were to be assigned. In this manner, the leaders of the work teams were expected to "dump their burdens," raise their level of ideological understanding, become thoroughly familiar with the policies and methods of the movement, and acquaint themselves in advance with the local economic and political conditions and problems of their respective keypoints.

In addition to the selection and intensive training of a core group of responsible senior officials from leading Party organs at each level, a substantially larger number of lower-level cadres and working personnel were recruited from Party and governmental offices, Army units, and schools and universities throughout the provinces to serve as "ordinary" members of the socialist education work teams. These ordinary personnel were also required to attend training sessions before their deployment, but their training was less rigorous and intensive, and generally lasted only from 10 to 14 days.

Work team personnel, once trained, were assigned to individual rural areas, which had been preselected as keypoints.[22] At each level within the provincial hierarchy of work team organization, responsible cadres were assigned to supervise operations. Ordinary members of the work teams (many of whom were not Party members) had little or no independent decision-making authority, and were required to accept orders from, and report directly on all operational matters to, the responsible cadres of their unit, who were in turn required to report on all matters of importance to their immediate superiors. In this way, a hierarchical chain of command and responsibility was established which led all the way from the individual work team member in a production team to the county-level "leading group" in charge of the Socialist Education Movement, and ultimately to the provincial, regional, and central Party apparatus.[23]

Once the work teams arrived at their rural squatting points, their major functions, as indicated earlier, were to investigate local political and economic conditions and, by striking roots and linking up with local poor and lower-middle peasants, to gather information on the attitudes and behavior of local cadres. A division of labor was generally observed. Routine political and ideological indoctrination work was conducted by local Party and Youth League branches, while the work teams mainly concerned themselves with visiting poor and lower-middle peasants and conducting the Four Cleanups among local cadres. It was the importance of this latter function that led to the widespread substitution of the term "four cleanup work teams" for the previously more widely used "socialist education work teams."

As might be expected, local rural cadres and peasants (in particular those who may have had something to hide) were not always pleased to play host to the work teams. And there was often a perceptible mood of anxiety and apprehension among the local populace when it was learned that a group of "outsiders" was about to arrive at a given commune or production brigade. For this reason, Party authorities generally attempted to avoid advance disclosure of the identity of those communes and brigades which had been preselected as keypoints. Nevertheless, and despite such precautions, the local "grapevine" in the countryside often accurately predicted the imminent arrival of a work team, with the result that a high state of tension and rumor-mongering often preceded such a visit.

Typically, the work teams began their Four Cleanup investigations by attempting to allay the tensions and fears of the local peasants. On the day of the work team's arrival, a mass meeting of all commune members in the keypoint unit was generally convened. At this preliminary meeting, the purpose of the work team's visit was outlined to the local peasants and cadres. The leaders of the work team attempted to put the local populace at their ease by stressing the positive functions of the Socialist Education Movement. The peasants were told that the work team had come to help them solve their economic problems, and that they had nothing to fear. At this preliminary stage, nothing was said about the goals of exposing and rectifying "four unclean" local cadres or initiating class struggles against the serious spontaneous capitalist tendencies of well-to-do local peasants.

Following the convocation of the initial mass meeting, the ordinary work team personnel were dispersed to individual production teams to strike roots with a few local poor peasants who had been preselected for their reputed political reliability. Acting under strict orders to practice the "three togethers" with the peasants, the work team personnel (generally one to three workers per production team) took up residence in the homes of these "roots." The work team members always brought their own bedding and eating utensils, and paid for their meals out of funds provided by the Party.[24]

Because many of the ordinary work team personnel were students or teachers fresh from the city—with little or no experience in rustic rural living—a certain culture gap existed between these "intellectual" outsiders and the local peasantry, many of whom were either totally or partially illiterate. Moreover, a large number of these urban intellectuals, by virtue of their relative elite status, had never experienced the physical burdens of farm labor, and many quickly became disillusioned with the discomfort involved in practicing the "three togethers" with the peasants. For these reasons, a certain amount of tension and hard feelings frequently arose between the local peasants and the urban squatters. Subsequently, Chairman Mao strongly criticized the behavior of some of the urban intellectuals who had gone down to the countryside to participate in the work teams: "Some professors were in the work teams, and they weren't as good as their assistants. . . . The professors have read too many books. . . . Can an intellectual fight after a few years of reading? . . . When these people go down, they obstruct the Four Cleanups. Their purpose is not to engage in the movement." [25]

In order to alleviate such problems, it was made mandatory in many areas for the work team members to regularly attend study sessions to help them overcome both their resistance to newly encountered physical hardships and their attitude of looking down upon the crude and culturally backward "country bumpkins." [26]

While the ordinary work team members were striking roots and generally attempting to ingratiate themselves with the local peasants, the responsible members of the work teams convened cadre meetings at the commune and production brigade headquarters. At these closed-door sessions, the major political tasks of the work teams were fully revealed for the first time. The local cadres were now told that the work teams had been sent down to investigate, expose, and rectify the economic and administrative malpractices of basic-level cadres and other "bad elements." The cadres were told that those who cooperated in the investigations by freely and voluntarily "dumping their burdens" and "taking a warm bath" (i.e., conscientiously admitting their errors and making financial restitution) would be treated leniently, while those who tried to cover up their own misdeeds, or the misdeeds of their friends and relatives, or who otherwise attempted to obstruct the work team's investigation, would be treated more severely.[27]

In the meantime, ordinary work team personnel, after a preliminary period of striking roots among the local peasantry, gradually began to solicit their candid opinions about the quality of the local cadres. Many peasants were at first reluctant to discuss their true feelings with the outsiders, fearing that if they said anything critical about the local cadres, the officials would retaliate against them after the work team had departed. "Work teams come and go," ran one common saying, "but the cadres remain. Who will protect us then?"

In order to overcome such natural reticence, work team members invariably began their inquiries by raising relatively minor problems. For example, if they raised a question about a local cadre who was suspected of corruption,[28] they would initially confine their questioning to problems concerning the cadre's leadership style or his manner of dealing with the peasants in day-to-day situations. No direct suggestions of graft or corruption were made by the work team members at this preliminary stage. In many cases this soft-sell approach worked, and the peasants gradually began to feel free to discuss the behavior of the local cadres in greater depth and detail.

The work teams also made a special effort to cultivate the friendship of younger peasants in the production team, since the youths were generally more willing to candidly discuss local problems than were their more cautious and conservative elders. The work team members thus made it a special point to join in various recreational activities along with the village youngsters.

When the first wave of rural work teams began their initial key-point investigations in the late winter and spring of 1964, their major targets of attack were corrupt elements among the ordinary (non-Party) cadres at the production brigade and team levels—the accountants, work-point recorders, and storehouse-keepers—together with the most notorious criminal elements among the local landlords and rich peasants.[29] The principal cadres (*chu-yao kan-pu*) at the commune and production brigade levels—the Party branch secretaries, commune and brigade leaders, militia chiefs, and Youth and Women's work directors (all of whom were Party members)—were generally exempted from investigation in this early period, as were the upper-middle peasants and less criminally inclined four category elements.[30]

In many instances, the work team leaders sought the cooperation of, and relied heavily upon, local principal cadres for assistance in the conduct of their investigations. As it turned out, however, this frequently proved to be counterproductive; the principal cadres were often either directly or indirectly complicit in the financial misdeeds of their basic-level subordinates, and by relying upon local Party elites for information, the work teams thus in many cases unwittingly contributed to the concealment, rather than the exposure, of corruption. As one refugee informant (a former ordinary work team member) put it:

> The brigade leaders and Party branch secretaries in our squatting point were put in charge of struggling against the accountants who had committed corruption. But since the embezzlement of public funds by basic-level accountants generally required the active assistance or tacit cooperation of these very same brigade leaders and Party branch secretaries, criticism of the accountants was usually quite superficial—only a "hurried glance." [31]

A second reason for the ostensible superficiality with which many rural work teams handled the investigation and rectification of basic-level "four unclean" cadres in this period lay in the reluctance of the work teams to antagonize the local authorities. As Professor Vogel had observed, "Cadres sent down to lower levels, being less familiar with local situations, were reluctant to push criticism of the local cadres too far for fear of undermining their authority, detracting from production, and perhaps even consolidating local resistance. They found it easier to avoid stirring up local sentiments." [32]

This same consideration—unwillingness to stir up what might prove to be a local hornets' nest—also operated in many instances to prevent the work teams from conscientiously exposing and criticizing the spontaneous capitalist tendencies of local peasants. For, again in Professor Vogel's words, the work teams often "sympathized with the plight of local peasants and were reluctant to curb private activities for fear of lowering still further the peasants' activism and standard of living." [33]

Throughout the first half of 1964, rural Four Cleanup work teams, in compliance with the provisions of the Second Ten Points, operated under a two to five percent quota system for punishing seriously unclean basic-level cadres and unreformed four category elements. With the county as a unit, a maximum of five percent of the local cadres and four category elements were targeted for struggle, although in the case of ordinary cadres a substantially larger percentage (often as high as 50–60 percent in a given keypoint brigade) were the recipients of significantly milder forms of criticism and "persuasive education." In general, the Four Cleanups movement in this period thus conformed to the established pattern of a "light breeze and gentle rain."

A major problem encountered by some work teams in their rural keypoint investigations (in addition to the aforementioned problems of peasant apprehensiveness, work-team conservatism, and cadre collusion) was the tendency toward irresponsible and perfidious denunciation of local cadres on the part of a small number of self-interested peasants. In some instances, peasants who for various reasons harbored personal or political antipathies against individual cadres took advantage of the protection afforded by the presence of the work teams to falsely (or exaggeratedly) accuse local officials of corruption, theft, or general misbehavior. In order to guard against such perfidy, all cases in which there was the suspicion of bad faith or impure motives on the part of the accusers were referred to higher-level authorities (usually at the county level, where the personnel files of local cadres and peasants were kept) for further investigation.

All cases involving allegations of corruption committed by Party members (as opposed to ordinary cadres) were also routinely sent upward for higher-level investigation and disposition. Finally, all cases involving economic or political crimes that were deemed upon initial investigation to be of a serious nature (whether committed by Party members, ordinary cadres, or four category elements) were similarly passed up to county-level Party authorities for final disposition. In this manner, the work teams were able in many cases to avoid assuming direct responsibility for making on-the-spot judgments—judgments that generally carried with them a certain amount of inherent political risk for the judges as well as for the accused, since there was always the possibility that they would hand down erroneous or unpopular verdicts, thereby rendering themselves vulnerable to future recriminations or disciplinary measures.[34]

In those instances where cases of cadre corruption were dealt with on-the-spot by work teams, the accused were initially confronted with their alleged crimes behind closed doors, in cadre meetings chaired by a responsible member of the work team. After the charges were read by the work team leader and the evidence was summarized, the accused was offered a way out if he would fully confess his misdeeds and pledge to return or compensate for all misappropriated funds or properties. If the charge was a relatively minor one, and if the confession was judged to have been sincere, the case was generally considered closed. On the other hand, if there was some doubt about the accused's sincerity, or if the accused continued to deny his guilt, subsequent open-door meetings would be held at which a limited number of local poor and lower-middle peasant representatives would be invited to participate in the hearing and the disposition of the case. Such meetings were generally informal, low-key affairs, at which both the "prosecution" and the "defense" were given the opportunity to present evidence, call witnesses, and cross-examine the opposition. In general, kangaroo-court tactics were not employed in these meetings, and mass "accusation rallies" and struggle meetings were held in only a small minority of cases.

Such was the essential nature of the initial keypoint stage of the

Socialist Education Movement in the first half of 1964. Work team investigations in this period were generally conducted in an atmosphere of relative calmness and discretion. The peasant masses had not as yet been fully mobilized, and the focus of the campaign was almost exclusively upon the rectification of petty economic corruption by ordinary rural cadres and habitual village troublemakers. By and large, the rural Party apparatus emerged unscathed from this stage of the movement.

For all of the above reasons, the first half of 1964 has been (retrospectively) identified as the period of the so-called "Small Four Cleanups" (*hsiao ssu-ch'ing*). With a few exceptions, to be discussed shortly, this stage of the movement was conducted by rural work teams in accordance with the relatively liberal and legalistic spirit of the Second Ten Points.

The Gathering Storm

The Small Four Cleanups lasted until the late summer of 1964, when suddenly, and without prior warning, Liu Shao-ch'i and his wife, Wang Kuang-mei, issued the call for a drastic intensification of the Four Cleanups campaign. This call, which was initially presented in the form of an investigation report delivered by Wang Kuang-mei in mid-July, and which was formalized with Liu's personal revision of the Second Ten Points some two months later, heralded the intensification of the Socialist Education Movement from an invigorating "light wind and gentle rain" to a full-scale political typhoon.

Two important but relatively unpublicized events immediately preceded the campaign's intensification. The first of these was the convocation of a working conference of top-level Party elites, at which Mao Tse-tung personally set down six operational criteria for evaluating the success or failure of the Socialist Education Movement. The second was the promulgation of a Central Committee directive governing the organization and functions of rural poor and lower-middle peasants' associations.[35]

Both events occurred in June 1964, although they went unreported at the time. Mao's "six criteria" for evaluating the Socialist

Education Movement were articulated at an enlarged meeting of the Standing Committee of the CCP Politburo, attended by the first secretaries of the six regional Party bureaus of the Central Committee. At this meeting, Mao asked:

What are the appropriate standards for measuring the work of the Socialist Education Movement? First, we must see whether the poor and lower-middle peasants have been truly mobilized. Second, we must see whether the problem of the "four uncleans" among the cadres has been thoroughly resolved. Third, have the cadres joined in physical labor? Fourth, has a good leading nucleus been set up? Fifth, when landlords, rich peasants, counterrevolutionaries, and bad elements who engage in destructive activities are exposed, are such contradictions merely passed up to higher levels [for disposition], or are the masses mobilized to strictly supervise, criticize, and, when appropriate, struggle against these elements and detain them for on-the-spot reform? Sixth, we must see whether production has increased or decreased [as a result of the movement].[36]

The significance of these six criteria lay not only in their manifest content, but also in their order of presentation. Mao has, of course, always been greatly concerned with the political mobilization of China's rural peasantry.[37] The fact that peasant mobilization was the first standard enumerated by Mao in his June 1964 statement is indicative of his continuing overriding concern with this question.[38]

As we have seen, Mao undoubtedly had reason to be concerned; for in the first half of 1964, mass peasant mobilization had *not* (despite numerous official protestations to the contrary) held a high priority among rural work team personnel, the majority of whom had confined their squatting-point activities at this stage to carrying out secretive investigatory work among a relatively small number of preselected peasant "roots." [39] Consequently, peasant mobilization had not occurred on a large scale; and mass struggles against corrupt cadres had in general been minimized—with major emphasis being placed instead upon quiet and discreet (i.e., closed-door) investigations, criticism, and discipline, under the tight control of the work teams, local Party organs, and higher authorities. In this manner (as we saw in our earlier discussion of the implications of the Second Ten Points), the rural masses were in effect, if not by design, at least partially "bound hand and foot."

The second major concern evinced by Mao in his six criteria for assessing the Socialist Education Movement was related to the previously noted tendency toward superficiality in the cleansing of aberrant basic-level cadres in the first half of 1964. In calling for the thorough resolution of the problem of the four uncleans among rural cadres, Mao was tacitly criticizing the prevailing practices of conspiratorial concealment of cadre corruption and "hurried glances" (i.e., excessive tolerance and deliberate overlooking of official malpractices) by work teams and local Party officials alike.

Mao's concern with the problems of cadre participation in productive labor and the setting up of solid leading nuclei in the villages need not be belabored here. We have already discussed the nature and roots of Mao's apprehension over the rise of such phenomena as bureaucratism, commandism, divorce from the masses, and insufficient class consciousness among rural cadres in the early 1960s. Nor need we dwell on Mao's concern that agricultural production should not be adversely affected during and as a result of the Socialist Education Movement.[40]

Mao's fifth criterion, which was directly related to the criterion of mass peasant mobilization, concerned the previously noted tendency toward buckpassing on the part of work teams and local Party officials in matters pertaining to the determination of guilt and punishment of four category elements and capitalistically inclined upper-middle peasants. Mao had undoubtedly become distressed over the evident lack of mass peasant participation in these matters, and his call for on-the-spot mass supervision, criticism, and struggle against these elements clearly reflected this concern.

Concurrently with the issuance of Mao's six criteria, the Party Central Committee issued a draft directive entitled "Organizational Rules of Poor and Lower-Middle Peasants' Associations." This directive, which set down for the first time concrete guidelines for the formation and functioning of a poor and lower-middle peasant class army in the countryside, was ostensibly geared to the attainment of the Maoist objective of mass peasant mobilization.[41] Nevertheless, the text of this directive contained a curious mixture of orthodox Maoist prescriptions for mass participatory democracy and (heterodox?) Liuist prescriptions for Party centralization and control.[42] For this reason, the June 1964 directive (authorship of which has never been officially attributed to Mao, Liu, or any other individual Party leader) is the most difficult to categorize of all the available socialist education directives.

On the Maoist side of the ledger, the Central Committee regulations of June 1964 called upon poor and lower-middle peasants' associations to actively scrutinize and oversee the administrative behavior of cadres at each level in the communes. Specifically, the peasants' associations were empowered to "assist the management committees and cadres at each level in seriously implementing the work of cleaning-up accounts, granaries, properties, and workpoints [i.e., the Four Cleanups]. . . . They must promptly expose and criticize such actions [on the part of cadres] as eating too much or owning too much, extravagance and waste, nepotism, corruption, theft, and destruction of public property." [43] And in order to provide protection for those peasants who seriously undertook to expose and criticize such cadre malpractices, the June 1964 organizational rules explicitly prohibited local cadres from striking retaliatory blows against those peasants who might criticize them: "If, due to their criticism of the work of the commune, production brigade, or team, or because of their criticism of individual cadres, [the peasants] should be attacked as a means of gaining revenge, they have the right to demand the support of the peasants' association." [44]

With respect to the exercise of peasant "dictatorship" over four category elements in the countryside (another orthodox Maoist principle), the Central Committee regulations called upon the poor and lower-middle peasants' organizations to "regularly assist public security departments in strengthening the supervision and reformation of landlords, rich peasants, counterrevolutionaries, and bad elements. . . . They must expose all illegal and destructive activities; and they must, in the process of productive labor, effectively strengthen the work of reforming these elements." [45]

On the question of how the peasants' associations were to deal with spontaneous capitalist tendencies on the part of upper-middle peasants whose political and socioeconomic status were different from those of the four category elements, the new Central Committee regulations prescribed (again in good Maoist fashion) a strong watchdog function for the poor and lower-middle peasant masses. Peasants' associations were instructed to "regularly pay attention to preventing and checking the spread of spontaneous capitalist tendencies," and they were urged to "wage struggles against the forces of capitalism." With respect to exposing and controlling such adverse phenomena as "going it alone," "abandoning agriculture to go into business," encroaching upon collective or public property, speculation, and profiteering, the peasants' associations were called upon to "criticize the people who commit these mistakes; and, where conditions are serious, they must promptly expose such acts and propose that the departments concerned [i.e., local militia units and public security forces] handle these cases." [46]

Equally important were the propaganda and (self-) educational functions to be performed by the peasants' associations. These organizations were given a mandate to "rouse the broad masses of commune members to cultivate the spirit of bitter struggle, the spirit of enthusiastic emulation, and the spirit of self-reliance [tzu-li keng-sheng]," and they were instructed to "educate their own members to care about collective production, love and protect public property, be exemplary in complying with labor discipline, . . . raise labor efficiency, and develop the function of taking the lead in production." [47]

In sum, the poor and lower-middle peasants' associations were given not only the right but also the duty to concern themselves with virtually every aspect of the economic, administrative, political, educational, and propaganda functions of the people's communes. No decision on any matter of public concern was to be arbitrarily taken by local administrative cadres without first being discussed with—and opened to emendatory suggestions by—the poor and lower-middle peasants. In this respect, the Central Committee regulations of June 1964 conformed rather closely to the spirit of Mao's principle of participatory democracy.

On the other hand (and somewhat contradictorily), however, the text of the June 1964 regulations made it perfectly clear that the peasants' associations were to be regarded as functional auxiliaries of the Party—subject to tight organizational control and discipline by the rural Party apparatus. Thus, for example, in the Preface to the Central Committee directive it was explicitly stated that

> Poor and lower-middle peasants' associations are *organized and led by the Chinese Communist Party*. Party organizations at all levels—especially basic-level Party organizations in the countryside—must actively lead and support the work of the peasants' associations, thus enabling them to become *a powerful arm of the Party* [*tang te yu-li fu-shou*] and a strong organization which unites the Party with the laboring people throughout the countryside.[48]

Moreover, of the six basic tasks of the peasants' associations enumerated in the June 1964 organizational rules, first position was given to the task of "actively responding to the call of the Party Central Committee . . . to be exemplary in complying with and executing the policies and commands of the Party." [49] In this respect, the Central Committee regulations conformed rather closely to the prescriptions for absolute, unquestioning obedience to Party authority and discipline which were the hallmarks of Liu Shao-ch'i's approach to the tasks of mass organization and social control.[50]

The peasants' association regulations of June 1964 represented a tacit (if ultimately untenable) compromise between the Maoist and Liuist views on the role of the peasant masses. For Mao as well as for Liu, the main question was how to control excesses of spontaneous capitalism and cadre malfeasance in the villages. Their disagreement, as Schurmann—and others, such as Schapiro and Lewis—have pointed out, lay primarily on the issue of whether such control should be imposed from *below* (through all-out mobilization of the peasant masses) or from *above* (through reliance on the formal Party apparatus).[51]

The Central Committee's organizational rules neatly skirted this issue by calling for both mass peasant mobilization and strict Party control. This was indeed a compromise; but it was at best an uneasy and in some ways an inherently self-contradictory one. The nature and ramifications of this contradictoriness were not long in becoming manifest, as the "light breeze and gentle rain" of the Small Four Cleanups gave way in the latter half of 1964 to a more profound and violent political storm—the "Big Four Cleanups."

More than any other Party leaders, Liu Shao-ch'i and his wife, Wang Kuang-mei, were instrumental in bringing about this transition. It is to an examination of their role in the Socialist Education Movement in the critical period of July–September 1964 that we now turn for clues to the origins, objectives, and implications of the Big Four Cleanups.

4 LIU SHAO-CH'I, WANG KUANG-MEI AND THE "T'AOYÜAN EXPERIENCE"

FOLLOWING THE PROMULGATION OF Mao's six criteria and the Central Committee's organizational rules in June 1964, the rural Four Cleanups campaign underwent a marked change of emphasis. The initial keypoint phase of the campaign, as we have seen, had focused upon the exposure and rectification of minor economic corruption by ordinary basic-level cadres in the areas of accounts, properties, granary inventories, and work-points. The emphasis in this early period had been on the persuasive education of offenders, rather than on organizational discipline. For various reasons, discussed in the previous chapter, this early phase of the movement had failed to make a significant impact upon either the local Party apparatus or the peasant masses in many rural keypoint districts.

In the summer of 1964 the campaign entered a qualitatively new stage, which subsequently became known as the Big Four Cleanups. The new stage was initiated at a conference convened in Shanghai in mid-July, attended by some 3,000 high- and intermediate-level Party cadres. At this conference Wang Kuang-mei, the urbane, sophisticated wife of China's Chief of State, delivered a lengthy (70,000 word) address in which she summarized her personal experiences in squatting at a point in the T'aoyüan production brigade in Funing County, Hopei. Known as the "T'aoyüan Experience" (*T'ao-yüan Ching-yen*), Wang's investigation report triggered off what was to become the most severe and intensive rural purge in the history of the Chinese People's Republic.[1]

The T'aoyüan Experience

Along with many other high-ranking Party officials, Wang Kuang-mei had been placed in command of a work team and dispatched to a rural squatting-point in the early winter of 1963–64, where she was to undertake keypoint investigations in conjunction with the launching of the local Four Cleanups campaign.[2] Wang's team arrived at T'aoyüan in late November 1963, and remained there until April 1964. Throughout this five-month period Wang assumed the guise of an ordinary cadre. In order to conceal her true identity from the local populace, she adopted the pseudonym Tung P'u, donned ordinary working clothes, and wore a gauze mask over her face much of the time.[3]

The Four Cleanups began in the T'aoyüan brigade in a manner not unlike that previously described. First, a mass meeting of brigade members was convened, at which the local peasants were informed that the work team had come to link up and practice the "three togethers" in order to help solve local economic and administrative problems. Next, individual members of the work team, including Wang Kuang-mei herself, dispersed to "strike roots" with a few local residents who had been preselected for their reputed political reliability. These "roots" (a total of 20 old peasants and retired cadres in the T'aoyüan brigade) were used as confidential informants in the preliminary investigatory stage of the movement. All this, of course, was in conformity with both the spirit of the Second Ten Points and with the prevalent practice of the period.

Unlike other rural work teams, however, Wang Kuang-mei's T'aoyüan team did not confine itself to superficial investigations or "hurried glances" at local four unclean cadres and four category elements. Moreover, Wang's work team neither enlisted the active support and cooperation of the local Party branch nor self-consciously limited the depth and breadth of its search for deviant behavior. Party cadres, ordinary cadres, four category elements and peasants with varying degrees of spontaneous capitalist tendencies were all considered fair game for criticism and rectification by Wang Kuang-mei and her cleanup-minded colleagues. No one (with the possible exception of the work team's 20 local "roots") was exempted from detailed scrutiny.

Wang's investigations were initially carried out in relative secrecy. Relying almost exclusively on her local informants, she quietly gathered extensive evidence on the attitudes and behavior of T'aoyüan's cadres and peasants before making public disclosures or soliciting mass public opinion. Because of the secrecy of these preliminary investigations, an atmosphere of general anxiety pervaded the T'aoyüan brigade in the early stages of the campaign.

In their preliminary investigations, members of the T'aoyüan work team reportedly uncovered evidence of widespread economic graft, corruption, and spontaneous capitalism in the brigade—centering around the leading cadres of the local Party branch and extending all the way down to the masses of ordinary commune members. In one official report of the T'aoyüan work team's activities in this period, for example, Wang Kuang-mei was quoted as having said:

> We have earnestly studied the situation of [class] struggle in the T'aoyüan brigade. The 20-odd principal cadres of the brigade and its constituent production teams are linked together by their common four unclean interests. . . . Cadres of the brigade openly take things, production team cadres steal, and the commune members are forced to sew up [the cadres'] trouser legs. . . . The four uncleans exist universally among the cadres. All of them, big or small, have problems and cannot be trusted.[4]

With respect to the discovery and exposure of spontaneous capitalist tendencies among the local peasantry, it was reported that the T'aoyüan work team was extremely critical of even the most minor forms of private enterprise. For example, it was claimed that in the fourth production team of the T'aoyüan brigade, some 66 forms of capitalism were exposed, including such petty offenses as selling too many chickens on the local market and devoting too much time and effort to the development of family sideline enterprises. In the entire brigade, a total of 155 peasants were reportedly required to dump 513 separate "burdens" (i.e., self-examinations). Failure to voluntarily confess reportedly resulted in the alleged offender being publicly chastised and shamed in loudspeaker broadcasts or on local wall posters.[5]

In sum, Wang Kuang-mei apparently concluded on the basis of her preliminary investigations that the overall political and administrative situation in the T'aoyüan brigade was extremely critical, that the majority of local cadres were seriously unclean, and that spontaneous capitalism was running rampant in the brigade. After reporting these conclusions to her husband, Liu Shao-ch'i, Wang received written instructions to take appropriate steps to publicly criticize, struggle against, and where necessary dismiss and replace the "rotten" cadres in the brigade.[6] In a letter addressed to Wang Kuang-mei by her husband in the spring of 1964, Wang's highly critical assessment of the political situation in T'aoyüan was reaffirmed. "The T'aoyüan Party branch," wrote Liu, "basically does not belong to the Party; . . . it is basically a two-faced counterrevolutionary regime." [7]

As a result of Wang's assessment of the situation, and Liu's subsequent instructions to take all necessary remedial measures, a total of 40 (out of 47) existing brigade and production team cadres in T'aoyüan—representing 85 percent of the total—were reportedly criticized by Wang's work team in the spring of 1964. Among those actually purged in this period were such principal cadres as the secretary and deputy secretary of the brigade Party branch, the brigade leader and deputy leader (who were concurrently members of the Party branch), and the brigade's storehouse-keeper, together with a number of ordinary (non-Party) cadres at both the brigade and production team levels. These seriously unclean cadres were replaced by people hand-picked by the work team and its local "roots." In addition, two deputy leaders of the work team were selected to remain in the brigade to serve as interim principal cadres, pending the recruitment of new local personnel.

In this manner, within five months Wang Kuang-mei effected a near-total turnover in the leadership of the T'aoyüan brigade. This turnover, moreover, was accomplished by the use of such pre-

viously frowned-upon techniques as the convocation of mass struggle rallies and public accusation meetings; and in a few cases, self-
confessions were reportedly extracted from the accused under
various forms of physical duress.[8]

Such was the essential nature of Wang Kuang-mei's notorious
T'aoyüan Experience—as reconstructed from a series of (profoundly hostile) accounts that appeared in print some three years
after the fact, during the Cultural Revolution. In her Shanghai
speech of July 1964 (which, according to Wang, had received Mao's
tacit approval),[9] Mme. Liu summarized the main points of her
recently concluded squatting-point investigation as follows: (1) the
political situation in the countryside was more critical than had
been anticipated at the outset of the Socialist Education Movement;
(2) the four uncleans among basic-level cadres were both more
prevalent and more serious than had at first been anticipated; (3) to
thoroughly expose and rectify the four uncleans, it was necessary
to bypass existing basic-level Party organs entirely and conduct
direct, discreet investigations among a small number of local
"roots"; (4) open-door investigation meetings were to be avoided at
the outset of the movement, since the peasants at this early stage
were generally afraid to express their true feelings in the presence
of local cadres; (5) it was necessary for work team members to
avoid bringing along subjective "frames" (k'uang-k'uang) a mental
set or predisposition based on secondhand information) when
squatting at points, since such a priori "frames" often proved to be
based on unreliable sources, and thus tended to interfere with the
objectivity of the investigation; (6) organizational discipline (i.e.,
demotion or dismissal) was a necessary supplement to persuasive
education in the rectification of four unclean cadres, since in the
absence of such discipline the lessons of socialist education were
deemed likely to be forgotten rather quickly; and (7) "human sea"
tactics—i.e., the deployment of large numbers of work-team personnel to a given keypoint unit—were advisable whenever serious
leadership problems were thought to exist in the unit.[10]

In the course of the vilification campaign against Wang Kuang-
mei in 1967 and 1968, a number of post-facto accusations were
raised in both the official and Red Guard media concerning her

alleged counterrevolutionary crimes in the T'aoyüan brigade.[11] Many of these charges dealt with nothing more serious than the claim that, for example, Wang had neglected the study of Mao's works. Or, there was the claim that since Wang could not tolerate the poor quality of the local food, she made secret arrangements to have lavish meals shipped in to T'aoyüan at state expense. Yet another relatively minor charge was that while she always gave the appearance of diligently laboring together with the local peasants whenever a photographer happened to be nearby, she quickly abandoned such dissimulative postures after the pictures had been taken. Such alleged offenses—even if true—may by and large be dismissed as being more in the nature of personal foibles than major political crimes.

On the other hand, however, a number of more serious—and, for our purposes, more relevant—charges have been raised against Wang Kuang-mei. For example, it was officially claimed that Wang had selected as her local "roots" a number of peasants and former cadres who were themselves corrupt, who harbored long-standing personal grievances against the existing cadres, and who therefore made false (or exaggerated) accusations against these cadres in the investigatory stage of the movement—thus leading Wang to seriously distort the scope and magnitude of the four uncleans in the brigade. Or, to cite another example, it was alleged that in an attempt to modernize and beautify the brigade, and thereby ingratiate herself with the local populace, Wang had spent a total of ¥644,000 (U.S. $250,000) in state funds on such "frivolous" projects as the construction of a paved road, two power pumping stations, three wells, and an irrigation canal in the brigade—thereby contravening Mao's dictum concerning the need for rural economic self-reliance. Finally, Wang was accused of having commandeered large quantities of chemical fertilizers and a number of tractors, insecticide sprayers, and a threshing machine from neighboring production brigades—all for the purpose of enhancing T'aoyüan's appearance of prosperity. Such actions were reportedly justified by Wang on the ground that "It doesn't matter if other brigades have their [agricultural] output reduced, but there will be trouble if T'aoyüan's output is reduced."

The aggregate effect of Wang Kuang-mei's "irresponsible economism" was allegedly to erode the revolutionary will of the peasants of T'aoyüan, since it served to foster the "revisionist" idea of relying on state investment, agricultural mechanization, and material incentives for economic development and a rising standard of living.

It was not for her alleged economism, however, that Wang Kuang-mei was most heavily criticized during the Cultural Revolution. Rather, it was for her reputed counterrevolutionary policy of "attacking the many in order to protect the few" (*ta chi i ta-p'ien, pao-hu i hsiao-ts'o*) in the course of her squatting experience at T'aoyüan (and elsewhere) that she and her husband were most severely attacked by the Maoists. In order to gain further insight into the nature and implications of this latter allegation, and to gain an appreciation of the relevant facts and circumstances surrounding its occurrence during the Cultural Revolution, it is necessary to examine the personal role played by China's Chief of State, Liu Shao-ch'i, in the Socialist Education Movement in the months following Wang Kuang-mei's Shanghai speech of July 1964.

Liu Shao-ch'i and the Cadre Question

According to Wang Kuang-mei's personal testimony in her self-examination of April 1967, "many people were against my going to T'aoyüan; only Liu Shao-ch'i . . . [and] Chairman Mao backed me up." [12] In retrospect, it may be hypothesized that the "many people" referred to in this statement were those provincial and subprovincial Party leaders upon whose territory Mme. Liu was intruding. In view of the nature of the subsequent T'aoyüan Experience, these Party leaders had good reason to be concerned. For Wang Kuang-mei completely bypassed them in conducting her investigations, and the wholesale purge of the local Party establishment in T'aoyüan that resulted from these investigations could only reflect poorly upon the quality of Party leadership at the provincial, special-district, and county levels. [13] Moreover, there is evidence to indicate that local Party leaders in Funing County and T'angshan special district (the location of the T'aoyüan brigade) had opposed

Liu Shao-ch'i and Wang Kuang-mei's recommendations concerning the need for a thorough housecleaning in the brigade.[14]

The fact of the matter was that Wang's inflammatory T'aoyüan Experience ran completely counter to the prevalent "light breeze and gentle rain" tactics which had previously characterized the keypoint stage of the Small Four Cleanups. Since few Party bureaucrats could be expected to appreciate having outsiders make waves in their local bailiwicks, their resistance to the recommendations of Wang and Liu was not particularly surprising—even less so since the key decisions in the T'aoyüan case had been made without their prior knowledge or consent.[15]

Clearly, Liu Shao-ch'i and Wang Kuang-mei had stirred up a great deal of intra-Party controversy as a result of Wang's T'aoyüan Experience. And it was in the period immediately following Wang's Shanghai speech of July 1964 that Liu Shao-ch'i began to openly advocate a hard line approach to the question of cadre rectification.[16]

In late July and August 1964 Liu and Wang traveled extensively throughout the south-central region of China on an inspection tour of provincial and local Four Cleanup keypoint districts. During the tour, which included an 18-day sojourn in Hunan Province in addition to a series of relatively brief stopovers in Kwangtung, Honan, and Hupeh Provinces, Liu and Wang repeatedly emphasized the need for all leading personnel involved in the Four Cleanups campaign to study the T'aoyüan Experience. And in order to propagate the T'aoyüan Experience, tape recordings of Wang Kuang-mei's Shanghai speech were distributed during this tour to Party leaders in each province, to be used as a policy guide in training future four cleanup work teams.[17]

Following Liu and Wang's inspection tour of south-central China, they returned to Peking. There, in August 1964, Liu delivered a series of speeches and informal talks on the question of the progress of the Socialist Education Movement. The major thrust of Liu's analysis of the current situation, as revealed in fragments from these talks published in various Party and Red Guard journals during the Cultural Revolution, was that political conditions in the Chinese countryside were on the whole extremely grim, and that drastic organizational measures were necessary to rectify the situation.

In one of his August 1964 speeches (delivered to a meeting of Party cadres in Peking), Liu stated that "Although we have been carrying out the Four Cleanups for a whole year . . . in many areas we have not yet penetrated deeply enough or thoroughly enough. . . . Not only have we failed to win any victories in the past year, we have lost the battle." The gravity with which Liu viewed this situation was clearly revealed in another passage from the same speech. "One-third of the leadership power in basic-level units," said Liu, "is not in our hands, with [the percentage being] more or less in various places." [18]

The major obstacles in the path of victory in the Four Cleanups campaign, according to Liu's assessment of the situation in the late summer of 1964, were two: on the one hand, large numbers of basic-level Party organs and cadres were seriously unclean or "degenerate"—not just economically corrupt but politically and organizationally putrified as well; on the other hand, even those rural Party officials who were not themselves seriously unclean were alleged to have "not yet learned how to struggle against the two-faced [manipulations] of landlords, capitalists, and degenerate elements. . . . That is why our Party members and cadres lose the battle . . . and cannot defeat our enemies." [19]

Liu was also highly critical of those higher-level Party officials who had demonstrated a lack of firm resolve to wipe out the four uncleans in the countryside. In an obvious reference to the prevailing tendencies toward leniency and superficiality on the part of four cleanup work teams, Liu stated that "At present, where [squatting-point] investigation reports are concerned, there is no 'leftism'; there is only rightism; there is only moderation. Since investigation reports only lead to further rightism, one may as well dispense with them." [20]

Liu Shao-ch'i's proposed solution to the twin problems of unclean (or incapable) rural political leadership, and superficiality ("moderation") in the implementation of the Four Cleanups by work teams, was to lay renewed stress upon the need for stern organizational discipline. Thus, in a conversation reportedly held be-

tween Liu and Li Hsueh-feng (a ranking member of the Secretariat
of the Party Central Committee) in early October 1964, Liu Shao-
ch'i stated that work team leaders "must not be afraid to dismiss
from office many [basic-level Party members and cadres]. Only dismissal can save a person and make him truly correct his mistakes.
Never mind the number dismissed. Those [Party members and
cadres] who ought to be dismissed must be dismissed." [21] And in
order to ensure that leadership of the work teams would be grasped
by reliable and experienced cadres who would not hesitate to conduct thorough investigations, even if this meant treading on sensi-
tive local toes, Liu proposed that "only those people who have
previously taken part in the Four Cleanups are qualified to make
investigation reports. It is necessary to wait and see for at least one
year. Only after one has done a good job of squatting at points [for
one year] in connection with the Four Cleanups may he be qualified to make an investigation report. [22]

In the above passages, Liu Shao-ch'i tacitly reveals his opposition
to the 2 to 5 percent quota system that had been written into the
Second Ten Points. Here also, Liu reveals the outlines of his "hard
line" on the question of the Four Cleanups (a line subsequently criticized during the Cultural Revolution as " 'left' in form but right
in essence").

It is not merely by way of isolated fragments from Liu's assorted
speeches and conversations of this period that his growing pessimism over the political situation in the countryside can be demonstrated. For in September 1964, Liu personally supervised a
major revision of Teng Hsiao-p'ing's Second Ten Points—a revision that served to alter fundamentally the existing moderate policy
line on the implementation of the Four Cleanups.

In summary, Liu Shao-ch'i's perception of the rural political situation in the late summer of 1964—on the basis of Wang Kuang-
mei's T'aoyüan Experience and his own subsequent inspection tour
of China's south-central provinces—was that the Socialist Education Movement on the whole had not been going well, that the
Four Cleanups had been conducted superficially in many (if not
most) keypoint areas, and that as a result there was a need for
greater firmness by rural work teams in dealing with the problems

of local political leadership in the countryside. These perceptions were all clearly reflected in Liu's Revised Second Ten Points.[23]

The Revised Second Ten Points

Although many sections of Teng Hsiao-p'ing's original Second Ten Points were retained verbatim in Liu's September 1964 revision, the fundamental tone of the revised draft was considerably different from the original. Many of the more legalistic and libertarian passages and nuances of the 1963 directive were now either totally deleted or significantly altered. Similarly, the earlier stress upon the primary goal of "unity and consolidation" of the rural cadres was greatly modified, with major emphasis now being placed upon the need for "criticism and struggle" as a precondition for such unity and consolidation. Gone, too, were the prevalent tones of optimism and confidence that had characterized both the First and Second Ten Points. In their place there now appeared a mood of pessimism and a grim determination to intensify the Four Cleanups campaign on all fronts.

This new determination was initially intimated in the revised estimate that the completion of the Socialist Education Movement throughout the country would require at least five to six years. In contrast, earlier estimates had projected the total duration of the movement at two to three years.[24]

In line with this new estimate, the Revised Second Ten Points adopted a hard line concerning operational methods to be employed in implementing the Four Cleanups. Although in broad terms no new work methods were introduced, the elaboration or modification of previously advocated methods indicated substantial differences. For example, new emphasis was placed on the need to have staunch work teams, led by politically reliable cadres, squat at points in the countryside for an extended period of time (à la Wang Kuang-mei). All provincial and municipal Party committees were now instructed to organize and train a number of specialized work teams, each of which was to conduct squatting-point investigations in at least two different keypoint areas, guiding the movement "from beginning to end" in each area. To overcome the prevalent

tendency toward superficiality in the conduct of such investigations, the minimum period of squatting at each keypoint was extended from three months to six. Moreover, the status of outside
work team personnel vis-à-vis local rural Party organs and cadres
was considerably upgraded with the statement that "the entire
movement should be led by the work teams." [25]

The work teams were no longer instructed to rely upon and
serve as "staff advisers" to the local cadres; and the September 1963
warning to work team personnel against "shunting aside" basic-
level Party organs and cadres was now deleted. In a similar vein,
earlier confident predictions that over 95 percent of the cadres
could be unified and consolidated by methods of education and
persuasion were now replaced by an ominous forecast that "prior to
the conclusion of the Four Cleanups movement, consolidation [of
the cadres] *can only be a hope.*" [26]

Liu Shao-ch'i's concern with correcting the previous tendencies
toward moderation and rightism in the Four Cleanups was clearly
revealed in his critique of the work teams' past performance:

> During the Four Cleanups campaign, for fear of "hurting the cadres'
> feelings," of [adversely] affecting the unity of the cadres, or of the cadres
> quitting work, work teams in some areas assumed a tolerant attitude to-
> ward cadres who had committed even serious mistakes. They were afraid
> to criticize, or to engage in struggle. . . . They thought . . . they had
> achieved unity. Yet the result was that they . . . achieved only a superfi-
> cial, temporary, and false consolidation . . . of the cadres.[27]

The new document was also highly critical of the prevalent tendency for work teams to strike mutually-supportive alliances with
basic-level cadres, a tendency that reportedly led to the suppression
of information about local political problems: "[If] the work teams
concern themselves only with circulating among the basic-level
cadres, it will be 'much ado about nothing' for a handful of people.
The movement will end in failure or reap very negligible results,
and the consequences may be quite serious. All this is borne out by
experiences gained . . . in various places during the past year." [28]

As we have seen, the September 1963 version of the Second Ten
Points had viewed the leftist deviation of excessive severity in the
handling of unclean basic-level cadres as being more harmful than

the rightist deviation of excessive leniency. In line with Liu's new assessment of the situation, this order was now reversed; the Revised Second Ten Points explicitly stated that lenient and superficial treatment of aberrant cadres was the more dangerous tendency.[29]

The September 1963 document had viewed petty economic corruption ("excessive eating, excessive possessions, and petty theft") as the most prevalent form of deviant behavior among rural basic-level cadres. The revised text of September 1964 took a much more serious view of the nature of the four uncleans:

> Many basic-level rural cadres have . . . not only committed the four uncleans economically, but have also failed to draw the line between friend and enemy, lost their own [class] standpoint, discriminated against the poor and lower-middle peasants, hidden their backgrounds and fabricated their personal histories, and so on, thus committing the four uncleans politically and organizationally. . . . Some have even degenerated into agents and protectors of class enemies. In addition, a certain number of landlords, rich peasants, counterrevolutionaries, and bad elements have sneaked into the [cadre] ranks. The problem, as we can see, is indeed serious.[30]

In this passage we see, for the first time, a tacit distinction being made between the "small four uncleans" (petty economic corruption in the areas of accounts, properties, granaries, and work-points) and the "big four uncleans" (major impurities in the political, organizational, and ideological, as well as economic behavior of rural Party members and cadres).

The key to the problem of thoroughly exposing and rectifying the "big four uncleans" among rural cadres—particularly among principal cadres in Party organs at the commune and production brigade levels—was held in the Revised Second Ten Points to be the "bold mobilization of the masses." Although a similar demand had been raised in the September 1963 directive, much greater emphasis was placed on this question in the revised version:

> Of all the various work items in the Socialist Education Movement, mass mobilization should be put in first place. . . . Some [work team] comrades are hesitant to mobilize the masses, having various kinds of concerns [e.g., "hurting the cadres' feelings"]. Others are opposed to mobiliz-

ing the masses, using a thousand and one excuses. They are all very wrong. . . . All those who have a wavering attitude toward the Socialist Education Movement first waver on the question of mobilizing the masses. All those who oppose the Socialist Education Movement first oppose the mobilization of the masses.[31]

As we have seen, one of the major problems to be overcome in mobilizing the peasants to candidly criticize their local leaders was the fear on the part of many peasants that once the work team had departed, local cadres (particularly those who had been criticized or otherwise made to lose face during the movement) would seek revenge against the people who had dared to speak out against them. In order to minimize this possibility, and thereby assuage the fears of the peasants, the Revised Second Ten Points called for the results of the Four Cleanups in each rural district to be continually "consolidated" (or rechecked) at regular intervals following the departure of the work team.[32]

Although the Revised Second Ten Points called for the bold mobilization of the poor and lower-middle peasant masses, it was stated that before the peasants could be truly mobilized, their class ranks would have to be purified so that "false" poor and lower-middle peasants who had "sneaked in" or who had otherwise been erroneously classified could be rooted out. Such class purification was to be led by the work teams, and was to include a thorough examination, and where necessary reassessment, of the class status and political background of every peasant household in each key-point village.[33] Once the purification of class ranks was completed in a given area, the work team was to "readjust" the local peasants' association by expelling those questionable elements who had sneaked into the organization:

In the past, there have been instances in which some upper-middle peasants, petty merchants, and even landlords and rich peasants were mistakenly classified as poor or lower-middle peasants. . . . This should be carefully rectified. We should strictly prevent false poor and lower-middle peasants from sneaking into the poor and lower-middle peasants' associations. . . . Anyone who is seriously questionable in political or historical background, . . . even if he is a poor or lower-middle peasant, should be barred from these organizations.[34]

With the questions of investigatory methods and procedures, relationships between outside work teams and local Party organs, and mass mobilization via "striking roots" and "purifying class ranks" having thus been dealt with in relatively great detail, the Revised Second Ten Points next prescribed an open-door method of rectification for all four unclean rural cadres—regardless of their Party status or the degree of seriousness of their mistakes. "Concerning cadres who have committed errors," stated the revised text, "we must let them make self-examinations before the masses and receive the criticism of the masses." This was in marked contrast to the earlier policy of having only seriously unclean or unrepentant ordinary cadres face the masses directly. Without open-door rectification, it was now claimed, "we are apt to ignore the seriousness of problems among basic-level cadres and not be stern enough in the education and criticism of cadres who have committed mistakes." [35]

Despite this new emphasis on the need for the peasant masses to participate directly in the criticism of aberrant cadres, the Revised Second Ten Points clearly indicated the need for work teams to restrain and control the mobilized masses: "Before the masses have been mobilized, we should stress mass mobilization; after they have been mobilized, we should stress the practical handling of problems. *This is a question of experience in controlling the mass movement. . . . All leading functionaries in the work teams should master this art.*" [36]

The September 1963 Second Ten Points had, as we have seen, established a number of procedural safeguards for insuring moderation and restraint in the judgment and determination of punishment for four unclean cadres.[37] No matter how well-intentioned these safeguards may have been, their net effect was to delay and dilute the rectificatory process by taking the power of final decision out of the hands of the local masses and work teams and putting it squarely into the hands of Party bureaucrats at the district and county levels. In the Revised Second Ten Points, such buck-passing was tacitly criticized with the acknowledgment that "our enemies . . . have utilized certain articles of our documents to carry out legalistic struggles against us." [38]

Although most of the legalistic safeguards that had appeared in the original version of the Second Ten Points were retained intact in the revised text, a new—and highly significant—provision was now added which called for all cases of cadre corruption to be fully investigated and disposed of (including the determination of punishments) "before the work team leaves the village." This provision applied equally to "ordinary" and "serious" cases, whose disposition required the prior approval of higher-level Party organs.[39]

The rationale for this new stress upon the need to complete the disciplinary phase of the Four Cleanups while the work teams were still in their rural squatting-points was made explicit with the allegation that "cadres in basic-level organizations who have committed serious mistakes are usually connected with certain cadres in higher-level organizations . . . *and are instigated, supported, and protected by them.*"[40] If this were true (and not even the Maoists have disputed Liu Shao-ch'i on this point),[41] then it stood to reason that only by maintaining their surveillance over the rectificatory process from beginning to end could the work teams ensure that four unclean cadres would receive appropriate organizational discipline.

On the question of how to deal with upper-middle peasants who had demonstrated spontaneous capitalist tendencies, the Revised Second Ten Points incorporated only minor changes in the permissive language that had characterized the original draft. Economic and political conflicts between the poor and lower-middle peasants on the one hand and the upper-middle peasants on the other were still viewed as "internal contradictions among the people," and the earlier warning against "opposing the upper-middle peasants as a whole" was retained in the revised draft. Such caution was considered necessary, as before, because "to push the upper-middle peasants to the side of the landlords and rich peasants would be most disadvantageous to us."[42]

Significantly, however, the September 1964 revised draft did not go so far in the direction of protecting and defending peasant privatism as the original version. Thus, for example, the earlier provision that "self-retained lands" in excess of the five percent legal limit should not be confiscated during the Socialist Education Movement was dropped from the new draft, as was the statement that four category elements should not "indiscriminately be considered as targets of our attack." Finally, the passage in the original text of September 1963 which had stated that habitual rural speculators, profiteers, and thieves were "originally working people, most of whom are somewhat different from the class enemy," was also deleted from the revised version. No longer was persuasive education advocated as the primary means of "consolidating" such "bad elements." Instead, on-the-spot mass criticism and struggle were now called for.[43]

Finally, on the question of Party reform, the Revised Second Ten Points was distinctly more hard line in its approach to the problem of rural organizational rectification than the September 1963 draft. For example, the total reregistration of all rural Party members was now called for—a step that had been left undecided a year earlier. Moreover, new stress was placed on the need for rooting out those Party members "who have committed serious or relatively serious mistakes . . . , who are constantly pessimistic and backward, and who show no improvement after repeated educational sessions. . . ." [44] And in order to augment the Party's organizational strength in the countryside, new emphasis was given to the need for recruiting into the Party a number of proven activist elements among the younger poor and lower-middle peasants during the course of the Socialist Education Movement.[45]

The New Hard Line: An Assessment

There can be little doubt that the Revised Second Ten Points, as an outgrowth of Wang Kuang-mei's T'aoyüan Experience, fundamentally altered the existing tenor of the Socialist Education Movement. The document's overriding concern with the problem of thoroughly exposing and rectifying the manifold political, organizational, and economic impurities of basic-level Party members and cadres stood in marked contrast to the major thrust of the original Second Ten Points, which had been primarily concerned with questions relating to spontaneous capitalism, the consolidation and demarcation of class lines among the peasantry, and the handling of four category elements. In this earlier version, the cadre question (i.e., the Four Cleanups) and the related question of the role of work teams had received only secondary stress as focal points of the rural Socialist Education Movement.[46]

During the Cultural Revolution, Liu Shao-ch'i was severely criticized by the Maoists for having undermined the correct orientation of the Socialist Education Movement by placing unduly heavy emphasis on the question of anti-cadre rectification and struggle—to the neglect of *class* struggle—in the Revised Second Ten Points. Whereas Mao Tse-tung had originally conceived of the Socialist Education Movement as an inoculative campaign designed to instill in the rural peasants and cadres a heightened awareness of the nature of the long-term struggle between socialism and capitalism, Liu Shao-ch'i allegedly sought to turn the movement into a struggle primarily between the four cleans and the four uncleans among Party members and cadres. For example, Liu explicitly stated (in one of his speeches of August 1964) that "What should first of all be solved in this movement is the contradiction between the four cleans and the four uncleans." [47] Although this statement did not appear verbatim in the Revised Second Ten Points, the main emphasis of that document was nevertheless clearly on the question of cleaning up the basic-level cadres and rural Party apparatus.[48]

In addition, by placing great stress on the need for outside work teams to lead and control the Four Cleanups movement from beginning to end, Liu subsequently incurred the Maoists' wrath for having "bound the masses hand and foot." This same charge, it will be recalled, was also leveled at Teng Hsiao-p'ing during the Cultural Revolution—though for manifestly different reasons. Whereas Teng's Second Ten Points had ostensibly constrained the mass movement by placing a host of dilatory, legalistic procedural safeguards in the path of direct action by the rural masses, Liu's Revised Second Ten Points, by granting, in effect, "all power to the work teams," completely reversed the procedure. Hence, if Teng's deviation is viewed as excessive legalism, then Liu's can only be interpreted as excessive authoritarianism.[49]

Most serious of all was the charge that Liu's Revised Second Ten Points, in painting a markedly grim picture of rural political conditions, in prescribing a "hard" organization line for the rectification of cadres, and in "binding the masses hand and foot" by placing authoritarian work teams in charge of the movement, had served to further the counterrevolutionary cause of capitalist restoration in China's countryside. So ultra-leftist was the tone of this document, ran the Maoists' argument, that in effect it served the ends not of the Party or of the masses, but rather of the class enemies. Put briefly, the most serious charge leveled against Liu Shao-ch'i's Revised Second Ten Points was that it was " 'left' in form but right in essence."

Before we can fully assess the credibility of this latter charge, it is necessary to examine the actual impact of the Revised Second Ten Points (and Mme. Liu's T'aoyüan Experience, which had provided the foundation for this revision) upon the course of development of the Four Cleanups in the autumn and early winter of 1964. If there was any single period in the four-year history of the Socialist Education Movement that can truly be called critical in terms of its effect upon subsequent intra-Party policy debates—in particular the growing schism between Mao Tse-tung and Liu Shao-ch'i—it was the four-month period between September 1964 and January 1965. For it was this period, which began with the adoption of the Revised Second Ten Points and ended with the promulgation of Mao's Twenty-Three Points, that marked the beginning of the end for "China's Khrushchev," Liu Shao-ch'i.

5 THE BIG FOUR CLEANUPS

THE LATTER HALF OF 1964 witnessed the initiation of what was in all probability the most intensive purge of rural Party members and cadres in the history of the Chinese People's Republic. Galvanized into action by the militant call of Wang Kuang-mei's T'aoyüan Experience and Liu Shao-ch'i's Revised Second Ten Points, four cleanup work teams at thousands of keypoints throughout the countryside began to crack down severely on cadre malpractices of all sorts. Indeed this was, as the Maoists have claimed, a period in which the work teams (and the local peasants' associations, which were controlled by the work teams) "attacked the many."

Just how many rural Party members and cadres were purged, demoted in rank, or otherwise subjected to organizational discipline in this period is open to question. Michel Oksenberg has estimated that "as many as 70 to 80 percent of subvillage leaders . . . may have been removed from office in some provinces." [1] It is likely, however, that this estimate is substantially overinflated. For one thing, county Party committees were generally expected to purge a maximum of five percent of the basic-level cadres during the campaign (although, as we have seen, this target had been made more flexible with Liu Shao-ch'i's demand that *all* aberrant cadres be given "appropriate punishment"). Moreover, while it is true that there were several reported cases of 50 to 80 percent of the cadres in a single keypoint village or production brigade being struggled against or purged during the latter part of 1964, countywide (and provincewide) averages probably did not greatly exceed the five percent target figure.[2]

If the official target figure of five percent is regarded as the lower limit of purgation on a nationwide scale, with the figure ten percent (see n. 2) regarded as the upper limit, then the maximum number of basic-level Party members and cadres actually purged in rural keypoint units during the Big Four Cleanups may have been on the order of 1.25 to 2.5 million.[3]

It will be recalled that Liu Shao-ch'i's Revised Second Ten Points had called for rural work teams to "boldly mobilize the masses" to undertake the task of exposing and criticizing all corrupt or otherwise unclean cadres. In the autumn and early winter of 1964, local peasants' associations, now subject to direct leadership and control by the work teams and—more important—guaranteed immunity by the work teams from cadre retaliation, were given the green light to openly struggle against those cadres who had been found guilty of the (big or small) four uncleans.[4]

According to a *People's Daily* editorial of the period, the keynote of this new stage of the Socialist Education Movement was to be the mobilization of poor and lower-middle peasants to "dare to supervise the cadres, dare to attack the enemy, and dare to oppose all bad people and bad deeds."[5] In theory this was not a radically new departure, since similar exhortations had appeared in both the First and Second Ten Points and in the Central Committee's June 1964 peasants' association regulations. In practice, however, Liu Shao-ch'i's newly articulated principle of work team hegemony over the campaign now served to energize the mass movement, since local Party organs in the countryside could no longer effectively divert, suppress, or otherwise blunt the thrust of the peasants' criticism. Moreover, the fundamental tenor of the Four Cleanups campaign had changed perceptibly in the direction of radicalization since the early summer of 1964, with the result that the official invitation to poor and lower-middle peasants to "dare to supervise the cadres" and "dare to oppose all bad people and bad deeds" was now—for the first time—taken up with a vengeance.

One of the earliest signs of the developing mass campaign of criticism against rural cadres was the publication of a letter from a poor peasant in Kwangtung Province to the influential regional Party newspaper, *Southern Daily*. After complaining about the prevalent practice among cadres of awarding themselves excessive work-points in the form of fixed subsidies, this peasant (encouraged, no doubt, by the local work team) went on to serve warning that "when the cadres are unfair we will criticize and supervise them; if they do not accept our criticism . . . we may fire them." [6] With the dikes thus opened, the floodwaters were not long in coming.

Financial supervisory groups of poor and lower-middle peasants, acting with the express consent of the work teams, soon uncovered numerous acts of misappropriation of public funds, acceptance of bribes, extortion, and personal extravagance on the part of basic-level cadres.[7] The most frequent peasant accusations against the cadres concerned the latter's method of recording work-points. In what must have been a humiliating experience for the cadres, "distribution teams" of poor and lower-middle peasants in some areas seized the cadres' work-point account books and conducted detailed examinations of the records contained therein. The peasants reportedly found numerous instances of secret subsidies, nepotistic favoritism, and out-and-out falsification of records. Often the cadres were discovered to have appropriated for themselves (or their families) as fixed subsidies as much as five percent of the total work-points of the brigade or production team, in disregard of the existing policy, which had set the maximum limit for such subsidies at two percent.[8] In an article appropriately entitled "Cleaning Up Work-Points and Cleaning Up Ideology," the editors of the *Southern Daily* stated that the practice of cadres misappropriating work-points was antisocialist and exploitative in nature, and should be "dug up at the roots." [9]

The besieged cadres in many cases reportedly attempted to fight back against their peasant detractors, claiming that "if the masses criticize the cadres, the cadres will not be able to lead them at all.

It's all right for higher levels to criticize cadres [i.e., behind closed doors], but if the masses do it, things will become chaotic." [10] A similar argument held that "we are relying too much on the poor and lower-middle peasants; it is not easy to do our work. . . . What's the use of having cadres if the peasants are going to run things?" [11] Such views were strongly and uniformly rebuked in the official media. And as a warning to those cadres who might be tempted to resist or hit back at their local critics, the *People's Daily* sternly announced that "the cadres must self-consciously and uninterruptedly accept criticism and supervision by their poor and lower-middle peasant brothers." [12]

In addition to being criticized, supervised, and dismissed for their alleged economic corruption, the rural cadres also came under heavy fire in this period for having allowed individual peasants to expand their private sideline occupations at the expense of collective undertakings,[13] for having aided the peasants in resisting the state plan for unified purchase of surplus grain,[14] and for having generally permitted spontaneous capitalist tendencies to go unchecked in the countryside.

Throughout the autumn of 1964, rural cadres were thus attacked from all directions, and their modest efforts at self-justification were summarily dismissed as attempts to "hoodwink the masses." Clearly, the prestige and status of the basic-level cadres were being seriously challenged, if not directly undermined.

Cleaning Up the Cadres

With Wang Kuang-mei's T'aoyüan Experience having been disseminated throughout the provinces for use as a programmatic guide in the training of work team personnel, and with the subsequent promulgation of Liu Shao-ch'i's militant Revised Second Ten Points, the Four Cleanups campaign reached its height of intensity in the late autumn of 1964. To illustrate the nature of the impact of the T'aoyüan Experience and the Revised Second Ten Points upon the conduct of the campaign in this period, a comparison with the previous period (the Small Four Cleanups) will prove helpful.

Beginning in the late summer of 1964, work teams in most key-point areas began to change their tactics and mode of operation. Instead of concealing the true purpose of their investigations, as before, the work teams now, upon entering a village or production brigade, openly declared at the very outset that their primary function was to clean up the local cadres—including the principal cadres. Moreover, instead of relying upon and cooperating with existing local Party leaders, the work teams in many areas summarily "seized power" from rural Party organs. According to a number of refugee informants, the work teams in the latter part of 1964 "controlled everything." Local Party branch and management committee cadres retained their routine administrative functions; but even in these matters they had to obtain the permission of the work team to conduct their day-to-day affairs.

As revealed in the diary of one former production brigade cadre who was personally criticized and struggled against during the Big Four Cleanups, the work team in his brigade (located in east-central Kwangtung) called a mass meeting of all brigade members on the day of its arrival in November 1964. All cadres, peasants, and even four category elements in the brigade were required to attend. At the outset of the meeting, the brigade leader nervously welcomed the arrival of the work team. Then the leader of the work team (a Northerner who did not speak Cantonese, and whose remarks therefore had to be translated for the local audience) gave a speech:

We have come to set fire to your leaders. We have come to help you clean up politics, ideology, economics, and organization. We have come to rectify cadres—particularly leading cadres—and not the masses. We intend to stay here until all the shortcomings and mistakes of your leaders are rectified. You masses must assist us in this. After this meeting you are to go back to your homes and write big character posters to expose the mistakes of your leaders. Do not let them slip away [kuo-kuan]. Among our cadres there are good ones and bad ones. The good must help the bad. Going into the water [hsia-shui] and bathing thoroughly is the only way bad cadres can become good cadres. . . .

Following this first mass rally, the leaders of each production team in the brigade were instructed to convene a series of evening discussion meetings in their own villages. At these meetings, which were attended by one or more members of the work team, the local peasants were invited to freely criticize the brigade's leading cadres. Written records of these meetings were kept by the work team personnel. Although the peasants were at first reluctant to criticize the leading cadres (for reasons previously explained), a great deal of persuasive argumentation was brought to bear by the work team members. For example, the work team leader informed the peasants that the purpose of criticism was to help, not hurt, the cadres. The peasants were also assured that the cadres were forbidden to refute the opinions of the masses. Most important, the peasants were told that "Whether or not you write wall posters is a question of whether or not you support Chairman Mao; the more you write, the more actively you support Chairman Mao." Party members and Youth League members were required to take the lead in writing wall posters, and their prolificacy and enthusiasm were regarded by the work team as a test of their loyalty and positivism.

After a week or ten days of writing wall posters, a second mass rally of brigade members was held. At this second meeting there was a general discussion of the problems that had been exposed in the previous period. Ordinary cadres whose errors were discussed at this second meeting were subsequently required to "go into the water and bathe" by writing self-examinations, which were initially delivered and evaluated behind closed doors by the members of the work team. Leading cadres at the level of Party branch secretary, brigade leader and deputy leader, and all financial cadres were uniformly required to read their self-examinations aloud at yet a third general meeting of the brigade members.[15]

At this latter mass meeting, the peasants (receiving their cues directly from the work team) passed judgment on the quality of the leading cadres' self-examinations. If the mistakes were judged to be minor (e.g., economic corruption amounting to less than ¥100), public repentance and a pledge to repay the misappropriated funds were regarded as sufficient disciplinary measures. In more serious cases, demotion in rank, dismissal, or expulsion from the Party was called for.[16] In the informant's brigade, three out of the seven leading cadres were found guilty of relatively serious errors (e.g., rape or the extortion of sexual favors from peasant women, embezzlement in amounts exceeding ¥100, and beating up local peasants). Two of the three were dismissed from their posts outright and placed on three years' probation within the Party, during which time they were to serve as ordinary commune members, with no official status or perquisites. The third was demoted from his position as deputy brigade leader to brigade cook, and was saved from more severe punishment only because his political history and class background were relatively good and he was able and willing to fully repay the amount that he had embezzled (¥230).

In addition, 19 ordinary cadres at the brigade and production team levels (out of a total of 33) were also criticized for various minor mistakes and shortcomings. If the errors were of an economic nature, full financial restitution was required (the cadres were allowed to pay back all misappropriated funds in small monthly installments). If there were minor ideological difficulties in connection with the cadres' work styles (tso-feng) or work methods (tso-fa), or if there were such problems as "divorce from the masses," commandism, or lack of a democratic work style, then voluntary public criticism and self-criticism was generally regarded as sufficient punishment—with the tacit undertanding that unless the individual truly mended his ways, he would be subjected to more severe treatment the next time around.

In order to extract self-confessions from recalcitrant unclean cadres, a great deal of persuasion was sometimes required. Particularly in the case of leading cadres, the work teams frequently kept local officials in continuous closed-door struggle meetings for hours—or even days—on end, during which time the cadres were strongly and repeatedly exhorted to confess their crimes. During these meetings, the stick of psychological coercion was often paired with the carrot of the promise of leniency if the accused fully and completely admitted his guilt. In one locality, the brigade Party branch's first secretary was continuously struggled against by members of the work team (who operated in shifts) for more than three days. The end came only when the secretary collapsed from exhaustion. After an interval of 12 hours, during which time he was allowed to sleep, the secretary was once again subjected to a nonstop third-degree interrogation. Eventually, the secretary fully confessed his crimes and was permitted to return home with the promise that his punishment would be lightened as a result of his "cooperation." In a number of similar instances of anticadre criticism and struggle in the autumn and early winter of 1964, the harsh methods of interrogation adopted by the work teams were in stark contrast to the "light breeze and gentle rain" tactics that had previously been employed during the Small Four Cleanups.

Another significant aspect of the Big Four Cleanups was the new emphasis upon rectification of commune-level Party and administrative organs. Previously, only basic-level cadres at the brigade and production team levels had been considered appropriate targets for keypoint investigations and criticism. Now, however, with the main focus of the campaign having been altered to encompass, among other things, the cleaning up of political and organizational impurities in the rural Party apparatus, commune-level officials found themselves, for the first time, directly under the gun. According to the recollections of a former lower-level cadre from southern Kwangtung, the anticadre struggle at the commune level began in the late summer of 1964, when

the members of the work team temporarily assumed positions of authority in the commune. They then began attacking the members of the commune management committee and the commune Party committee. There were about ten such leading cadres in each commune, and about 80 percent of these were subjected to serious struggles. Although these commune leaders did not form a tight-knit clique, they did share their work with each other and therefore most of them were implicated in the problems of the others. These commune leaders were not struggled against in public, but simply gathered together at commune headquarters for meetings with the work team cadres. Once the Party secretaries and management committee members [were confronted with the accusations and evidence gathered by the work team], they realized their situation and were willing to write confessions. The worst offenders, those who were the most unpopular in the commune, were taken around to the brigades and production teams where they were criticized more severely in public. . . . It took about one month to carry out these struggles against the Party secretaries and members of the commune management committee. About 40 percent of these commune leaders were removed from their positions and sent back to become ordinary peasants. Others were transferred away from the commune or demoted in rank.

Although coercion of any kind had been explicitly forbidden in both the First and Second Ten Points, many cadres found themselves the objects of considerable abuse when their crimes were publicly revealed to the local peasants. According to one informant, "Those [cadres] with the most serious problems were put on little stands, and the masses demonstrated around them. . . . Many of the peasants were obviously worked up and some of the cadres were afraid of physical violence. Although ordinarily there was to be no hitting or physical punishment, sometimes angry peasants did hit the cadres."

Indeed, coercion (or, in some cases, the threat of coercion, whether explicit or implicit) was a major element in the implementation of the Big Four Cleanups in many rural areas. According to a number of refugee informants, apprehensive cadres in many villages, fearing public struggle, attempted to leave the countryside before their misdeeds could be exposed. In some cases, the fleeing cadres were caught by local public security personnel and returned to their villages, where the enraged masses would set upon them and beat them. In other cases, cadres committed suicide rather than be publicly struggled against or assaulted.[17]

According to numerous refugee informants, the rural cadres were justified in feeling terrorized. Corruption of all kinds, from the petty misappropriation of work-points to more serious acts of extortion or embezzlement, was quite widespread in the countryside. Never before, however, had such a thoroughgoing attempt been made to fully expose and criticize such corruption. During previous campaigns (including the Small Four Cleanups), many cadre misdeeds had been covered up, many peasants had been afraid to criticize their leaders, and work teams had been content to skim the surface in their squatting-point investigations. Now, however, the situation had changed. The rural Party apparatus was clearly on trial, and the cadres knew that their day of reckoning had come.

But if large numbers of rural cadres were terrorized by the intensity of the Big Four Cleanups, their superiors at the county, special district, and provincial levels undoubtedly experienced similar trepidation. In the Revised Second Ten Points, Liu Shao-ch'i had made the observation that "cadres in basic-level organs who have committed serious mistakes are usually connected with certain cadres in higher-level organizations." There are few grounds for questioning the validity of this observation, since many lower-level Party officials clearly did have higher-level patrons and supporters within China's provincial Party hierarchies. The exposure of serious mistakes at the basic levels thus could only reflect poorly upon the quality of higher-level Party leadership. A good illustration of this point is provided by the hitherto unpublicized case of the implementation of the Big Four Cleanups in the Shengshih production brigade of Shahsi commune, Chungshan County, Kwangtung.

The Shengshih Affair

From 1960 to the summer of 1964, the Shengshih brigade, a relatively prosperous farming village located in the Pearl River Delta about 75 kilometers south of Canton, had received widespread publicity in China's mass media as a model production brigade—a provincial standard bearer in both politics and production.[18] In the early spring of 1963, shortly after the advent of the Socialist Education Movement, the brigade was personally cited by the First Secretary of the CCP Central-South Party Bureau, T'ao Chu, as an advanced unit.[19] A year later, in the spring of 1964, when the keypoint stage of the (Small) Four Cleanups was initiated in Kwangtung province, Provincial Party First Secretary Chao Tzu-yang personally squatted in the brigade, praising the cadres and peasants of Shengshih as "models of revolutionization." [20] And in June of 1964, an emulation campaign was launched throughout Kwangtung province under the slogan "learn from Shengshih brigade." [21]

The First Secretary of the Shengshih brigade Party branch, a veteran cadre named Ch'en Hua, had similarly been the recipient of a great deal of public praise as a "five good" cadre during the early stages of the Socialist Education Movement. Secretary Ch'en was on many occasions publicly extolled as a national labor model, and he was rewarded for his achievements in the late spring of 1964 by being granted a private audience with Chairman Mao in Peking.[22]

When the Big Four Cleanups began in the late summer of 1964, a new work team was sent to the Shengshih brigade (the first work team, headed by Provincial Party First Secretary Chao Tzu-yang, had departed some months earlier). According to two refugee informants who had intimate knowledge of the events of this period, the new work team secretly "struck roots" with two old peasants in the brigade who privately challenged Ch'en Hua's qualifications as a model cadre. According to these two, Ch'en Hua had over a period of several years committed numerous acts of rape, corruption, extortion, and "suppression of the masses." But since Ch'en ruled the brigade with an iron fist, and since he reportedly had spies (erhmu: lit., ears and eyes) everywhere, the local peasants had in the past been reluctant to expose his misdeeds to outsiders for fear of subsequent retaliation.

After the new work team reported the allegations of the two old peasants to the commune Party committee secretary, an investigation meeting was convened in which Ch'en Hua was privately confronted with the accusations of the two peasants. Ch'en was duly (if superficially) criticized by his commune-level superiors for his "improper work style" and for "failing to deeply penetrate the masses." With this mild rebuke, the case was considered closed.

Shortly thereafter, however, the work team was called away for further study and training (presumably to study Wang Kuang-mei's T'aoyüan Experience, which was currently being promoted throughout the province in the aftermath of Liu and Wang's inspection tour of south-central China). Taking advantage of the work team's temporary absence, Ch'en Hua reportedly had the two peasants who had informed on him beaten up by a group of his local henchmen. The rest of the peasants in the brigade ostensibly knew what had happened and why, but were apparently afraid to say anything for fear of their own physical safety.

When the work team returned after several days' absence, the two old peasants refused to reveal what had happened to them (they had presumably been warned against doing so). However, they secretly wrote a letter directly to the Kwangtung provincial Party committee explaining the facts and circumstances of the case. The case was then turned over to the Chungshan County Party committee for further investigation. When leading cadres from the county came to Shengshih brigade to check up on the story, the local peasants refused to speak to them for fear of being observed by Ch'en Hua's spies. When the county investigation team left the area, having failed to corroborate the complaint, the two old peasants were beaten again, this time after hemp bags had been placed over their heads so that they would not be able to identify their assailants.

Subsequently, the local work team again contacted the two peasants and advised them to address their complaints in writing to the Party center in Peking. Otherwise, they said, the work team's hands would be tied, as no one would dare to speak out to corroborate the peasants' story, and as the subprovincial Party establishment clearly lacked the enthusiasm to carry the investigation any further. The two peasants thereupon wrote directly to the General Office of the Party Central Committee (*Chung-yang Pan-kung Shih*). And within a few weeks, yet another work team was dispatched to investigate the Shengshih affair. This latter investigatory group, which was sent directly from Peking, was headed by Wang Kuang-mei herself.

Bypassing the special-district, county, and commune Party headquarters altogether (for obvious reasons), Wang's work team proceeded unannounced from provincial headquarters in Canton directly to the Shengshih brigade. Accompanying her were a number of officials from the Peking Public Security Bureau and the Kwangtung Provincial Public Security Department. As had previously been the case in her T'aoyüan investigation, Wang Kuang-mei concealed her identity and the nature of her mission from the cadres and peasants of Shengshih.

While the members of Wang's work team quietly set about striking roots and practicing the "three togethers" with the local peasants, Ch'en Hua somehow discovered the true identity and source of authority of the newly arrived outsiders.[23] As soon as secretary

Ch'en found out that the work team had come directly from the Party center, he apparently realized that the game was up, and he quickly put into operation a plan for escaping from the brigade. Taking a few members of his local clique (*hsiao-t'uan*) with him, he set out by motorboat, under cover of darkness, for Hong Kong, which lay some 40 kilometers away, across the Pearl River.

Wang Kuang-mei and her work team colleagues (many of whom, as mentioned previously, were trained in police work) were prepared for this eventuality, and Ch'en Hua's motorboat was intercepted by a Chinese shore patrol boat within minutes of its departure. Ch'en and the other members of his clique were thereupon returned to the brigade, where they were publicly struggled against and subjected to varying degrees of punishment. Ch'en was killed when he either threw himself or was forcibly thrown upon a high-voltage electrical transformer at the brigade headquarters.[24] Other members of Ch'en's local clique were given long prison or labor-reform sentences.[25]

The Shengshih affair clearly proved highly embarrassing (and potentially career-damaging) to Party officials at the provincial and subprovincial levels in Kwangtung, many of whom (including the regional and provincial Party first secretaries) had gone on record praising Ch'en Hua as a model cadre.[26] Indeed, the story of Wang Kuang-mei's visit to the Shengshih brigade was never revealed in the media—not even during the Cultural Revolution.

It need not be assumed that middle- and top-level leaders in Kwangtung had been active conspirators in Ch'en Hua's alleged misdeeds. On the contrary, they were acutely embarrassed—most likely because Ch'en had managed to put one over on them. Nevertheless, it can be strongly argued that without the active intervention of Wang Kuang-mei's central work team, it is highly unlikely that Ch'en's misdeeds would have been fully exposed and punished.[27]

Provincial and local officials in Kwangtung clearly had a vested interest in keeping the Shengshih affair quiet. Only by bypassing these Party authorities, thereby circumventing such vested interests, could the scandal be fully exposed and the situation rectified. This, then, provides a cogent illustration of Liu Shao-ch'i's previously noted observation concerning the connection between unclean basic-level cadres and their higher-level patrons and protectors. This also helps to explain why the previous Small Four Cleanups, which had been implemented by work teams in full cooperation with local Party authorities, had failed to "lift the lid" off numerous cases of cadre misbehavior in the countryside.[28]

The Shengshih affair points up the existence of a natural tendency on the part of self-interested Party bureaucrats to share a common interest in minimizing the harsh effects of the cadre rectification drive of late 1964. These bureaucrats, particularly at the subprovincial levels, had a great deal to lose if all the dirty linen in their own closets were to be fully aired and conscientiously cleansed. For this reason, it was only by circumventing local Party establishments at the commune, county, special district, and—on occasion—provincial levels that the thorough exposure and rectification of the four uncleans could be insured. Such was the fundamental lesson of the Big Four Cleanups.

In making this end run around local Party establishments, however, four cleanup work teams frequently (and for obvious reasons) incurred the undisguised wrath of Party officials in the provinces, many of whom felt (not without some justification) that they were being slighted or—even worse—treated as unreliable. For example, when Wang Kuang-mei conducted yet another of her celebrated squatting investigations in Paoting special district, Hopei, in the late autumn of 1964, she came into open conflict with local Party committeemen at the special district and county levels—and even went so far as to recommend that certain leading cadres on these committees be replaced for insubordination.[29]

Many provincial and subprovincial leaders apparently felt that the Big Four Cleanups was going too far, that too much uncontrolled havoc was being wrought in the countryside, and that the work teams were overstepping the bounds of propriety in bypassing the existing Party machinery. Such discontent in the provinces came to a head in late October 1964, when a work team dispatched by the Shansi provincial Party committee undertook to discredit and seize power from the leadership of the nationally famous Tachai production brigade. Although this incident went unreported at the time, in retrospect there can be little doubt that the attempted purge of Tachai's cadres—including national model Party branch secretary Ch'en Yung-kuei—was one of the key events that precipitated a showdown between Liu Shao-ch'i and Mao Tse-tung on the question of the proper aims and instrumentalities of the Socialist Education Movement.

The Tachai Affair

The Tachai brigade, located in the mountainous hinterland of Hsiyang County, Shansi, is perhaps the most celebrated rural production unit in all of China. Since the early 1960s, the brigade and its Party branch secretary, Ch'en Yung-kuei, have been the recipients of more favorable publicity in the mass media than any other single village or cadre, respectively. The national reputation of Tachai and of Ch'en Yung-kuei received a significant boost during the early and middle stages of the Socialist Education Movement when the brigade was lauded for its martial spirit of self-reliance in overcoming natural adversities and for the diligence demonstrated by its cadres in conscientiously participating in productive labor.[30]

Tachai was originally a "poor and backward" mountain village, comprising some 380 peasants living in crude, handwrought caves. The hillside lands were highly unfertile and extremely vulnerable to the vicissitudes of climate and to soil erosion. Through several years of hard work, diligence, austerity, and self-reliance, the brigade reportedly achieved spectacular increases in its annual grain yield—from 150 *chin* per *mou* of cultivated land in the pre-1949 period to over 800 *chin* per *mou* in 1964.[31] In this manner the brigade earned the reputation as a national model production unit.[32] For his part, Ch'en Yung-kuei was rewarded for his reputed selflessness and devotion to duty early in 1964 by being elected a deputy to the Hsiyang County People's Congress. In October of that year, he was selected to attend the forthcoming session of the National People's Congress in Peking as a provincial representative from Shansi.[33]

In late October 1964, at the height of Ch'en Yung-kuei's rise to national prominence, a work team was dispatched to the Tachai brigade to launch the Big Four Cleanups among local cadres. Although the specific details of the work team's investigation are rather obscure, the broad outlines are quite clear.[34]

As reconstructed from a number of official CCP publications that appeared during the Cultural Revolution, some two to three years after the events in question, the Big Four Cleanups in the Tachai brigade closely followed the precedent established by Wang Kuang-mei's T'aoyüan Experience. Upon its arrival at Tachai, the work team seized power from the brigade Party branch and management committee, convened a mass meeting of brigade members at which the local peasants were instructed to write wall posters thoroughly exposing and criticizing the misdeeds of their leading cadres, and quietly struck roots with a few preselected confidential informants in the area.

According to Ch'en Yung-kuei's personal account of the work team's activities in this early period of its investigation, upon entering the brigade

the work team directed the spearhead of struggle against the revolutionary cadres at the basic levels. . . . When the movement began, they considered the unity of our Party branch and of the poor and lower-middle peasants as an unnatural phenomenon. They said they had never seen such a thing before, and that therefore there must be problems. . . . Over a two-month period they called numerous meetings and forums, compelling the poor and lower-middle peasants to attack the cadres and to expose the "inside story" of the brigade Party branch. . . . They kicked out the Tachai Party branch committee . . . and set up in its place a special production group. . . . They labelled anyone opposing them as "active counterrevolutionary elements" or "degenerate elements. . . ." In this way they sought to haul down Tachai's red banner.[35]

At issue in the Tachai affair was the question of the legitimacy of Tachai's credentials as a model agricultural production unit. Apparently, there was considerable skepticism in higher Party circles concerning the credibility of Tachai's self-reported grain production figures for the previous several years—figures that were cumulatively nothing short of spectacular.[36]

Following the preliminary mass mobilization stage of the Four Cleanups, members of the Tachai work team reportedly concen-

trated their efforts on the task of debunking Tachai's inflated por-
duction claims:

They charged the Tachai brigade with owning more land than it had reported because they said it was impossible to raise such a high output of
grain as Tachai claimed on its arid, hilly land. A special land surveying
team made up of more than 70 cadres from the provincial, special district,
county, and commune authorities . . . was formed to look into the matter.
This team spent over 50 days conducting careful surveys. . . .
Next the work team alleged that the records of Tachai's grain output
must be inaccurate. They organized another investigation, ploughed
through the records, checking with each household and rechecking the
[grain] stores. . . .
Then the work team raised doubts about the amount of grain the
brigade reported it had sold to the state . . . and put forth the charge that
the people of Tachai didn't eat well enough.[37]

As a result of its investigations and surveys, in early December
1964 the Tachai work team reportedly concluded that "There are
grubs in the staff of the red banner of Tachai. If they are not
eliminated, the banner cannot be raised high." And Tachai was
consequently reclassified from an "advanced" unit to a "brigade
with serious problems." [38]

While it is impossible for an outsider to judge the truth or falsity
of Tachai's reported production figures with confidence, a careful
examination and cross-comparison of some 35 public media reports
concerning Tachai, which were published in the period 1961–1969,
reveals a number of glaring inconsistencies. These inconsistencies
tend to indicate that someone may indeed have been guilty of a certain amount of sleight-of-hand in manipulating Tachai's gross, per-
mou, and per-capita production statistics. For example, one report
officially stated that Tachai's per-*mou* grain production in 1953 had
been 140 *chin*, while a subsequent report inexplicably "adjusted"
this figure to 240 *chin*.[39] Similarly, whereas in 1961 it had been
claimed that the total land area currently under cultivation in the
brigade was 710 *mou*, three years later that figure was retroactively
revised upward to 840 *mou*.[40]

Whether or not Tachai's production claims in the early 1960s
were fraudulent, the fact remains that in late 1964 there existed a

group of higher-level Party officials who suspected them to be fraudulent, and who acted upon that suspicion by having a work team thoroughly investigate the question of Tachai's agricultural acreage and output. Later, during the Cultural Revolution, Ch'en Yung-kuei would claim that the work team's investigation actually served to clear his good name by proving conclusively that "the records accorded completely with actual production. . . . The brigade's reports for the years in question were entirely correct." [41] Nevertheless, there is some question as to the veracity of this claim, made three years after the fact by a self-interested participant in the struggle. For in retrospect, it appears that what actually saved Ch'en Yung-kuei's good name in the winter of 1964–65 was not that the Tachai work team could find no legitimate grounds for criticizing him, but rather that Chairman Mao intervened directly in his behalf against the work team.

In mid-December 1964, at precisely the time that the Tachai work team was attempting to discredit the leading cadres of the brigade Party branch, Ch'en Yung-kuei left the brigade to take his place on the Shansi provincial delegation to the First Session of the Third National People's Congress in Peking, a position to which he had been duly elected some two months earlier. Upon his arrival Ch'en requested—and received—a private audience with Mao Tse-tung.[42] At this meeting Ch'en apparently succeeded in convincing the Chairman that the Tachai work team had overstepped the bounds of legitimate investigation in initiating an unjustifiably harsh struggle against the brigade's leaders.

According to Ch'en's personal account of his meeting with the Chairman, "Chairman Mao was best able to understand us [i.e., the cadres of Tachai], and he showed the greatest concern for us. At the crucial moment of the struggle, he received me in audience and gave me important instructions concerning work in Tachai. . . . To us this was the greatest encouragement, the most intimate concern, and the most powerful support." [43] There is no cause to question the veracity of Ch'en Yung-kuei's account of the firm support lent him by Mao Tse-tung at this critical juncture. For immediately following their meeting, Ch'en's political stock was given an enormous boost when he was selected to serve on the highly prestigious Praesidium of the National People's Congress.[44] Following this, Ch'en quickly received a second major shot in the arm when, on December 22, Premier Chou En-lai, in delivering his "Report on the Work of the Government" to the National People's Congress, singled out the cadres and peasants of Tachai for high praise:

Premier Chou cited the experiences of the Tachai Agricultural Production Brigade in Hsiyang county, Shansi, . . . as a concrete example of our achievements in economic construction through self-reliance. . . . On the question of revolutionizing Party and government organs and cadres at all levels, the Premier said that . . . all our Party and government organs and the broad mass of our cadres should learn from the thoroughly revolutionary spirit and style of work of . . . the people of Tachai, and advance along the road of revolutionization.[45]

To round out his spectacular political comeback, on December 26 Ch'en Yung-kuei was given the rare privilege of personally addressing the assembled delegates to the National People's Congress.[46] In this address (an abridged version of which was subsequently published in the January 1965 edition of *Red Flag*), Ch'en spoke of the numerous political, ideological, and economic achievements scored by the cadres and peasants of Tachai. According to an official press release issued on December 26 by the New China News Agency,

Ch'en Yung-kuei, taking "Self-Reliance is a Magic Wand" as his theme, introduced the delegates to the moving experiences of Tachai's commune members in conscientiously executing the policies set down by the Party Central Committee and Chairman Mao with respect to the need for self-reliance in overcoming difficulties one at a time, policies which have led to the rapid transformation of the [poor and backward] face of Tachai.[47]

The ultimate gesture of Maoist support for Ch'en Yung-kuei was made at the end of December, when a large photograph of Ch'en's smiling face appeared alongside that of the Chairman on the front page of the prestigious *People's Daily*. Accompanying the picture was a brief news item quoting Mao's most recent instruction: "In agriculture [we must] learn from Tachai." [48]

Having built a political bridge directly to the supreme leader in Peking, Ch'en Yung-kuei returned to Tachai in mid-January 1965, where he reportedly received a hero's welcome. The Tachai work team, on the other hand, finding the political ground completely cut out from under its investigation, soon beat a hasty retreat from the brigade. In the words of Ch'en Yung-kuei, in the aftermath of his triumphant return from Peking "We stretched our chests, fought a determined struggle, and finally drove away that work team which had vainly tried to chop down the red banner of Ta-chai." [49]

The broader implications of the Tachai affair were not long in becoming manifest. For concurrent with the convocation of the Third National People's Congress in late December 1964, Mao Tse-tung convened an extraordinary working conference of the Party Central Committee. At this conference Mao delivered four talks on the subject of the Socialist Education Movement. In these talks he sharply criticized the prevailing orientation of the Big Four Cleanups and demanded a wholesale reordering of the campaign's priorities. [50]

Mao Takes Command

Although Mao neither explicitly mentioned the Tachai affair nor personally criticized Liu Shao-ch'i and Wang Kuang-mei by name in his statements to the Central Committee working conference, he nevertheless sharply challenged the appropriateness of various policies that had been promoted by Liu and Wang, including the practice of "attacking the many." For example, in a thinly-veiled reference to the Tachai affair, the Chairman scolded: "Four Cleanups means . . . cleaning up *a few people*. Where there is something unclean, clean it up; where it is clean, no cleaning up will be necessary. There must be some clean people! *Where there are no lice on a person, how can you find lice?*" [51]

Mao went on to argue that Four Cleanup work teams must not indiscriminately struggle against basic-level cadres—even those cadres guilty of petty corruption. While conceding Liu's claim that graft and corruption were widespread phenomena in the countryside, he strongly questioned the wisdom of insisting upon stern organizational discipline and total financial restitution in all cases of official malfeasance. In a conversation with an unidentified comrade, the Chairman thus called for the rapid "liberation" (i.e., rehabilitation) of most offenders:

Chairman: Among the four unclean cadres, the majority are those who have committed 40, 50, or 100 yüan of corruption or graft. When we liberate this batch, we will then be in the majority [sic]. . . .

XX: That may not be so. There are many with corruption amounting to hundreds of yüan, and those who have committed graft and corruption involving several thousand yüan or 1,000 catties of grain are also numerous. Perhaps we should liberate those who have committed graft amounting to 1,000 yüan, and simply ask them to repay the money.

Chairman: What can you do since you cannot squeeze out all the toothpaste? It may be possible for them to keep some. How can you squeeze it so clean? *Let's be lenient!* . . . *We need not talk about thoroughness.* . . .

XX: How much should be returned and repaid?

Chairman: The toothpaste can't be squeezed clean. . . . Just label them "elements" and *leave some way out for them.* Don't involve their families. *The labels can be removed at some point.* Among those whose labor is good, no label as corrupt elements should be given.[52]

Mao's rationale for dealing liberally with four unclean elements lay in his apparent belief that the vast majority of economic corruption was small in scale and did not involve sabotage by class enemies. Hence, struggling against such elements was deemed to be both unnecessary and unwise—unnecessary insofar as the contradictions concerned were nonantagonistic, and unwise insofar as it was politically impractical to struggle against such a large segment of the rural population: "On the question [of dealing with corrupt elements] I am somewhat on the right. *There are so many . . . that they might constitute 20 percent of the people.* . . . How many people would there be if 20 percent were marked out in a population of 700 million? I am afraid there would be a tide toward the left." [53]

The Chairman coupled his call for moderation in the rectification of four unclean cadres with a tacit rebuke to Liu Shao-ch'i for the latter's neglect of the overriding issue of class struggle between the proletariat and the bourgeoisie. "The name of this movement," chided Mao, "is the *Socialist* Education Movement, not the *Four Cleanups* Education Movement or the *Intertwining Contradictions* Education Movement." [54]

Next, Mao sternly rebuked "certain comrades" who were alleged to be insincere in calling for mass democracy in the countryside. In an oblique—but nonetheless pointed—reference to Liu's practice of using work teams to control the process of mass mobilization, the Chairman stated: "Though you repeat day after day that there must be democracy, there is no democracy; though you ask others to be democratic, you are not democratic yourselves." [55] Drawing an analogy between the Socialist Education Movement and a military assault against an enemy fortress, Mao drove home his point about mass democracy: "When you cannot capture a fortress, you summon the [ordinary] soldiers, fighters, and squad leaders to hold a [mass] meeting and discuss strategy. Then you will find the way. That is . . . democracy." [56]

Mao's strongest criticism of his comrades was contained in a series of remarks delivered on January 3, 1965. In them, the Chairman criticized the practice, popularized by Liu and Wang Kuang-mei, of engaging in "human sea tactics"—i.e., sending large work teams (often comprising as many as 10,000 to 20,000 people) to individual rural keypoint counties. Referring to the activities of a work team which had been led by Wang Kuang-mei in Hsin-ch'eng County, Hopei, Mao took up the attack:

18,000 people were concentrated in a county of 280,000 people. . . . Why didn't you rely on the 280,000 people of that county? . . . If you had relied on the right people, it would have been sufficient to send a dozen or more people to each county. . . . Some 10,000 to 20,000 people were mobilized in a small county to undertake the movement like a torrential rain. . . . Terrible! Such a waste of time! . . . It is impossible to engage in human sea tactics.[57]

Mao also disputed the Liuist contention (first presented in the Revised Second Ten Points) that Four Cleanup work teams should be made up exclusively of politically reliable people from good class backgrounds: "The work teams are not all that clean," stated the Chairman. "Is it necessary to dismiss all questionable persons? Not necessarily. There may be corrupt people and speculators in the work teams. . . . [Since] they have experience with corruption and speculation, they are indispensable. . . . For now, the work teams need not be so pure."

Next, Mao rebuked Teng Hsiao-p'ing for advocating the method of discretely "striking roots" in the countyside:

K'ang Sheng: Striking roots and linking up was discovered by Old Teng. . . .

Chairman: True, this was invented by Old Teng! Mystifying! Don't announce the purpose of our visit! Of course we must announce what we wish to do: production, distribution, and work-points—these are matters to which we must devote ourselves. . . . Whether to clean up or not must be discussed by the masses. . . . Striking roots and linking up is too placid without any mass movement. . . . You said you, would strike roots and link up, but what roots and what links? It was all so placid, which means that you did not rely correctly.[58]

Mao also scolded another of his comrades, Liu Tzu-hou (First Secretary of the Hopei provincial Party committee and a close associate of Liu Shao-ch'i), for spending too much time studying and popularizing the T'aoyüan Experience and the Revised Second Ten Points at his rural squatting point in the Paoting district of Hopei: "It took you forty days to study the documents. Why should they be studied for so long? I don't recommend this." [59]

Liu Tzu-hou (who was subsequently denounced as an "agent" of Liu Shao-ch'i and Wang Kuang-mei) also came under attack for following the Liuist policy of placing the peasant masses under the tight control of work teams. Criticizing work team dominance of the mass movement as "obstructionist," Mao argued that the peasants must be permitted to play a more active and spontaneous role in launching the struggle against class enemies. Liu Tzu-hou tried to defend himself against the Chairman's barbs, but to no avail:

Chairman: When you go out to develop and engage in a mass movement, or to lead a mass struggle, the masses will do as they wish, and they will create their own leaders in the course of the struggle. . . . Whether one is a professional or an amateur, one can only learn by fighting. . . . In short, what I mean is that we must rely on the worker-peasant masses. . . .

Liu [Tzu-hou]: The poor and lower-middle peasants had plenty of ideas, and though we also offered some, primarily they were their ideas. . . . After the masses had been mobilized to a certain extent, it was necessary for the work team to control the temperature, and be adept at observing the situation, deciding when to attack and when to retreat. . . .

Chairman: It is necessary to give the masses a free hand. It is no good if you trust only the work teams, but not the masses. . . . [Work teams] have obstructed the Four Cleanups.[60]

In line with his firm opposition to the prevailing practice of directing the spearhead of the Four Cleanups against ordinary cadres at the basic levels, Mao repeatedly stressed that the Socialist Education Movement was primarily a *Party* rectification campaign. Dividing four unclean cadres into "wolves" (i.e., Party powerholders) and "foxes" (i.e., ordinary cadres), Mao argued that "The crucial problem is Party rectification. . . . The problem is to catch the wolves first and the foxes later. It will be impossible if we don't start with the powerholders." [61]

On the question of the political reliability of Party organizations in the countryside, Mao's December 1964 assessment was somewhat less negative than it had been the previous August, when he had concurred with Liu Shao-ch'i's pessimistic conclusion that one-third of the Party organs throughout the country were either controlled by or had fallen under the influence of class enemies. "Let's discuss Party committees," exhorted the Chairman in a statement of December 20. "I believe the rightists are a minority, and those who are ultra-right constitute only a small portion. The left is also a minority. The middle-of-the-roaders are more numerous, and they have to be won over." [62]

Although Mao did not appear overly concerned with the existence of political impurities in basic-level Party organizations, he was deeply perturbed about the deteriorating quality of Party leadership at the middle and upper levels, particularly at the provincial level: "Some provincial committees have become rotten, such as your committee in Anhwei, yours in Kweichow, yours in Tsinghai, and yours in Kansu! (some said Yunnan also) Yunnan is an 'individual' case, and has not yet reached that point." [63]

In the above passages, we see how the focus of Mao's immediate concern shifted in late December 1964 (following his meeting with Ch'en Yung-kuei) from cleaning up petty graft and corruption in the countryside to rectifying "Party powerholders who take the

capitalist road"—i.e., those leading officials who had used Four
Cleanup work teams to distort, obstruct, or otherwise impede the
implementation of Mao's instructions concerning the development
of a mass movement of class education in the Chinese countryside.
In these passages we see also an ominous portent of things to come.

The Twenty-Three Points

Mao's extreme dissatisfaction with the state of the mass movement was fully revealed in a major new directive promulgated by
the CCP Politburo at the conclusion of the Central Committee
working conference in early January 1965. Entitled "Some Problems Currently Arising in the Course of the Rural Socialist Education Movement," this directive—known in CCP parlance as the
"Twenty-Three Points"—constituted a formal critique of many of
the principles and policies popularized by Liu Shao-ch'i and Wang
Kuang-mei.[64]

The emendatory nature of the Twenty-Three Points was initially revealed in the preface, wherein it was stated that "If the
present document should contradict previous Central Committee
documents concerning the Socialist Education Movement, then this
document shall uniformly be regarded as the standard." [65] Following this caveat, the January 1965 resolution bluntly acknowledged
that "a great many problems . . . exist in our work." First to be
mentioned among such problems was the question of priorities in
the Socialist Education Movement.

It will be recalled that in the late summer of 1964, Liu Shao-ch'i
had stated that "What should first of all be solved in this movement
is the contradiction between the four cleans and the four uncleans."
The Twenty-Three Points emphatically derided Liu's formulation
of the problem as "un-Marxist–Leninist":

> The contradiction between the four cleans and the four uncleans . . .
> does not clarify the fundamental nature of the Socialist Education Move-
> ment. . . . If we take a literal point of view, the so-called [contradiction
> between the] four cleans and the four uncleans could be applied to any so-
> ciety in past history. . . . Since [this] approach does not explain the nature
> of today's contradictions, [it] is not a Marxist-Leninist way of looking at
> things.[66]

After criticizing Liu Shao-ch'i's policy of placing major stress upon the four cleans–four uncleans question, the document went on to assert that the true objective of the Socialist Education Movement was the resolution of the overarching contradiction between socialism and capitalism. Only this latter viewpoint, which emphasized the fundamental *class* nature of the contradictions and antagonisms existing in Chinese society (as opposed to more limited questions concerning the honesty or dishonesty, rectitude or corruptness, of individual Party members and cadres) was adjudged by the Maoists to be correct:

> Presenting the nature of the movement [as the contradiction between socialism and capitalism] comprehends the essence of the question and is Marxist-Leninist. It is decidedly in accord with the scientific theories of Comrade Mao Tse-tung . . . concerning the continued existence, throughout the entire transitional period, of class contradictions and class struggle between the proletariat and the bourgeoisie, and the struggle between the two roads of socialism and capitalism. If we forget this . . . we will go astray.[67]

In line with this revised definition of the essential nature of the Socialist Education Movement, the Twenty-Three Points sought to redefine the primary targets of the Four Cleanups campaign. Previously, as we have seen, Liu Shao-ch'i had regarded corrupt basic-level rural Party members and cadres as the primary (though not the exclusive) targets of criticism and struggle. Now, however, it was specifically held that "The keypoint of this movement is to rectify *those powerholders within the Party who take the capitalist road.*"[68] While no individual Party members were identified by name or otherwise singled out for criticism as bourgeois powerholders in the January 1965 resolution, it was clear that this term applied to leading cadres at all levels within the Party apparatus, from the basic levels up to and including the Central Committee itself:

> Among those powerholders within the Party who take the capitalist road, some are out in the open and some remain concealed. Of the people who support them, some are at lower levels and some at higher levels. . . . Among those at higher levels, there are some people in the communes, districts, counties, special districts, and even in the work of provincial and Central Committee departments, who oppose socialism.[69]

When Liu Shao-ch'i was first officially reviled as China's "number one Party powerholder taking the capitalist road" in the spring of 1967, during the height of the Cultural Revolution, it was implied that Mao's January 1965 reference to the existence of bourgeois powerholders and their supporters within the Party Central Committee had been explicitly intended as an attack against Liu for his " 'left' in form but right in essence" Four Cleanups policies.[70] While there is no evidence to support the Maoists' post facto contention that Liu was subjected to direct *personal* criticism by Mao at the Central Committee working conference of December 1964, there is abundant (albeit circumstantial) evidence in the text of the Twenty-Three Points that Liu's *policies* were indeed under heavy fire.

As we have seen, both Liu and his wife, following the lead of Teng Hsiao-p'ing, had openly advocated that Four Cleanup work teams should conduct preliminary investigations in their rural squatting-points by discretely striking roots with a small number of preselected peasant informants. This practice was expressly criticized in the Twenty-Three Points with the statement that "The work teams . . . must not be secretive; [they] must not be mysterious, and must not confine their activities to a small minority of the people." [71]

In similar fashion, Liu's highly negative assessment of the quality of rural cadre leadership was countered in the Twenty-Three Points with the assertion (which has since come to be regarded as a hallmark of Maoist cadre policy) that "There are four possible types of cadres: good, relatively good, those with many problems, and those whose mistakes are of a serious nature. *Under normal conditions, cadres of the first two types constitute the absolute majority.*" [72] And in order to discourage the work teams from unilaterally "shunting aside" or seizing power from local Party organs and cadres (a practice which, as we have seen, had been widely adopted in Four Cleanups keypoint units in the autumn and early winter of 1964), the work teams were now instructed to "rely on the great majority of cadres (including cadres who have dumped their burdens), and gradually realize a three-way alliance [*san chieh-ho*] among the cadres, masses, and work teams." [73]

In contrast to Liu Shao-ch'i's policy of placing work teams in total control of the movement from beginning to end, the Twenty-Three Points stressed the need for work teams conscientiously to implement the Party's mass line work style in their conduct of the campaign. Thus, while it was conceded that "cadres must be supervised both from above and from below," it was nevertheless held that "The most important supervision is that which comes from the masses." [74] And instead of temporarily empowering the work teams to replace "rotten" or otherwise corrupt cadres in those basic-level units where the quality of Party leadership was found to be critically impure, the Twenty-Three Points explicitly delegated such authority to the poor and lower-middle peasants' associations: "In those places where basic-level organizations have atrophied or become paralyzed, and before a new leadership nucleus has been established, we may implement [the policy of] all power to the poor and lower-middle peasants' associations." [75]

Liu Shao'-ch'i's policy of requiring all corrupt cadres to make full financial restitution as a condition for their liberation by the work teams also came in for criticism in the Twenty-Three Points. "Economic indemnities should not be randomly or unsystematically imposed," stated the January 1965 resolution. "At the same time, such indemnities must accord with the actual conditions and with reason. In cases where the problems are not serious, . . . if the masses so agree, the indemnities may be reduced, delayed, or even cancelled." [76] And in order to facilitate the rapid consolidation of over 95 percent of the rural cadres, it was now held that "cadres who have committed minor four unclean mistakes, even though they may have many problems, . . . ought to be quickly liberated." [77]

In similar fashion, the Liuist practice of using human sea tactics in the Four Cleanups campaign was explicitly criticized: "We should not rely on human sea tactics. We must not concentrate excessively large work teams within a single county, commune, or brigade. . . . This will help us follow the mass line." [78] Instead, renewed stress was placed on the need for work teams to mobilize the masses in the countryside freely and unreservedly, so as to overcome the phenomenon of "being like women with bound feet." [79]

Finally, and in direct contrast with Liu Shao-ch'i's extremely grave and pessimistic assessment of rural political conditions in the late summer and autumn of 1964, the Twenty-Three Points confidently asserted that

> Practice proves that so long as the whole Party penetratingly and correctly . . . continues to grasp the principles of class struggle, continues to rely on . . . the poor and lower-middle peasants, revolutionary cadres, . . . and other revolutionary elements, and continues to pay close attention to uniting more than 95 percent of our people and 95 percent of our cadres, then the many problems which exist . . . in the countryside will not only be easy to discover, but will also be easy to resolve. [80]

Liu, Mao, and the Twenty-Three Points: An Assessment

The Twenty-Three Points marked a clear departure from the dominant hard-line organizational policies of the previous period. The new directive redefined the basic aims and instrumentalities of the Four Cleanups and shifted the spearhead of the campaign away from the initiation of harsh, destructive criticism and struggle against rural cadres. Higher-level work teams, which had previously assumed full control of the movement, were now ordered to share the command function with local cadres and with the peasants' associations. No longer were rural Party organs and administrative personnel to be peremptorily shoved aside or bypassed; no longer were the peasant masses to be "bound hand and foot" or subjected to authoritarian manipulations by outside investigatory personnel. No longer, in short, was rural rectification to be imposed from above. Henceforth, the Four Cleanups was to be a "revolution from below"—a class-oriented mass movement of poor and lower-middle peasants, revolutionary cadres, and other revolutionary elements aimed at exposing and rectifying bourgeois powerholders and their supporters at all levels of organization within the Party hierarchy. [81]

In Liu Shao-ch'i's first "self-criticism" of October 1966, the text of which appeared initially on Peking wall posters in December of that year, Liu substantially (albeit reservedly) confirmed the Maoists' charge that in certain respects both the T'aoyüan Experience and the Revised Second Ten Points had been " 'left' in form but right in essence":

> In 1964 I committed a mistake which was " 'left' in form but right in essence." . . . In the summer of 1964 I felt that some features of the Second Ten Points had hampered efforts to arouse the masses, and I therefore made some revisions and published a revised draft on September 18. . . . I held conferences with the various ministries in Peking and emphasized the need for leaders at various levels to firmly strike roots in the rural areas. This was, of course, correct, but mistakes were made in emphasizing this excessively, and in making it absolute. In addition, I also stated at that time that the Four Cleanups campaign was not taking deep root or being thoroughly implemented, and that there were many failures. Owing to my overestimation of immediate struggles, I made some mistakes. . . . Some comrades [i.e., the Maoists] said that the Four Cleanups could be truly carried out by the masses, while others considered this inappropriate. This latter notion was actually a denial of the Chairman's thought. It was a mistaken idea and had a very bad influence. . . .
>
> Around that same time I trusted too much in the general summation of experiences made by Wang Kuang-mei. I spread these experiences throughout the country and in Peking. This gave a very bad impression to many comrades. As a matter of fact, Wang Kuang-mei's experiences were at that time mistaken.
>
> Being unable to realize my own mistakes, at the central conference in [August] 1964, I said that contradictions between the four cleans and the four uncleans were intertwined with contradictions within and outside of the Party, while making no explanation about the substantive nature of the movement as explained in the Twenty-Three Points. This was not Marxism-Leninism. At this point I had forgotten the logic of class struggle, as upheld by our Party for the past dozen years. That is why I committed the mistake of being " 'left' in form but right in essence."
>
> My mistake was corrected after Chairman Mao enacted the Twenty-Three Points. . . . The Twenty-Three Points placed the emphasis of the movement on rectifying powerholders within the Party who took the capitalist road, and stipulated that the targets of the movement should be strictly limited to a very small number of bad people. . . .[82]

The current Maoist version of history holds that the mistakes committed by Liu Shao-ch'i in the latter half of 1964 were clearly perceived by the Chairman as constituting a major political offensive by bourgeois powerholders within the Party, and that the Chairman responded to this offensive, smashing it and discrediting its leaders (most notably Liu Shao-ch'i) by personally enacting the Twenty-Three Points.[83] In many respects the Twenty-Three Points, with its formulation of a new theoretical framework for the Socialist Education Movement, its more moderate and optimistic assessment of the nature and severity of the cadre question, and its primary emphasis upon populistic mass mobilization rather than strict organizational control in the countryside, did indeed mark a major shift in the orientation of the Big Four Cleanups. Moreover, as we have seen, there can be little doubt that many of Liu Shao-ch'i's policies were directly challenged both in Mao's remarks at the Central Committee working conference of late December 1964 and in the text of the Twenty-Three Points.

On the other hand, however, there is no evidence to substantiate the Maoists' claim that Liu came under *personal* attack as a bourgeois powerholder in this period or that this attack (if indeed it occurred) succeeded in smashing Liu's "counterrevolutionary line." Not only was Liu Shao-ch'i not personally mentioned in the Chairman's commentaries of December and January, but Liu continued to exercise considerable power within the Party Central Committee well after January 1965. Indeed, he was publicly identified in the mass media as late as October 1965 as Chairman Mao's "closest comrade in arms." [84]

The suspicion thus arises that the Maoists' post facto allegations concerning the efficacy of the Twenty-Three Points in crushing the revisionist line of the heretic Liu—allegations that were first made almost two and one-half years after the fact, during the height of the Maoists' Cultural Revolutionary vendetta against Liu—were substantially exaggerated in order to discredit Liu and bolster the revolutionary prestige of Chairman Mao.[85] Liu may indeed have been guilty of committing certain errors during his stewardship of the Socialist Education Movement in 1964. But the errors in question did not become *crimes* until 1967.

6 TRANSITION: THE ROAD DIVIDES, 1965–1966

In MID-JANUARY 1965, Four Cleanup work teams throughout rural China were recalled to their urban training headquarters for intensive study of the Twenty-Three Points. When they subsequently returned to their communal squatting-points there was a noticeable decrease in both the scope and intensity of attacks against rural cadres. This decrease was clearly reflected in the mass media, as the number of reports of anticadre criticism and struggle fell off dramatically in the last half of January and early February 1965.

There appear to be at least three interrelated reasons for this relatively sudden shift in cadre policy. The first was Chairman Mao's personal concern, as reflected in the Twenty-Three Points, with the problem of ensuring correct ideological orientation in the "struggle between two roads." Equally important, however, was that as a result of the previous high tide of "attacking the many" a condition of leadership demoralization and paralysis had arisen in a sizeable number of rural areas. This condition, coming as it did on the eve of the crucial spring planting season, threatened to adversely affect China's rural economy unless something could be done to bolster the cadres' flagging morale. The third factor in the shift to a more conciliatory cadre policy was the occurrence of a serious war-scare in China in the spring of 1965. Precipitated by the dramatic escalation of American air strikes over North Vietnam in February and March of that year, and by a consequent fear on the part of Peking's leaders that the war might soon spill over into Chinese territory, a new "patriotic mobilization campaign" was initiated, centering around the task of unifying and consolidating the rural peasants and cadres for national defense and productive purposes.

These three factors—Maoist ideology, economic expediency, and military contingency—combined to bring about a visible relaxation of the Four Cleanups campaign in the first half of 1965. We have already examined the nature and implications of the first of these factors in connection with Mao's dispute with Liu Shao-ch'i over the proper orientation of the campaign. The second factor, the problem of restoring cadre morale, was clearly underlined in the following investigation report broadcast by a provincial radio station in late February:

> While encountering many good people and good deeds among the cadres, we also found that there are a number of cadres in the countryside who adopt a passive attitude towards organizing the new upsurge of farm production. Among them are cadres who, because they had shortcomings in work in the past and were criticized both by the upper levels and by the masses, are now afraid to do anything, being frightened of making more mistakes. . . . Cadres who have been criticized for their shortcomings must not be afraid to do anything; they must liberate their thinking and work boldly. . . . It should be emphasized that the great majority of cadres are loved and supported by the peasants.[1]

To reverse the potentially dangerous trend toward paralysis of basic-level leadership, a number of conciliatory gestures were made to rural cadres in the spring of 1965. For example, it was now officially ordained that basic-level cadres were entitled to receive "adequate subsidization" for their performance of non-production-related administrative work (kung-tso). Previously, as we have seen, a dominant propaganda theme in the mass media had been that rural cadres were being widely corrupted by receipt of illegal income in the form of excessive work-point subsidies, and that such subsidies should henceforth be sharply reduced. In the autumn and winter of 1964–65, however, the mobilized poor and lower-middle peasants, acting under the supervision of outside work teams, had been somewhat overzealous in their drive to clean up cadres' work-point accounts. Not only the excess work-point appropriations of the cadres, but also their legal allowances had in many cases been forcibly cancelled or extracted through the imposition of financial indemnities. In order to placate the embittered cadres, the *People's Daily* now declared that "Rural basic-level cadres have responsibilities other than labor to fulfill. . . . Commune members should understand that it is right and proper to give basic-level cadres a definite amount of allowance. . . . The cadres should be adequately subsidized." [2]

Although ostensibly in accord with the Maoist decision to shift the spearhead of the Four Cleanups campaign away from the basic-level cadres, the new conciliatory cadre policy of 1965 was sometimes carried to extremes that were patently un-Maoist in effect if not in intent. For example, in Shensi Province it was officially held that "The most important task of our rural cadres is to lead the peasants to make a success of production. All cadres who have led an increase in production are good cadres." [3] This statement clearly contravened the Maoist categorical imperative, which holds that politics must always "take command" over purely instrumental considerations in the management of the economy. [4]

In contrast to the interrelated factors of Maoist ideology and economic expediency, it is rather more difficult to assess the importance of military considerations in producing the new climate of tolerance and moderation that characterized the Party's cadre policy in 1965. On the one hand, it is generally regarded as axiomatic that in times of external crisis a sense of national unity and solidarity is essential to the success of patriotic appeals for the full mobilization of human and material resources. Thus, William Dorrill (among others) has argued that "[the] perceptible decline in the militancy of the [Four Cleanups] struggle during the first half of 1965 . . . constituted no more than a minimal tactical response to the immediate need to spur production and cement national unity in preparation for possible warfare in Vietnam." [5]

On the other hand, however, it is demonstrably true that the initial change of emphasis in cadre policy from "struggle" to "consolidation" actually predated the outbreak of a serious war-scare in China by more than a full month. Hence, extreme caution must be exercised in attempting to attribute this change of policy primarily to external factors. What is more likely, therefore, is that the military emergency of February-March 1965 served to reinforce and accelerate the implementation of soft-line policies that had already been articulated.

An additional—and perhaps most important—aspect of the "external threat" factor as it influenced the development of the Four Cleanups campaign in the first half of 1965 was the increasingly active role played by local people's militia (*min-ping*) forces and regular Army personnel in the conduct of the campaign. According to a number of refugees, militia cadres in rural China (the majority of whom were demobilized servicemen) were given significantly expanded leadership duties and responsibilities beginning in February and March. And a large number of militia cadres were elected to serve as commune or production brigade functionaries to replace civilian cadres who had been severely criticized or discredited during the hard line stage of the Big Four Cleanups.[6] Moreover, according to these same refugee sources, the number of PLA personnel serving on rural Four Cleanup work teams also rose noticeably in the spring of 1965.[7]

The wholesale entry of the PLA and the people's militia into the rural political arena clearly represented more than a simple reflex response to the threat of external aggression. For it also marked the emergence of a new Maoist strategy in the drive to control the forces of capitalism and bourgeois ideology in Chinese society—a strategy that was subsequently to figure prominently in the initial stages of the Cultural Revolution.

By placing his stamp of approval on the use of the Army as a civilian propaganda force, Mao Tse-tung in effect executed an end-run around the Party apparatus. In Mao's view, the Party itself had become increasingly decadent and unresponsive to the imperatives of class struggle (witness his January 1965 critique of Liu Shao-ch'i's Four Cleanups policies and his reference to the existence of high-level bourgeois powerholders within the Party). Mao's deliberate upgrading of China's military establishment in the first half of 1965 may thus be viewed, at least in part, as a reflection of his mounting concern over his personal loss of influence within the Party.[8] As Franz Schurmann has pointed out, "Mao Tse-tung had lost *de facto* control of the Party at that time. . . . Nevertheless, Mao appears to have had one organizational channel for conveying his opinions, namely the military." [9]

Whether or not Mao had actually lost control of the Party by the winter of 1964–65, the fact remains that the Socialist Education Movement underwent some rather curious vicissitudes in the first half of 1965. For one thing, despite the noticeable easing of pressures on basic-level cadres in the period following the promulgation of the Twenty-Three Points, there was no indication that this relaxation was accompanied by a major shift in the orientation of the Four Cleanups campaign to new targets at higher levels within the Party, as had been called for by Chairman Mao.[10]

In retrospect, it appears that the absence of extensive purging within the Party apparatus at the middle and top levels in 1965 may have been directly related to the decline of Mao's personal influence at the Party center. It seems relatively clear that Mao did, in fact, desire such a purge, but that bureaucratic inertia and deliberate obstructionism prevented the campaign to rectify high-level bourgeois powerholders from getting off the ground.

Equally significant, Mao's loss of personal influence led to a considerable amount of normative conflict in the provinces over how the Socialist Education Movement was to be conducted. In some provinces, such as Honan, where bona fide Maoists were in control of the provincial Party apparatus, the twin themes of "struggle between the two roads" and "all power to the poor and lower-middle peasants" were strongly emphasized in 1965.[11] In other provinces, however, these Maoist themes were either totally ignored, severely attenuated, or replaced by more instrumental (and in some cases decidedly un-Maoist) themes.[12]

In one of the more remarkable illustrations of interprovincial divergence in the orientation of the Socialist Education Movement in the first half of 1965, the text of a speech delivered in mid-June by Central-South regional Party boss T'ao Chu on the subject of the future outlook for the movement was released to the public in radically different versions in Kwangtung and Hunan respectively. As broadcast in Hunan, the speech contained several passages that warned of the serious danger of a capitalist restoration in the countryside and pointed to the existence of "a number of unresolved problems in ideology, politics, organization, and economics"— problems that were held to be "unfavorable to the consolidation and development of the rural socialist battlefront." In Kwangtung, on the other hand, all references to such unfavorable conditions were excised from the public broadcast of T'ao Chu's speech, with the result that T'ao's overall assessment of the current rural political and economic situation took on a decidedly rosier hue.[13]

Divergences in outlook and policy line were by no means limited to the provinces, however. A number of key central Party media also evidenced considerable ambivalance and confusion in the first half of 1965 in their editorial statements concerning the proper normative standards and operational guidelines for the Socialist Education Movement. For example, in a *People's Daily* editorial of late May, which openly called for a radical expansion of the targets of class struggle in the countryside to include the "capitalist tendencies of the upper-middle peasants," it was simultaneously (and somewhat contradictorily) held that individualistic economic behavior by middle peasants was not to be regarded as evil in itself, since such behavior allegedly served a "progressive economic function." [14]

One final example will help to confirm the existence of a relatively high degree of controversy, contradictoriness, and confusion within higher Party circles in the first half of 1965. In May of that year, shortly after the First Secretary of the Kwangtung Provincial Party Committee called for the initiation of a "large-scale mobilization and discussion" among the peasant masses in order to lay the political and ideological groundwork for a new "leap forward" in agricultural production, the editors of the *People's Daily* poured cold water on this idea by declaring that "We must not launch mass movements in a big way, hold rallies, or engage in large-scale discussions for everything." [15]

Using Amitai Etzioni's analytical typology of power and compliance in complex organizations,[16] we may tentatively identify the focal points of intra-Party controversy in the first half of 1965 in terms of an inherent conflict among three distinct (and in many respects incompatible) approaches to the tasks of cadre rectification and social mobilization in rural China. The first approach, characterized by a high degree of reliance upon *normative power* (i.e., mass mobilization through persuasive education and indoctrination among cadres and peasants), corresponds to the Maoist policy of intensifying ideological struggles between the two roads by placing "politics in command." The second approach, marked by a greater dependence upon *coercive power* (i.e., strict organizational discipline imposed from above upon unclean cadres and "backward" peasants), comprehends the essence of Liu Shao-ch'i's hard-line socialist education policies, as manifested during the Big Four Cleanups in the latter part of 1964. The third approach, which rests upon a pragmatic recognition of the need for bringing positive socioeconomic inducements to bear in the struggle for consolidation of the rural "socialist battlefront," is characterized by a high degree of reliance upon *remunerative power* (i.e., utilitarian concessions to the material demands and aspirations of the peasants and cadres).[17]

For various reasons, some of which have already been discussed, the third (utilitarian) approach began to emerge as the dominant modality in the conduct of the Socialist Education Movement in the early summer of 1965. In addition to the proliferation of conciliatory appeals for cadre support and cooperation mentioned earlier, the mass media throughout China began in May and June to place heavy emphasis on the need for Party organs in the countryside to give greater attention to improving the peasants' level of material well-being. The radical view that most—if not all—forms of private economic activity in the rural areas were by nature capitalistic (and therefore ideologically unacceptable) was now derided in the Party press as "metaphysical"; individual peasant sideline occupations—such as raising vegetables, poultry, and livestock for private commercial sale—were now given the Party's official stamp of approval; and rural cadres were now exhorted to effect a better balance between labor and leisure, so as to avoid overworking the peasants. Finally, a rising "ultra-leftist" trend toward the egalitarian leveling of peasant incomes in some rural areas was offically criticized for having served to stifle the initiative and activism of the highly productive middle peasants.[18]

Mao Counterattacks

Although the shift to remunerative (instrumental) power did not necessarily contravene the tactically flexible tenets of orthodox Maoism, there can be little doubt that as Mao viewed internal political and socioeconomic developments in China in the summer of 1965 he became increasingly distressed over the apparent failure of his thesis on class struggle to take firm hold within the Party hierarchy. Party bureaucrats in many provinces were placing not politics but production in command; and a number of Mao's own colleagues at the Party center were beginning to openly challenge the appropriateness of the Chairman's prescriptions for escalating the "struggle between the two roads." For example, at a Central Committee working conference of September 1965, Peking Mayor P'eng Chen openly asserted that "everyone is equal before the truth" and "everyone has the right to speak," and that therefore "even the Chairman himself should submit to criticism if he is wrong." At the same meeting, Party propaganda director Lu Ting-yi made a speech in which he criticized Stalin's "cult of personality"—a speech Mao reportedly interpreted as a challenge to his own position.[19]

Apparently, Mao had good reason to be upset with P'eng Chen. For in the first half of 1965 P'eng had strongly opposed the class-struggle orientation of Mao's Twenty-Three Points. According to Red Guard accounts of P'eng's squatting experience in T'ung County, Hopei, beginning in January 1965 P'eng had "grabbed the leadership of the Four Cleanups movement and . . . pushed his revisionist line that 'production is everything' ":

He encouraged corrupt cadres to agitate for a reversal of verdicts . . . and he paid no attention to the violent struggle of the poor and lower-middle peasants against cadres who failed to pass the Four Cleanups test. . . . As a consequence, a heavy storm of verdict reversal blew in T'ung County. . . . [He] substituted production for class struggle . . . and said "the central task of the work team is to grasp production. . . . The success or failure of the Four Cleanups depends on this. . . ." After the publication of the Twenty-Three Points, P'eng Chen distorted it as an "anti-leftist" document and shamelessly slandered the Socialist Education Movement in the preceding stage as having committed "leftist" mistakes.[20]

If these allegations are true, then the Maoist charge that P'eng Chen was in close collusion with Liu Shao-ch'i during the Four Cleanups is patently false, since P'eng was ostensibly bitterly opposed to the "leftist" mistakes committed during Liu's stewardship of the movement in late 1964. On the other hand, P'eng's ostensible "rightist" deviation does put him in a position of close proximity to the extreme liberalism of Teng Hsiao-p'ing, as manifested in the Second Ten Points.

To break the grip of oppositionist elements at the Party center—a grip that in Mao's view had led to dangerous ideological drift and backsliding in the Socialist Education Movement—Mao was compelled to resort to extraordinary measures. At the Central Committee working conference of September 1965 he asked "what are we to do about revisionism which crops up at the Party center?" With Peking having been "locked up tight" by the opposition so that, in Mao's own words, he "couldn't get a needle in edgewise," the Chairman answered his own question by opting once again for an end-run strategy. Thus, in the autumn of 1965, Mao turned to Lin Piao's PLA and various "loyalist" elements in the regional and provincial Party apparatus for support in mounting his assault upon bourgeois powerholders in the Party.[21]

The Maoist counterattack came in the last three months of 1965 and took the form of a two-pronged drive to "revolutionize" Party committees at the county level and above and to promote the "living study and application" of the thought of Mao Tse-tung throughout China.[22]

Beginning in October 1965, an open-door rectification (k'ai-men cheng-feng) of leading Party cadres at the county level was implemented in an effort to transform these intermediate-level functionaries from deskbound bureaucrats who "look at flowers from horseback" (*tsou ma k'an hua*) to conscientious servants of the people.[23]

Many of the various complaints lodged by the Maoists against the county Party committee secretaries in the fall and winter of 1965–66 were of a nature familiar to students of Chinese communist bureaucracy, including allegations about excessive devotion to routine administrative duties, excessive concentration on compiling formal written reports and statistical data, and the convocation of too many lengthy and unproductive cadre meetings and conferences. Exclusive or near-exclusive stress by county Party committees on the goal of increasing agricultural production by any available means, irrespective of the opinions or class interests of the poor and lower-middle peasants, was similarly criticized on the grounds that such a posture tended to undermine the command position of political and ideological imperatives, and thereby opened the door to revisionism. Excessive requests by county Party cadres for state aid and long-term loans for purchasing chemical fertilizers and farm machinery, and for financing rural capital construction projects, were criticized as contravening the Tachai spirit of self-reliance. Finally, the county Party secretaries were scored for their conservative unwillingness to seize the initiative in creatively solving concrete problems, a posture that allegedly stemmed both from "fear of making mistakes" and from the "negative behavior of looking for stability." [24]

The significance of the open-door method of rectifying county Party committees lay in the use of basic-level cadres and peasant activists as instruments for exposing the shortcomings of their political superiors. Previously, as we have seen, the open-door method had been used by work teams to solicit peasant criticism of cadres at the basic levels. Now, however, it was used for the first time to expose the shortcomings of county-level functionaries.[25]

The proposed remedy for the various behavioral and attitudinal problems uncovered in the course of the new rectification movement consisted of a heavy dose of ideological indoctrination in the form of prolonged and systematic Mao-study. Leading cadres at the county level were urged to overcome their incorrect attitudes and work styles by studying the writings of Chairman Mao and applying the lessons derived therefrom to the concrete problems encountered in the course of carrying out their official duties. At the same time, they also were directed to simplify or streamline existing administrative structures and procedures—a step that would enable them to spend more time at the front lines of production, where they were expected to work alongside the masses, "bringing with them the works of Chairman Mao, hoes, and earth baskets."

Although the county revolutionization movement of 1965–66 was termed a "serious rectification drive" within the Party, there is no direct evidence indicating that substantial numbers of power-holders at the county level were actually purged in this period. Many ordinary staff members of the functional departments of the county Party committees were reportedly transferred to the lower levels for an indefinite period; but this does not in itself indicate a systematic purge. Indeed, the very mildness of the disciplinary measures prescribed for aberrant county-level cadres lends credence to the idea that the county revolutionization movement was actually a relatively mild campaign that, in effect, served to protect leading Party cadres against a more severe assault by the Maoist minions.[26]

The Mao-study movement of 1965–66 was by no means confined exclusively to county-level Party cadres. As early as August 1965, Mao-study activities had also been initiated among the peasants and basic-level cadres in the countryside.[27]

A resolution adopted by the Central-South Regional Bureau of the Central Committee on January 16, 1966, called for the systematic unfolding of a mass campaign to study Chairman Mao's works.[28] In stating that the Mao-study movement was an integral part of the Socialist Education Movement, the resolution also indicated that the People's Liberation Army (PLA) and the four cleanup work teams were to constitute the "backbone force" of the new drive.[29]

The decision to turn the conduct of the Mao-study movement over to the PLA and to the work teams represented a clear departure from the former division of labor, under which ideological work had been conducted primarily by local Party committees and Youth League branches, while work teams had generally confined themselves to investigating political and economic conditions and gathering information about the attitudes and behavior of local cadres. Now, however, the scale of priorities had visibly changed, and Mao-study was officially elevated to a dominant position in the hierarchy of socialist education goals.[30]

A major purpose of the rural Mao-study movement, as it reached a pre-Cultural Revolution peak in the early spring of 1966, was to clarify the relationship between politics and production. The following summary of the proceedings of a three-level cadre conference held in Kiangsu Province in March 1966 is instructive in revealing the nature of this problem:

> Many comrades stressed that "giving prominence to politics" [*t'u-ch'u cheng-chih*] must come first. However, others said: "Rather than waste time chatting about politics, we should take loads of manure to the fields. . . . So long as we have grain, cash and work-points, everything is fine. So long as production work is done well, politics is good." During the discussion, many comrades cited evidence to show that those units which gave prominence to politics and put Mao Tse-tung's thinking in command were continuously increasing production. "Otherwise," they said, "even if some successes were scored in production, they would not last very long." . . . The discussion lasted six days, at the end of which all the participants understood the importance of giving prominence to politics and to the thought of Mao Tse-tung. . . . Most basic-level cadres in the county now keep a copy of Chairman Mao's works on them at all times, studying whenever they get a spare moment. [31]

The somewhat contrived and stereotyped didacticism of this passage tends to obscure the fact that the prevalence of the so-called "pure production viewpoint" (*tan-ch'un sheng-ch'an kuan-tien*) posed a serious challenge to orthodox Maoist policies in the countryside. The fact that this viewpoint was evidently still quite prominent among cadres at the commune, production brigade, and production team levels even after three years of socialist education was undoubtedly a source of considerable anxiety to ideologues at the Party center.[32]

Ironically, the very work teams initially charged with leading the rural Mao-study movement were themselves soon to become prime targets of that movement. Apparently, they too had resisted giving prominence to politics. For example, in announcing that 10,000 work teams had recently been dispatched to the rural areas of

Kwangtung Province to conduct spot-testing work in the new Mao-study phase of the Socialist Education Movement, a *Southern Daily* editorial of mid-February 1966 conceded that "in the actual work of running test points, there have been all sorts of erroneous ways of doing things, the common characteristic of which is not giving prominence to politics." [33] The editorial went on to assert:

> The primary question here is one of world outlook. Every work team member must think about his own aim in running test points. . . . with an individualist aim, one will go on a devious road, taking notice only of production instead of politics, . . . thinking only of one's own reputation and prestige instead of the demands and aspirations of the masses. . . . We hope that all cadres going down to run points will remold themselves . . . by launching a revolution in their own minds, waging struggles against individualist thoughts and against all sorts of bourgeois thinking and work styles.[34]

In reading through official press and radio reports of the period from October 1965 to April 1966, one cannot help but get the impression that the initiation of the rural Mao-study movement reflected a growing awareness on the part of the central leadership (or at least the Maoist elements in the central leadership) that the Four Cleanups campaign had fallen far short of achieving the anticipated results.[35] The major premise of the Socialist Education Movement—the Maoist claim that class struggle, once grasped, works miracles—had clearly proven to be overly optimistic, and a number of so-called "old, great, and difficult problems" (*lao ta nan wen-t'i*) in the countryside consequently remained unresolved.[36]

By the late spring of 1966, the rural Mao-study movement was in full swing. A major new feature of the movement in this period was the initiation of a large-scale drive to recruit new rural Party and Youth League members and basic-level cadres, both to replace those officials who had been purged during the Four Cleanups and to increase the organizational strength of the Party at the basic levels.[37]

Unmasking the Bourgeois Powerholders

When the Cultural Revolution began in earnest in May 1966 with the Maoist denunciation of Peking Mayor P'eng Chen, there was little indication that the new campaign was related to the Socialist Education Movement in any but a tangential way. P'eng Chen's major crime, it seemed, was his attempt to defend a number of his subordinates against the charge that they had written a series of profoundly anti-socialist, anti-Maoist literary tracts in the early 1960s. And in any event, the focus of the Cultural Revolution in its early phase was clearly the rectification of "revisionist influences" in urban academic and cultural circles.[38]

It soon became apparent, however, that the targets of the Cultural Revolution were to be expanded to encompass P'eng Chen-type "freaks and monsters" in all sectors and at all levels of Chinese society—including the countryside. Thus, an open letter addressed to the peasants of Hupeh Province by the Hupeh Provincial Poor and Lower-Middle Peasants' Association Committee in late June militantly exhorted: "Comrades! We must unmask all anti-Party, anti-socialist . . . freaks and monsters *in the whole country, the whole province and in our own localities and home units. Whether they are in the towns or the villages, below us or above, we must strike them all down and uproot them.* The poor and lower-middle peasants must carry the Great Cultural Revolution through to the end." [39]

Initial rural reaction to this type of exhortation was relatively cautious.[40] The Socialist Education Movement was, after all, still the major order of unfinished business in the majority of China's villages; and in these areas the four cleanup work teams continued to carry out the movement much as before, with primary emphasis on Mao-study activities.[41]

By the end of June, however, the news of Chairman Mao's personal approval of the use of wall posters by the masses to expose and criticize bourgeois powerholders had spread to the villages.[42] Emboldened by the Party center's exhortation to launch a "full airing of views and great debates" among the worker-peasant masses,[43] the peasants in some (mainly suburban) areas soon turned to an energetic, if at times unprincipled, verbal assault upon local "freaks and monsters"—including, for the first time in some instances, leading Party cadres at the commune and production brigade levels.[44]

The brief flurry of political agitation in China's rural areas in the early summer of 1966 necessitated an attempt to clarify the relationship between the Socialist Education Movement and the Cultural Revolution. Previously, the nature of this relationship had been only briefly hinted at, and then in such a way as to gloss over potential points of overlap or conflict between the two movements.[45] But, with rural Party organs and four cleanup work teams alike apparently immobilized by the somewhat contradictory imperatives of the two movements (e.g., Mao-study vs. revolutionary "big contending"), further clarification was required.

Such clarification was initially provided in the celebrated "Sixteen Points" adopted by the Central Committee's Eleventh Plenum on August 8.[46] In that document, the relationship between the two movements was defined in terms of the complementarity of their respective foci. Whereas the Socialist Education Movement was described as "currently being conducted in rural villages and urban enterprises" (i.e., in basic-level production units), the Cultural Revolution was said to take as its keypoint the "cultural and educational units and leading Party and governmental organs in the large and medium-sized cities." [47]

That the two movements, though differing in focus, were clearly intended to complement each other was indicated in the assertion that "The Great Cultural Revolution enriches and elevates the Socialist Education Movement . . . [and] adds momentum to the movement in cleaning up politics, ideology, organization, and economics." [48]

Despite the ostensible identity of purpose ("to rectify a small handful of bourgeois powerholders") of the two movements at this stage, however, and despite their professed complementarity of focus, the Socialist Education Movement and the Cultural Revolution were nevertheless explicitly intended to be kept separate and distinct. Thus, the Sixteen Points concluded its brief discussion of the Socialist Education Movement by stating that the Cultural Revolution would *not* be launched in those villages and urban enterprises "where original arrangements for the [socialist education] movement are appropriate, and where the movement is going well." As for those "certain localities" which did not fall into this category, the Sixteen Points merely indicated (somewhat obscurely) that the Cultural Revolution could be used as a "focal point" to "add momentum" to the Socialist Education Movement.[49]

The Maoists' August 1966 decision to mutually insulate the two movements was reaffirmed in a number of official policy statements over the next few months. Premier Chou En-lai, in a speech to a Red Guard rally in Peking on September 15, explicitly enjoined the Red Guards from entering industrial plants and rural areas to "exchange revolutionary experiences." He told the assembled youths that the revolution in these places would proceed according to original arrangements for the Four Cleanups.[50]

In November and December there was a shift in this policy. The Maoist leadership now called for a universal extension of the Cultural Revolution into factories and farms. At this point, the insulation of the Socialist Education Movement ended, and the Party media officially called for the Four Cleanups to be channeled into the mainstream of the Cultural Revolution.[51]

A Central Committee directive dated December 15 stated that no new work teams would be sent to the countryside during the Cultural Revolution. And, as if to confirm the fact that the four cleanup work teams had been the subject of significant intra-Party controversy, the directive ominously stipulated that a general reevaluation of the results of the Four Cleanups would be conducted in the near future as part of the Cultural Revolution.[52] Henceforth, the Socialist Education Movement was to be supplanted in all areas and in all respects by the Cultural Revolution.

7 REVERSING THE VERDICTS: THE JANUARY REVOLUTION

IN THOSE VILLAGES which had already conducted—or were in the process of conducting—the Socialist Education Movement when the December 15 Central Committee directive officially terminated that campaign, the political situation was extremely complex and confused. In these areas, four cleanup work teams, acting under the supervision of higher-level Party committees, had carried out investigations leading directly to the purging of substantial numbers of basic-level cadres and the labeling of numerous four category elements. Since the December directive in effect froze the work teams while explicitly promising that the results of their investigations would be reexamined, there was some question as to whether the victims of the Four Cleanups would now be permitted to appeal the judgments in their own cases. Lacking firm official guidelines on this question, many of the recently purged cadres and newly labeled four category elements apparently took advantage of the Central Committee's conspicuous silence on the subject of the propriety of the four cleanup work teams to denounce them as counterrevolutionary and to demand a wholesale "reversal of verdicts" in the countryside.[1]

Ostensibly freed from the watchful eye of the work teams, and spurred on by the official exhortation to "seize power" (to-ch'üan) issued by the Maoists shortly after the New Year, various dissident elements throughout the countryside launched an unprecedented attack against rural powerholders of all kinds in January and February of 1967. In addition to demanding the reversal of previous verdicts and the overthrow of local Party officials, the insurgents in some areas sought to recall the four cleanup work teams to their original rural squatting points—this time to be the targets of criticism and struggle rather than the initiators.[2]

By the end of January, the situation was serious enough to warrant the issuance of a new Central Committee directive. Promulgated on January 25, this directive constituted the first formal Maoist defense of the (now defunct) Socialist Education Movement against the derogations of various retribution-minded victims of that movement. In stating categorically that "great achievements have been made in the Four Cleanups," and in implicitly retracting the earlier promise to reexamine the results of the Four Cleanups during the Cultural Revolution, the directive was clearly aimed at limiting the scope of rural insurgency.[3]

Although it was officially conceded that "some comrades" in the four cleanup work teams had committed mistakes in their work, it was nevertheless held that such mistakes were the fault not of the work teams themselves, but rather of "the person who originally put forward the erroneous line that was 'left' in form but right in essence"—i.e., Liu Shao-ch'i.[4] According to this new interpretation it was inappropriate for rural peasants and cadres to retain or recall work teams for struggle, and it was held that individual complaints against the work teams were to be registered by writing to higher-level Party authorities rather than by taking direct action.

Finally, the January 25 directive declared a near-total injunction against the reversal of work-team–imposed verdicts in the countryside: "It is necessary to safeguard the achievements of the Four Cleanups. Those Party cadres taking the capitalist road who have been dismissed from office, and the landlords, rich peasants, counterrevolutionaries, bad elements, and Rightists who have been labeled, are absolutely not permitted to reverse the verdicts passed on them, nor are they allowed to make trouble."[5]

A *Red Flag* commentary published in early March 1967 shed further light on the purpose of this injunction by acknowledging that it was precisely those rural cadres and four category elements who had been labeled or struggled against during the Four Cleanups who were now in the vanguard of the movement to reverse verdicts and overthrow all those in authority.[6] In calling for the total repudiation of this "adverse current," the *Red Flag* commentary repeated claims, initially made at the time of the Eleventh Central Committee Plenum the previous August, that the Socialist Education Movement had been conceived by Chairman Mao himself and thus constituted a "great revolution" in which the enthusiasm of the masses had been greatly raised and the enemies of socialism dealt a "severe blow." Various allegations raised by dissident elements to the effect that the Four Cleanups had "made a mess of things" were dismissed as "utterly vicious attacks by the class enemy," and the four cleanup work teams were generally exonerated of responsibility for making mistakes on the grounds that "an overwhelming majority of them acted according to Chairman Mao's instructions. They ate, lived, labored, and struggled together with the poor and lower-middle peasants, developed a profound proletarian friendship with them, and contributed their part to the Four Cleanups movement." [7]

The problem with both the January Central Committee directive and the March *Red Flag* commentary was that neither document provided concrete guidelines for differentiating between those cadres and four category elements who had been rightfully struggled against during the Four Cleanups, and those who had been wrongly criticized or labeled. Moreover, in upholding the general propriety of the Four Cleanups, a major loophole had been introduced—the admission that certain mistakes had been committed by the work teams left open the possibility that errors of *omission* as well as *commission* had occurred, and that some cadres who had managed to slip through (*kuo-kuan*) during the Four Cleanups might now find themselves classified as bourgeois powerholders during the Cultural Revolution.[8]

It soon became apparent that the political situation in the countryside was far too complex and multifaceted to be handled in terms of the rather crude, simplistic, and ambiguous guidelines proposed in January and February. In addition to the areas of ambiguity mentioned above, at least three other factors served to complicate the issue. In the first place, the Four Cleanups had not been systematically completed in many—indeed in the majority—of China's rural villages.[9] Hence, no reliable precedents were available to the "revolutionary masses" in these areas to help them distinguish in principle between proletarian and bourgeois powerholders. In such a situation, the call to "safeguard the achievements of the Four Cleanups" could have little or no relevance as a guide to behavior.

Secondly, the initiation of an all-out campaign of vilification against Liu Shao-ch'i in the early spring of 1967 brought with it the official allegation that large numbers of "good and comparatively good" rural cadres had been *erroneously* overthrown in the middle stages of the Four Cleanups—a revelation that at least partially controverted previous claims concerning the overwhelming success of the Socialist Education Movement.[10] Nor were the grievances of those cadres who (rightly or wrongly) felt themselves to have suffered injustice at the hands of four cleanup work teams salved by the Central Committee's January 1967 ruling that they could take their complaints in writing to higher-level Party organs. First, the Party apparatus was itself suspected of complicity in the misdeeds of the work teams; in addition, the January Revolution had succeeded in virtually paralyzing Party organs at all levels in the provinces—thus rendering them useless as potential courts of appeal.

Even more significantly, the major substantive issues of factional conflict in the villages were in many cases only loosely (if at all) correlated with questions of broad political or ideological principle. Although local power struggles were routinely rationalized (by all parties concerned) in terms of proletarian revolutionaries vs. bourgeois powerholders, the extreme variability of local political conditions in China, together with the partial noncongruence of the various concrete issues that divided the village populace into competing factions, rendered reality considerably too complex to be interpreted in simplistic dichotomous terms, or in terms of undifferentiated ideological exhortations.[11] Because of this, and because in the midst of revolutionary upheaval pragmatic considerations of self-interest frequently tend to outweigh abstract considerations of principle as a motivational force, the question of the overall propriety or impropriety of the Four Cleanups was in many villages irrelevant to the existing situations of factional conflict.

For all these reasons, the Party center's call to "safeguard the achievements of the Four Cleanups" was largely ineffective as a technique for discriminating between appropriate and inappropriate seizures of power, between justifiable and unjustifiable reversals of verdicts. It was in this situation of uncertainty that the People's Liberation Army was called on to assume the role of arbiter in the more serious cases of rural factional conflict.[12]

Since the four cleanup work teams were often the immediate focus of factional controversy in the rural areas, one of the primary tasks of the PLA arbitration teams was to attempt to neutralize the work team issue as a source of local conflict. Armed with a broad Central Military Commission mandate to take all steps necessary to suppress physical violence,[13] PLA representatives in the countryside directed those four cleanup work teams which had been retained or recalled to the villages for purposes of struggle to disband and leave the countryside. This action was formally endorsed in a Central Committee resolution of February 17, which specifically required all work teams dispatched in the period since the initiation of the Cultural Revolution in May 1966 to return to their home units.[14]

Maoist praise for the overall achievements of the Socialist Education Movement continued to be publicly articulated until the late autumn of 1967.[15] At that point, however, it was officially acknowledged that during the final stages of the movement—i.e., in the nine-month period from the formal initiation of the Cultural Revolution in May 1966 to the final recall of all work teams in February 1967—large numbers of revolutionary cadres and peasants had been erroneously labeled as counterrevolutionary elements by the work teams.[16] Consequently, in the autumn of 1967 a series of executive orders was issued in the name of the Cultural Revolution Group of the Central Committee. These orders had the effect of nullifying virtually all verdicts imposed by rural work teams in the period after the initiation of the Cultural Revolution.[17] And in a rather blatant retroactive distortion of the historical record, it was now officially claimed that the Socialist Education Movement had been terminated on May 16, 1966 (the date of the Central Committee circular attacking P'eng Chen), rather than the following December 15 (the date of the Central Committee directive ordering an end to the Four Cleanups).[18]

Thus the book was closed on one of the most bizarre and complex—and as yet only imperfectly understood—episodes in the entire history of the Chinese People's Republic. Amid growing confusion over just who had done what to whom and why, the Socialist Education Movement gave way to the full fury of the Cultural Revolution, and the struggle to rectify the ever-elusive bourgeois powerholders soon reached new levels of violence and disorder.[19]

Retrospective

With the benefit of hindsight, it is apparent that the oft-repeated Maoist assertion that the Cultural Revolution was a direct outgrowth and generic extension of the Socialist Education Movement, while containing certain elements of truth, is misleading—and therefore subject to modification—in at least five respects.

1. It is apparent that if (as the Maoists have claimed) the Twenty-Three Points of January 1965 served as an open declaration of war against high-level capitalist roaders within the Party, then the outcome of that war—at least in its pre-Cultural-Revolution phase—must have been a bitter disappointment to Mao.[20] Not only did the Party apparatus at the middle and upper levels emerge relatively unscathed from the Four Cleanups, but Mao's own credibility and hegemony at the Party center increasingly were called into question during the later stages of the movement in 1965. In this respect, it can be argued that the Cultural Revolution constituted Mao's response to a critical loss of personal authority during the Socialist Education Movement.

2. Closely related to the first point is the fact that the extraordinary Party committee revolutionization campaign of October 1965–March 1966, together with the concomitant nationwide Mao-study movement, were clearly designed as emergency emendations

to, rather than linear extensions of, the Socialist Education Movement. That these two campaigns were essentially salvage operations is clearly indicated by the official acknowledgement that "class struggle . . . is being rekindled even in those areas which have gone through systematic socialist education" and the subsequent admission that a number of "old, great, and difficult problems" remained unresolved in the later stages of the movement.[21]

3. The premature, precipitate termination of the Socialist Education Movement in December 1966, when viewed in the light of subsequent allegations that large numbers of "revolutionary" cadres and peasants had been erroneously labeled as counterrevolutionary elements by work teams in the period after May 16, 1966, leads to the conclusion that, at least in Mao's eyes, the Four Cleanups had become predominantly conservative (if not counterrevolutionary) in essence in the period of overlap between the initiation of the Cultural Revolution in the late spring of 1966 and the termination of the Socialist Education Movement in mid-December.[22] This conclusion is reinforced by two additional considerations: first, the Maoists' retroactive (and otherwise inexplicable) decision to regard May 16 as the terminal date of the Socialist Education Movement; and second, the corollary decision that limited the regime's official defense of the great achievements of the Four Cleanups to those "correct" verdicts imposed by work teams *prior to May 16*, while at the same time it explicitly sanctioned the reversal of all "erroneous" verdicts imposed *after* that date.[23]

4. Available evidence tends to indicate that by the spring of 1967 few, if any, of the major operational instrumentalities of the Socialist Education Movement remained in effect. Provincial, special-district, county, and municipal-level Party committees, which had assumed major responsibility for directing the overall implementation of the movement, were now themselves either discredited or virtually paralyzed under the impact of the January Revolution. Basic-level rural cadres, who had once been the major target of the Four Cleanups, were now officially exempted from being struggled against or overthrown on the grounds that they were not really powerholders at all.[24] And Party-led work teams, which had been the primary instrument for carrying out the Four Cleanups in

the villages, were now disbanded and—in those areas where intra-mural political conflict was particularly serious—replaced by PLA arbitration teams.

5. Most importantly, it must be noted that a major contradiction between the Socialist Education Movement and the Cultural Revolution lay in the widely differing organizational bases of the two movements (elitist work teams vs. large-scale mass organizations), their divergent operational methods (tight Party control vs. mass organizational autonomy), and their totally different primary target groups (corrupt basic-level cadres vs. higher-level bourgeois power-holders). As a Party-organized and -controlled *revolution from above*, the Socialist Education Movement thus proved to be fundamentally incompatible with the new Cultural Revolution, which was by nature a *revolution from below*, a revolt of the masses directed primarily against powerholders within the Party itself.

Party organizations in the provinces (along with the work teams under their jurisdiction) understandably proved reluctant to serve as willing instruments of their own destruction during the Cultural Revolution; nor were they content to sit passively by in the face of a rising tide of officially sanctioned mass criticism and repudiation. These considerations undoubtedly help to explain the ostensibly conservative behavior of Party work teams in the period after May 16, 1966, when CCP organs were under attack throughout the country. Under fire, the Party establishment simply defended itself as best it could, with all means at its disposal—including the work teams.[25] This, in turn, served to confirm Mao's suspicion that the Party apparatus was self-serving and unresponsive to the legitimate demands of the revolutionary masses. Hence it became critically important, in Mao's view, to "unbind" the masses—i.e., to free them, albeit temporarily, from the iron discipline of the Party machine headed by Liu Shao-ch'i and Teng Hsiao-p'ing.

8 CONCLUSION

DURING THE CULTURAL REVOLUTION, Mao's supporters sought to demonstrate the existence of a counterrevolutionary conspiracy led by Liu Shao-ch'i and Teng Hsiao-p'ing—a conspiracy aimed at sabotaging the socialist revolution in China's countryside and paving the way for a capitalist restoration. The conspiracy theory was first suggested by Mao Tse-tung himself, in a wall poster (*ta-tzu pao*) written in early August 1966: ". . . in the last fifty days or so [i.e., June–July 1966] some leading comrades have enforced a bourgeois dictatorship and struck down the surging movement of the Great Proletarian Cultural Revolution. . . . Viewed in connection with the rightist tendency of 1962 and the erroneous tendency of 1964, which was 'left' in form but right in essence, shouldn't this prompt one to deep thought?" [1] Although it was not clear at the time precisely to whom the term "some leading comrades" referred, the subsequent circulation of Liu Shao-ch'i's notorious self-examination of October 1966 left no doubt as to the identity of the principal culprit. In that document, Liu confessed (under duress?) to having committed a series of mistakes—in 1962, in 1964, and again in 1966; it could hardly be regarded as coincidental that the three errors acknowledged by Liu corresponded precisely with the three main deviations cited by Mao in his wall poster.[2]

As for Teng Hsiao-p'ing's role in the alleged conspiracy, the former Party Secretary-General was held directly responsible for promoting a climate of extreme permissiveness in the post-Great Leap Forward economic crisis, for being excessively tolerant of spontaneous capitalist tendencies during the Socialist Education Movement (particularly with respect to his authorship of the Second Ten Points in September 1963), and for conspiring, with Liu, to sabotage the Cultural Revolution in its initial mass movement stage in the period after May 16, 1966.

Before evaluating the substance of the main charges against Liu Shao-ch'i and Teng Hsiao-p'ing, let us briefly recapitulate the errors in question and place them in their appropriate context.

1. The "rightist deviation of 1962." In 1960–61, liberal policy guidelines were formally adopted by the Party Central Committee on such questions as the role of material incentives, free markets, and private plots in agriculture. Pursuant to this liberalization, in 1962 an attitude of extreme permissiveness prevailed in many rural areas; and large numbers of peasants were permitted—and even encouraged—to "go it alone" in farming, to enter into individual household contracts for grain production and delivery, and to privately reclaim substantial amounts of wasteland. These latter practices (as opposed to the legitimate policy guidelines from which they ostensibly derived) were strongly criticized by the Maoists during the Socialist Education Movement. Subsequently, during the Cultural Revolution, Liu Shao-ch'i and Teng Hsiao-p'ing were repeatedly accused of having deliberately and maliciously promoted these practices as part of a concerted attempt to restore capitalism in China.[3]

2. The "erroneous tendency of 1964." This refers to the extensive purge of basic-level cadres that occurred in the countryside in the autumn of 1964, under the aegis of Wang Kuang-mei's provocative T'aoyüan Experience and Liu Shao-ch'i's subsequent pessimistic and hard-hitting Revised Second Ten Points. The Maoist allegation that the deviation in question was " 'left' in form but right in

essence" was derived, as we have seen, from the notion that although Liu's cadre policy was ostensibly hard-line and uncompromising, its very toughness was such that the crucial distinction between the two categories of contradictions (antagonistic and nonantagonistic) was obscured, thereby resulting in excessively harsh and indiscriminate struggles against large numbers of cadres—many of whom had committed only minor ("common") violations and offenses. Moreover, by promoting an authoritarian policy of "all power to the work teams" in the course of the Four Cleanups, Liu allegedly sabotaged the Maoist mass line, which called for the poor and lower-middle peasants to be "masters of their own house." [4] Hence, an ostensibly orthodox ("leftist") political rectification drive to clean up administrative corruption allegedly produced certain second-order consequences that were distinctly unorthodox ("rightist") in thrust. The crux of the Maoist allegation is that such consequences were deliberately and maliciously induced by China's "number one bourgeois power-holder." [5]

3. *The "bourgeois dictatorship of 1966."* When work teams were dispatched by the Party center to conduct investigations into the rising mass movement of the Cultural Revolution in certain schools, universities, and cultural organs in June and July of 1966, their initial response to the radical antiauthoritarianism of the rebellious students was to protect and defend embattled Party officials, administrative cadres, and teachers in these institutions. In some cases, the work teams not only defended the leaders of the institutional establishments to which they were assigned, but also initiated criticism and struggle against the young rebels for their anarchistic tendencies. The phenomenon of defending local establishment leaders by struggling against their critics became known in the lexicon of the Cultural Revolution as "attacking the many to protect the few," and was attributed by the Maoists to Liu Shao-ch'i and Teng Hsiao-p'ing, who were admittedly responsible for dispatching the work teams in question during Mao's absence from Peking in the period immediately after May 16, 1966. [6]

Maoist allegations concerning the existence of a conscious counterrevolutionary conspiracy linking up each of the aforementioned deviations into a common fabric of sabotage and deceit must be scrutinized from two distinct perspectives: first is the *factual* question concerning the veracity of events described in the accusations; second is the *interpretive* question of what conclusions or inferences are appropriately drawn from the available evidence. It is, of course, entirely possible that while specific allegations raised by the Maoists might be factually accurate, the inferences drawn from such facts might nevertheless be unwarranted. Indeed, it is our primary contention that such is the case—that while Liu Shao-ch'i and Teng Hsiao-p'ing did advocate at various times policies that were of dubious contemporary ideological (i.e., Maoist) orthodoxy, they were neither plotting thereby the restoration of capitalism nor acting in a conspiratorial manner.

Concerning the events of the post-Great-Leap era, Parris Chang has convincingly argued that there must have been a substantial intra-Party consensus concerning the necessity of introducing liberal economic and administrative reforms in the countryside in the early 1960s.[7] Not only is there no record of Maoist opposition to such reforms being voiced at the time of their advent; but more significant, the CCP's major programmatic directive of this period, the "Sixty Articles on Commune Management" (adopted in 1961 and revised in 1962)—which sanctioned such permissive measures as commune decentralization, private plots, and free markets—was subsequently defended by Mao himself. Indeed, the Sixty Articles remains to this day the primary operational guide to rural administration in China.

There can be little doubt that Liu Shao-ch'i and Teng Hsiao-p'ing viewed the Great Leap Forward as a major catastrophe; nor can there be any doubt that they participated actively in the process of dismantling the Leap in 1960–62. But the economic crisis of the period was so severe that this viewpoint and this participation were not politically or ideologically culpable at the time. Even Mao himself was forced to acknowledge that "some mistakes in our practical work" had occurred, giving rise to "some hardships."[8]

What distinguished Liu and Teng from Mao in this respect, therefore, was not their common realization that something had gone wrong, but rather their significantly divergent diagnoses of *why* the

Great Leap had gone astray and their respective prescriptions for *what to do about it*.

The Collapse of the Great Leap

In January 1962, Liu Shao-ch'i reportedly stated that 70 percent of the Leap's failure was due to human error (poor planning, overzealous cadre leadership, etc.), while 30 percent was due to natural causes (floods, drought, etc.). Mao, on the other hand, argued that the percentages should be reversed. This disagreement represented something much more significant than a minor numerical quibble: it reflected a fundamental division between two distinct—and largely incompatible—cognitive orientations toward the Chinese countryside.

In our analysis of the Socialist Education Movement, we noted the stark contrast between Mao's characteristically optimistic assessment of the potential for revolutionary transformation of the vast majority of China's rural cadres and poor and lower-middle peasants and Liu's bleak and distrustful pessimism. This contrast can be traced back at least to the mid-1950s, when Liu reportedly opposed Mao's policy of rapid, total collectivization of the peasantry on the grounds that the material conditions for full collectivization (e.g., agricultural mechanization and electrification) did not yet exist. Clearly, Liu failed to share Mao's unconditional faith in the efficacy of mass mobilization as a stimulus to material progress. From this basic cognitive cleavage flowed many of the specific policy and operational differences that characterized the Maoist and the Liuist "lines" in the early and mid-1960s.[9]

Specifically, it follows from Mao's positive, populistic outlook that given favorable climatic conditions and stepped-up political education and mass mobilization, the economic and administrative difficulties of the post-Leap period, as well as the widespread problems of cadre and peasant demoralization, should have been relatively easy to overcome and that the extreme permissiveness of the early 1960s should therefore not have been extended or permitted to become institutionalized once the immediate crisis had passed— as it appeared to have passed by the time of the Tenth Plenum in

September 1962. Liu's essentially negative outlook, on the other hand, quite naturally led to predictions of continued serious difficulty in the absence of greatly strengthened Party discipline at the basic levels and renewed determination to thoroughly clean up corrupt practices in the countryside.

It is quite conceivable that Liu in fact did condone such practices as "going it alone" and "contracting production to individual households" in 1962—much as Lenin had done during Russia's NEP in the early 1920s. (Indeed, the similarities in cognitive orientation and work methods between Liu and Lenin are too striking to be ignored: both men had a profound distrust of the peasantry, which they considered stupid, brutish, and hopelessly petit-bourgeois; both were strict advocates of Party discipline and centralized authority; and both permitted significant tactical concessions to peasant self-interest in the face of severe economic crises.)

Nevertheless, and despite Liu's tolerance of rural private enterprise in the early 1960s, it by no means follows that Liu carried out a counterrevolutionary conspiracy. For one thing, as we have seen, both Liu's 1964 Revised Second Ten Points and Wang Kuang-mei's T'aoyüan Experience were if anything rather *intolerant* of excessive peasant privatism.[10] In this regard, it is undoubtedly true that Liu's 1964 hard-line stance stemmed from rather different concerns than did Mao's own anticapitalist mandates of 1962–63, since Liu was apparently less worried than Mao about the possibility of class enemies making a comeback in the villages. What bothered Liu most of all was the lack of strong Party discipline and honest cadre leadership in the communes; in his view, widespread corruption, rather than sabotage by a small number of class enemies, was the root of the problem. Such differential perceptions of malaise inevitably led to differential prescriptions for rectification.

Secondly, and closely related, Liu's orientation toward authority led him to favor strong tutelary Party control over the rectification process. As Jack Gray has pointed out,

in the protracted struggle of the Socialist Education Movement, in which there was ample room for policy disagreements of a familiar, indeed almost predictable, kind over collectivism versus rural private enterprise, such potential controversies were overshadowed by the question of the means by which collectivism should be re-asserted. The division was concerned with whether this should be done by administrative fiat from above, or by popular effort from below.[11]

In contrast to both Mao and Liu, Teng Hsiao-p'ing appears to have regarded economic permissiveness as an acceptable strategic principle, rather than merely a tactical expedient. His 1962 statement, "Black cats, white cats, what does it matter? So long as they can catch rats, they are good cats," together with his 1963 Second Ten Points, which evidenced extreme liberalism on the subject of the tolerable limits of private enterprise in the countryside, reveal a general lack of concern with the long-term implications either of cadre corruption or class struggle. Above all, Teng seems to have been concerned with establishing routinized bureaucratic norms and procedures and with regularizing the channels of communication between higher and lower levels within the Party—in short, with perfecting the instruments of "rational" public administration.

Moreover, the Maoist contention that P'eng Chen was a close collaborator of Liu Shao-ch'i during the Four Cleanups is controverted by P'eng's reported strong opposition to Liu's "ultra-leftism" of 1964. Most likely, P'eng worked closely with Teng Hsiao-p'ing in promoting a policy of leniency and moderation with respect to cadre corruption and "capitalist tendencies" in the countryside. (See pp. 142–43, above.)

With Liu and Teng adopting widely divergent positions on such questions as the tolerable limits of private enterprise, the seriousness of cadre corruption, and methods for rectifying wayward cadres and four category elements, Maoist allegations concerning the existence of a conscious conspiracy are difficult to sustain. And this becomes all the more apparent when one considers that neither Teng Hsiao-p'ing nor P'eng Chen played a significant role in the so-called "erroneous tendency of 1964" to which Mao alluded in his August 1966 wall poster. On the contrary, Liu Shao-ch'i implied in his October 1966 self-examination that he undertook to revise the Second Ten Points in September of 1964 precisely because he had become dissatisfied with the excessively legalistic and dilatory provisions of Teng's initial draft.[12] And P'eng Chen, in turn, was highly critical of Liu's "ultra-leftism," taking the lead in promoting the reversal of verdicts against unclean cadres in the first half of 1965.

Finally, it has become reasonably clear in retrospect that whatever the nature of Teng Hsiao-p'ing's mistakes, they were never regarded as being so serious as Liu's. It is perhaps ironic that Teng, a true liberal on the question of spontaneous capitalist tendencies, was ultimately rehabilitated, while Liu, a more orthodox collectivist, has remained in total disrepute.[13]

1964: The Few and the Many

We have already examined in detail Liu Shao-ch'i's role in the sequence of events that culminated in the issuance of the Maoist Twenty-Three Points in January 1965. Let us turn now to the allegation that Liu's true purpose in initiating a hard-hitting anticorruption campaign in 1964 was to "protect a few" higher-level bourgeois powerholders within the Party—an allegation central to the Maoist claim concerning the existence of a plot to sabotage the Socialist Education Movement.

How credible is this allegation in the light of existing evidence? Certainly, both Wang Kuang-mei's T'aoyüan Experience and Liu's Revised Second Ten Points reflect a pessimistic political outlook not inconsistent with the idea that Liu was prepared to dismiss large numbers of rural Party members and cadres as an object lesson; and there is certainly ample evidence that many cadres were, in fact, purged at precisely the time that Liu was alleged to have been subverting the movement. However, the case against Liu begins to break down when it is asserted that in "attacking the many" (i.e., basic-level cadres) Liu's true intent was to "protect a few" (i.e., higher-level powerholders).

The strongest piece of evidence tending to controvert this latter charge is the text of the Revised Second Ten Points itself. As we have seen, in that document Liu took a very serious view of the problem of higher-level instigation, support, and protection of corrupt cadres at the basic levels. And in order to fully expose and rectify such collusive practices, the Revised Second Ten Points demanded that: "In such cases, we must go to the origin and get hold of the responsible persons. *No matter to what level the cadres belong, or what positions they hold,* if they have collaborated with undesirable basic-level cadres and committed bad acts, they should be subjected to open criticism before the people. . . . In more serious cases, appropriate punishment should also be meted out." [14]

Far from constituting an attempt to protect higher-level power-holders in the Party, the above exhortation would seem to indicate Liu's deep concern over the problem of thoroughly and completely stamping out unclean practices among Party officials at all levels. Nor is there any apparent reason why Liu Shao-ch'i should have found it necessary—or even expedient—to adopt such devious means as a massive diversionary purge to protect anyone higher up in the Party. As far as is known, neither Liu nor any of his known associates were under suspicion at this time. (Not until December 1964, following the Tachai affair, were there any overt signs of Mao's displeasure with Liu or any other high-ranking Party power-holders—but this was *after* the full force of Liu's anticorruption campaign had already been felt in the countryside.) In short, it is extremely difficult to see *whom* Liu might have been trying to protect, and *why* he should have had to go to such drastic lengths to do so. In the absence of an established motive for such alleged deception, we must treat the Maoist interpretation of the events of this period with some skepticism.

If we reject as unsubstantiated the Maoist charge that Liu sought to "protect the few" in the latter half of 1964, we are faced with the necessity of providing a credible alternative explanation for why the charge was raised in the first place; i.e., we need to establish a motive for Maoist distortion. To fully explore this crucial question, it is necessary to examine the context in which the charge of "attacking the many to protect the few" first arose.

The Work Team Debacle of 1966

We have already noted that many of the work teams dispatched to investigate the political situation of the Cultural Revolution in urban schools and universities in the summer of 1966 committed the "rightist" error of suppressing anticadre, anti-Party dissent. Thus, the Central Committee's Sixteen Point Decision of August 1966 explicitly criticized certain work teams for having "organized counterattacks against the masses who put up wall posters against them" and for spreading such reactionary ideas as "opposition to the leaders of a unit or a work team means opposition to the Party and socialism." [15]

It is important to bear in mind that in this and other official statements of the period, the major error of the Cultural Revolution work teams was said to have been their use of coercion to silence mass criticism of the Party establishment.[16] Yet, such repressive actions were clearly and substantially different from the actions of the four cleanup work teams in 1964. In the earlier period, work teams had instigated the peasant masses to struggle *against* local cadres; in the later period, the situation was exactly reversed: work teams suppressed the masses in order to protect the cadres. In other words, *the deviations committed by work teams under Liu Shao-ch'i's direction in 1964 and 1966 respectively were almost diametrically opposite in nature.* In 1964, the "many" were attacked (leftism); and in 1966, the "few" were protected (rightism). Yet, in the spring of 1967 these two radically divergent phenomena were lumped together by the Maoists under the single rubric, "attacking the many to protect the few."

In order to explain this rather enigmatic development, it must be recalled that the initial months of 1967 were marked by widespread and severe assaults by Red Guards and "revolutionary rebels" on the machinery, symbols, and personnel of Party organizations throughout China. Indeed, the January Revolution witnessed the most radically antiestablishmentarian upheavals of the entire Cultural Revolution. In the face of this mass insurrection, large numbers of basic-level cadres in China's urban and rural areas became severely demoralized. Many expressed their alienation and discontent by simply lying down on the job and refusing to carry out their official duties and functions.[17]

In an attempt to reassure the cadres and bolster cadre morale, as well as to help restore social order and labor discipline in farms and factories, the Maoist regime, in the late winter and early spring of 1967, began to promote a conspicuously soft line of unity and conciliation toward cadres. It was at this point that basic-level cadres were given assurances that they were not powerholders and therefore were not legitimate targets of rebel attacks. And it was also at this point that the first of many prohibitions against further power seizures by Red Guards and revolutionary rebels was issued by the Central Committee.[18]

It was in this context of an attempt to reverse the tendency toward incipient anarchy fostered by the January Revolution that fierce public attacks were launched against Liu Shao-ch'i. Instead of placing the blame for the radical excesses of the previous period on the shoulders of the Red Guards and revolutionary rebels (where it most probably belonged), the regime now accused Liu and his so-called "black gang" of having incited the masses to criticize and overthrow basic-level cadres in a diversionary attempt to shield the true anti-Party, antisocialist villains—a handful of top-level bourgeois powerholders. It was at this point—and only at this point—(April 1967) that the phrase "attacking the many to protect the few" was first used to describe Liu's alleged deviations of 1964 and 1966.[19]

The Maoists' blatant retroactive reinterpretation of the nature of Liu Shao-ch'i's errors was apparently necessitated by the gravity of the problems facing the regime in the spring of 1967. The raising of charges concerning "attacking the many to protect the few" may thus be viewed as part of an attempt to check the anarchistic tendencies of the previous months and to restore cadre morale. The creation of a major scapegoat for revolutionary excesses in the person of "China's Khrushchev" was part and parcel of this effort.[20]

The "Two-Road Struggle": A Postscript

At the time of the Tenth Central Committee Plenum of September 1962, Mao Tse-tung had ample cause to feel that something had gone wrong with China's socialist revolution. Economic recovery from the grain crisis of 1959–61 was well underway, but recovery had its price—the reemergence of private enterprise (both legal and illegal) in the countryside, the restoration of individual material incentives, a marked increase in the incidence of graft and corruption among cadres, the flourishing of unorthodox ideas in the intellectual sphere, the routinization and bureaucratization of the Party apparatus, and the concomitant relaxation of ideologically prescribed behavioral norms throughout society.

Under the aegis of the slogan "Never forget class struggle!" Mao introduced at the Tenth Plenum a series of policies designed to halt—and ultimately reverse—these trends. These policies were incorporated into the Socialist Education Movement, which largely comprised a series of time-tested methods and techniques of political mobilization: promulgating intensive propaganda stressing the twin themes of the superiority of collective production over private enterprise and the dangers inherent in permitting spontaneous capitalist tendencies to go unchecked; arousing the political hostility of the poorest (and hence in theory the purest) peasant classes against the four category elements and other purveyors of bourgeois mentality in the countryside; requiring cadres to participate directly in productive labor on a regular basis; sending higher-level personnel (work teams) to squat at the basic levels to conduct systematic investigations of local political and economic conditions; and rectifying aberrant cadres through a combination of education, criticism, and (in extreme cases) struggle.

The policies adopted by the CCP after 1962 did, in fact, achieve a certain measure of success. Excessive capitalist tendencies in the countryside were at least partially curbed; a great deal of cadre corruption was exposed and rectified; a measure of orthodoxy returned to intellectual life; and political indoctrination attained remarkable levels of intensity in all sectors of society. These results were all accomplished under the leadership of the existing Party establishment, headed by Liu Shao-ch'i and Teng Hsiao-p'ing.

But China could not be remade in the Maoist image overnight. And the establishment itself was beginning to creak and groan under the combined weight of bureaucratic inertia and institutional ossification. Postrevolutionary entropy had set in, and it became progressively harder for Mao to move the establishment in the desired direction. Various statements—such as the Chairman's Jan-

uary 1965 interview with Edgar Snow, in which he viewed the outcome of the revolution as being in doubt for several genera-
tions—indicated that the prospect of a long-term struggle
increasingly preoccupied China's highest leader.[21]

The launching of the Cultural Revolution once again reflected
Mao's perception that all was not well with his revolution. But
where the causes of concern at the time of the Tenth Plenum had
been relatively clear and objective, the motivating factors at this
later date were apparently more personal. In 1966 and 1967, the
old formulas and slogans were once again invoked—class struggle,
the mass line, devotion to the people, etc.—but they were now accompanied by drastically different tactics. The "light breeze and
gentle rain" Mao had advocated in 1962–63 was replaced by the
storm and fury of the power seizure, as Mao seemingly was no
longer willing to recognize or credit the manifold difficulties faced
by Party leaders in their attempts to cope with the conflicting
demands of politics and production, of cleaning up the cadres and
consolidating them.[22] Instead of honest mistakes, Mao increasingly
saw willful perfidy and sabotage. This may help explain why, in
contrast to the depersonalized adversities of 1962–63, Mao perceived only highly personalized adversaries—"demons and monsters"—in 1966–67. In the former period, capitalist tendencies could
be comfortably described as spontaneous in origin; in the latter
period, such tendencies were held to be the conscious creation of a
few top-level "renegades, traitors, and scabs."

There is no small irony in this perceptual reversal. For it can be
argued that it was precisely because of Mao's underlying positivism—his unbroken faith in the revolutionary potential of the
worker-peasant masses—that he was forced to resort to the creation
of scapegoats to explain the shortcomings of the Socialist Education
Movement.

Having concluded that the Party apparatus could not adequately
cope with the bourgeois tendencies deeply rooted in Chinese society, Mao in 1966 placed his hopes for revolutionary renewal on the
mobilized masses—the Red Guards and revolutionary rebels.
These latter groups, however, fell far short of the Maoist vision of
selflessness. In addition to their obvious lack of discipline and their

evident distrust of all authority, they frequently demonstrated as much preoccupation with the symbols and perquisites of power as any bureaucrats. Consequently, Mao was compelled to rely increasingly upon the one institutional force capable of restoring social order and discipline—the People's Liberation Army. And when the dust of the Cultural Revolution slowly began to settle in 1968–69, it was not the mobilized masses who emerged triumphant, nor even an ostensibly revolutionized Party apparatus, but rather the Army—a situation Mao could not have foreseen, and one that undoubtedly proved to be a source of considerable disappointment to him, as subsequent events (including the purge of Defense Minister Lin Piao) have confirmed.

In the final analysis, Mao appeared to be up against the most tenacious of all revisionist influences—self-interest. In the mid-1970s, the outcome of this historic confrontation remained in doubt; and the crucial question "*Quis custodiet ipsos custodes?*" remained unanswered.

NOTES

INTRODUCTION

1. *Hung-ch'i. (Red Flag)* no. 13–14 (1963), p. 11.

2. The slogan "Black cats, white cats . . ." was attributed to Party Secretary-General Teng Hsiao-p'ing, who was purged during the Cultural Revolution and later rehabilitated in 1973.

3. *Jen-min Jih-pao (People's Daily;* hereafter cited as *JMJP*), November 23, 1967. A translation of this important article, entitled "Struggle between Two Roads in China's Countryside," appears in *Peking Review,* no. 49 (December 1, 1967).

4. *Ibid.* 5. *Ibid.,* September 6, 1967. 6. *Ibid.,* November 23, 1967.

1. THE SOCIALIST EDUCATION MOVEMENT

1. For a detailed discussion of China's domestic political situation in the period immediately preceding the Tenth Plenum, see Charles Neuhauser, "The Chinese Communist Party in the 1960's: Prelude to the Cultural Revolution," *The China Quarterly,* no. 32 (October–December 1967), pp. 1–36.

2. *Peking Review,* no. 39 (September 29, 1962). 3. *Ibid.*

4. The text of this speech, dated September 24, 1962, was made available through Japanese sources in 1968. The full text is translated in *Chinese Law and Government: A Journal of Translations,* 1, no. 4 (Winter 1968–69), 85–93.

5. *Ibid.,* p. 87.

6. These so-called "Lienchiang documents" comprised a series of internal Party communications—directives, reports, and statistical tables. A full translation of this important collection appears in C.S. Chen, ed., *Rural Peoples' Communes in Lienchiang* (Stanford: The Hoover Institute, 1969).

7. *Ibid.*, pp. 216–19.   8. *Ibid.*, p. 200.   9. *Ibid.*, p. 159.

10. *Ibid.*, p. 210.   11. *Ibid.*   12. *Ibid.*, p. 191.

13. *Ibid.*, pp. 210–11.   14. *Ibid.*, p. 204.

15. Quoted in *ibid.*, pp. 205–6. Although the date of Chou En-lai's speech was not disclosed, the context in which his address was quoted indicates that it was most likely delivered in December 1962 or January 1963.

16. These are the only available fragments from Mao's February 1963 address. They are quoted in the "First Ten Points" of May 20, 1963 (see pp. 21–28).

17. *JMJP*, January 1, 1963.   18. *Ibid.*, January 11, 1963.

19. *Ibid.*   20. *Ibid.*

21. *Hung-ch'i* no. 2 (January 27, 1963). Each of the above slogans possessed impressive Maoist bona fides, dating back to the Party rectification movement of 1942–44.

22. *JMJP*, January 25, 1963.   23. *Ibid.*, February 23, 1963.

24. *Ibid.*, February 18, 1963.   25. *Ibid.*, February 23, 1963.

26. On this point, see also Ezra F. Vogel, *Canton Under Communism* (Cambridge: Harvard University Press, 1969), pp. 301–2.

27. See, for example, *JMJP*, January 1 and March 30, 1963.

28. See, for example, *Nan-fang Jih-pao* (*Southern Daily;* hereafter *NFJP*), November 3, 1962; and *JMJP*, January 5, 1963. The previously cited case of the *hsia-fang* movement in rural Kwangtung provides a good illustration of the widespread tendency for provincial and local Party officials to stress the production-related, rather than the political goals of the campaign.

29. This statement, together with a number of other comments made by the Chairman during the course of the Socialist Education Movement, appears in an important collection of Mao's previously unpublished writings and commentaries, *Mao Tse-tung T'ung-chih shih Tang-tai tsui Wei-ta te Ma-k'o-ssu Lieh-ning Chu-i-che* (*Comrade Mao Tse-tung is the Greatest Marxist-Leninist of the Contemporary Era*) (August 1969). A translation of this collection appears under the title "Miscellany of Mao Tse-tung Thought (1949–1968)," in *Joint Publications Research Service* (hereafter *JPRS*) no. 61,269 (February 20, 1974), Part 2.

30. Mao Tse-tung, "Speech at the Hangchow Conference" (May 1963), in *ibid.*, p. 319.

31. *Ibid.*, p. 320.

32. For a full translation of this document, see Richard Baum and Frederick C. Teiwes, *Ssu-Ch'ing: The Socialist Education Movement of 1962–1966* (Berkeley: Center for Chinese Studies, 1968), Appendix B.

33. *Ibid.*, Article IV.   34. *Ibid.*, Article III.

35. A partial text of this note was reproduced in the CCP's Ninth Comment on the Open Letter of the Central Committee of the CPSU ("On Khrushchev's Phoney Communism and its Historical Lessons for the World"), published in *JMJP*, July 14, 1964. An additional passage from Mao's note was appended to Article X of the First Ten Points.

36. First Ten Points, Article X.

37. Mao Tse-tung, "Instruction on the Commune Education Movement" (May 1963), in "Miscellany of Mao Tse-tung Thought," p. 315.

38. Mao Tse-tung, "Speech at the Hangchow Conference," in *ibid.*, p. 323.

39. First Ten Points, Article VIII.   40. *Ibid.*   41. *Ibid.*

42. The CCP's use of peasants' associations as an instrument for rural mass mobilization dates back to the mid-1920s. This technique had proved particularly effective in the Party's land reform movement of 1949–52. However, with the advent of agricultural cooperativization and collectivization in the mid-1950s, the peasants' associations quickly fell into disuse and atrophied.

43. First Ten Points, Article VIII.

44. *Ibid.*, Article V.   45. *Ibid.*, Article VIII.

46. Mao Tse-tung, "Instruction on the Commune Education Movement," in "Miscellany of Mao Tse-tung Thought," p. 315. Later on in this same passage, Mao exhorted: "don't act as though it is enemy against enemy, no" (*ibid.*, p. 317).

47. First Ten Points, Article VIII.

48. There is a curious and unexplained contradiction between the official praise for Honan Province contained in the above passage and Chairman Mao's pungent criticism of Honan contained in his earlier cited "Speech to the Hangchow Conference." (See page 20.) This contradiction suggests that Mao may not have been the sole author of the First Ten Points, and that significant intra-Party discord may have existed even at this early stage of the movement.

49. First Ten Points, Article VIII.

50. *Ibid.*, Article IX. In laying down this requirement, the First Ten Points cited the "advanced experience" in cadre participation in labor achieved by Party officials in Hsiyang county, Shansi—location of the "model" Tachai production brigade, to be discussed later.

51. *Ibid.*, Article VI.   52. *Ibid.*, Article X.

53. That the drafters of the First Ten Points were at least as concerned with *raising* questions of methods and techniques as with providing universal and concrete guidelines for their solution was indicated by the inclusion, in the preface to that document, of Mao's celebrated essay, "Where Do Man's Correct Ideas Come From?" and by the injunction (in Article X) for Party committees at all levels to give high priority to the tasks of conducting "squatting-point" investigations and research at the basic levels.

54. *NFJP*, May 25, 1963.   55. *Ibid.*, August 24, 1963.

56. *Ibid.*, May 25, 1963.

57. *Ibid.*, May 28, 1963. Here, as before, the conspicuous lack of any reference to the investigatory and supervisory functions of the peasants' organizations vis-à-vis Party branches is significant.

58. *NFJP*, May 25, 1963.   59. Vogel, *Canton Under Communisim*, pp. 314–15.

60. *JMJP*, May 20, 21, 22, 25, and 27, 1963. The phenomenon of cadres being

"divorced from production" was regarded in these "Talks" as a manifestation of bureaucratism and a betrayal of the Party's mass line—the first step on the road to Soviet-style revisionism.

61. See, for example, *JMJP*, June 2, 4, and 18, 1963.

62. *Hung-ch'i*, no. 13–14 (July 10, 1963).

63. *Ibid.* Altogether, ten advantages of cadres participating in productive labor were cited in the preface to the *Hung-ch'i* investigation report. These were, in order of presentation: "(1) cadres, in taking part in labor with the masses, will identify themselves . . . with the laboring people, and the masses will regard the cadres as 'bosom friends' . . . ; (2) By consistently taking part in labor, cadres will retain the true character of the laboring people . . . and resist the influence of bourgeois ideology . . . ; (3) For rural cadres, participation in labor will help them strengthen their class-consciousness and class feeling and carry out in a better way the Party's class line . . . of relying on the poor and lower-middle peasants . . . ; (4) The example of active participation in labor by cadres will stimulate the labor enthusiasm of the masses . . . ; (5) . . . the cadres will nurture a greater love for the fruits of labor, and will become good, frugal administrators of the socialist economy; (6) Cadre participation in labor will bring about a revolution in customs and habits and help create new conventions which honor labor and frown upon idleness . . . ; (7) Cadres' participation in labor will exert an influence on the younger generation, who will grow up . . . following the road of industry and thrift and acquire an ardent love for the collective; (8) Basic-level cadres, by taking part in labor, will know more about production conditions . . . ; (9) Constant participation in collective labor will make it more convenient for cadres to carry out scientific experiments . . . ; (10) By identifying themselves with the masses in labor, cadres will be able to give timely explanations of Party policies and lines to the masses, and will be able to implement them in a better way. . . ."

64. *Ibid.*

65. *Ibid.* These figures represent an average for the fourteen rural areas discussed in the *Hung-ch'i* investigation report. The absence of established labor norms for production team cadres is due to the fact that the vast majority of team cadres were regarded as "non-divorced from production" (*pu t'o-li sheng-ch'an:* i.e., full-time laborers). Exceptions to this status were granted to those team cadres who doubled as brigade Party branch or management-committee members.

66. The third "fix" was the provision that cadres should spend their entire annual quota of labor-days working at a "fixed point"—i.e., a particular production team—rather than wandering around from team to team.

67. *JMJP*, August 18, 1963.   68. *Ibid.*

69. *Ibid.*, June 2, 1963. The reference to "taking a warm bath" in the last sentence of this statement alludes to the demand raised in the First Ten Points that rural cadres "wash their hands and bodies" in the course of the Socialist Education Movement.

70. *Ibid.*, August 18, 1963.   71. *Ibid.*

72. *Radio Chengchow*, Honan, June 11, 1963. For an explanation of various systems used in rural China to allocate, tally, and assess work-points, see Andrew Nathan,

"Paying the Chinese Farmer," *Far Eastern Economic Review*, February 27, 1964, pp. 457–58; and Chen Mai Fun, "Paying the Peasants," *Far Eastern Economic Review*, November 3, 1966, pp. 263–64.

73. *Radio Changsha*, Hunan, July 19, 1963.   74. *Ibid.*

75. According to one former county-level cadre I interviewed, official corruption of one sort or another at the basic levels in the countryside was so pervasive in the early 1960s (due to economic hardships which arose during the "three hard years" of 1959–61) that Party officials simply didn't want to stir up a hornet's nest by conscientiously investigating the basic-level cadres. Moreover, the organizational and personal relationships between basic-level cadres and their superiors at the commune, district, and county levels were so strong that to expose and rectify "four unclean" cadres at the basic levels would have been to set off a virtual chain reaction of unseemly revelations, recriminations, and scandals all along the subprovincial Party hierarchy. This interpretation tends to agree with that of Liu Shao-ch'i, as revealed in the text of his revised version of the "Second Ten Points" of September 1964. See chapter 4.

76. This impression of widespread official reluctance to initiate the Four Cleanups in the summer of 1963 is confirmed in the classified refugee interview files of the Union Research Institute, Hong Kong. In these files for the year 1963, some two dozen rural refugees tell of their experiences with the Socialist Education Movement; yet no mention is made of the existence of a Four Cleanups campaign in this period. Indeed, aside from the two provincial radio braodcasts (from Honan and Hunan) cited earlier, I discovered only one additional reference to the existence of the campaign in this period: the report of a former resident of Huiyang county, Kwangtung, concerning the recent initation of an experimental "Three Cleanups" movement in his district. See *Hsing-tao Jih-pao* (Hong Kong), July 6, 1963.

77. It is estimated that in 1963 at least half of China's total rural population of 500 million was under 25, with the 16–25 group accounting for perhaps 35–40 percent of this subtotal, or approximately 100 million people. The importance of this large group of youngsters far outweighed their numerical strength, however, for in addition to being the most literate and best educated group of rural inhabitants, from their ranks would ultimately come the leadership of China's "revolutionary successor generation." Hence the Party's great concern over the manners and mores of China's rural youth.

78. For documentation concerning the implementation of the rural "recall and compare" campaign in the summer of 1963, see *JMJP*, June 10, 1963; *NFJP*, June 28, 1963; and *Chung-kuo Ch'ing-nien Pao* (*China Youth News*; hereafter, *CNP*), May 25, June 13, and June 27, 1963.

79. On this point, see Vogel, *Canton Under Communism*, pp. 306–7.

80. *CNP*, May 25, 1963. As related to the author by a number of peasant refugees, the "recall and compare" movement was sometimes laughingly derided by previously affluent (and therefore more hostile) peasants as "recalling past sweetness and comparing it with present bitterness."

81. *CNP*, June 27, 1963.

82. Michel Oksenberg, "The Institutionalization of the Chinese Communist Revo-

lution: The Ladder of Success on the Eve of the Cultural Revolution," *The China Quarterly*, no. 36 (October–December 1968), p. 75.

83. This hypothesis, which is admittedly impressionistic, is derived from interviews conducted by the author with a number of former Party officials at the middle- and lower-levels. Although it is impossible to test this hypothesis using rigorous and controlled methods, the hypothesis is borne out directly by official accusations raised against numerous Party officials during the course of the Cultural Revolution, accusations to the effect that these officials had been afraid to mobilize the masses, had been unwilling to accept "new things" for fear of upsetting their settled routines, and had placed the goal of personal comfort ahead of "grasping revolution."

84. A similar conclusion was reached by Vogel *(Canton Under Communism)*. For further analysis of the increasing trend toward the routinization of Party life in the early 1960s, see Vogel, "From Revolutionary to Semi-Bureaucrat: The 'Regularization' of Cadres," *The China Quarterly*, no. 29 (January–March 1967), pp. 36–60; Michel Oksenberg, "Local Leaders in Rural China, 1962–1965," in A. Doak Barnett, ed., *Chinese Communist Politics in Action* (Seattle: University of Washington Press, 1969), pp. 155–215; and Oksenberg, "The Institutionalization of the Chinese Communist Revolution."

85. *Radio Nanchang*, Kiangsi, September 11, 1963.

86. See, *inter alia, Radio Nanning*, Kwangsi, July 15, 1963; *Radio Nanchang*, Kiangsi, July 8, 22, and August 25, 1963; and *Radio Hofei*, Anhwei, September 7, 1963.

87. *Radio Nanchang*, Kiangsi, July 8, 1963. During the Cultural Revolution, many regional and provincial party officials were criticized for having similarly placed "production in command" in their rural squatting-points during the Socialist Education Movement. See chapter 6.

2. THE SECOND TEN POINTS

1. The full text of this directive is translated in Richard Baum and Frederick C. Teiwes, *Ssu-Ch'ing: The Socialist Education Movement of 1962–1966* (Berkeley: Center for Chinese Studies, 1968), Appendix C.

2. P'eng Chen's contribution to the Second Ten Points was initially hinted at by Liu Shao-ch'i in the latter's notorious "self-criticism" of October 1966. Teng's role as principal architect of this document was later officially confirmed in *JMJP*, November 23, 1967.

3. See, for example, Charles Neuhauser, "The Chinese Communist Party in the 1960's: Prelude to the Cultural Revolution," *The China Quarterly*, no. 32 (October–December, 1967), pp. 12–13; also Ezra F. Vogel, *Canton Under Communism* (Cambridge: Harvard University Press, 1969), pp. 315–16. For a summary of official statements concerning the alleged heterodoxy of the Second Ten Points, see *JMJP*, November 23, 1967.

4. Baum and Teiwes, *Ssu-Ch'ing*, Appendix C (Preface).

5. *Ibid.*, Article II.   6. *Ibid.*   7. *Ibid.*, Article VI.

8. *Ibid.*, Article VII.   9. *Ibid.*, Article IV.

10. *Ibid.*, Article II. The "Five-Anti Movement" mentioned in this passage was the urban equivalent of the rural Four Cleanups. In January 1965 the two movements were officially merged, and the term "Five-Anti Movement" was subsequently dropped.

11. *Ibid.*

12. *Ibid.* Articles I and II. Questions as to the nature, composition, and specific functions of the work teams were not discussed in the Second Ten Points. They will be examined in chapter 3.

13. *Ibid.*, Article II.   14. *Ibid.*

15. It is important to bear in mind that the majority of basic-level cadres in rural China—including the great majority of production team cadres and most brigade-level accountants, storehouse-keepers (*pao-kuan yüan*), and work-point recorders— were *not* members of the CCP. For example, in Kwangtung province, a 1960 survey revealed that out of a total of one million or more rural cadres at the commune, brigade, and production team levels, only about 400,000 were Party members. See Vogel, *Canton Under Communism*, pp. 371–72; and *NFJP*, January 14, 1960.

16. Second Ten Points, Articles I and VIII. According to the testimony of a number of former rural cadres, this "closed door" method was applied to CCP members because of the regime's reluctance to expose the mistakes and shortcomings of Party cadres to the public at large—since to do so would be to cause these key elite personnel to "lose face" in the eyes of the masses, thereby reducing their effectiveness as leaders.

17. *Ibid.*, Articles I and VI.

18. A fifth substantive category, cadre participation in productive labor, also received major stress in the Second Ten Points. But since the September 1963 directive contained no fundamentally new policy guidelines concerning this subject, we shall not examine this question in detail in the following discussion.

19. Second Ten Points, Article IX.

20. *Ibid.* Although this policy of leniency toward class enemies appears on the surface to be rather permissive, it does not necessarily go against the grain of Maoist thought, which has always stressed the necessity of "providing a way out" for class enemies. See, for example, Article XV of the Twenty-Three Points of January 1965, discussed in chapter 5, below.

21. Second Ten Points, Article III.

22. *Ibid.* The "60 Articles" on commune management and administration, revised and adopted by the CCP Central Committee at the Tenth Plenum in September 1962, stipulated that the amount of "self-retained land" in a given village should not exceed five percent of the total arable land of that village. In the Lienchiang documents, discussed earlier, it was revealed that in some villages as much as 30 to 40 percent of the total land area had been either privately held or "contracted to households." The Second Ten Points reaffirmed the correctness of the "60 Articles" on this question, but in so doing failed to provide for the confiscation of private lands in excess of the five percent limit, except in those cases where "the area in excess of the stipulated limits is comparatively large." In such serious cases, it was held that viola-

tors should be "persuasively educated"—rather than coerced—into returning the excess land.

23. Second Ten Points, Article III. 24. *Ibid.* 25. *Ibid.*

26. It is this quality of tolerance that has led some observers to regard the Second Ten Points as "revisionist." See pp. 57–59.

27. Second Ten Points, Article III.

28. It will be recalled that in orthodox Maoist thought, the middle peasants are by definition a force to be "united with," though never "relied upon." Because of the middle peasants' observed tendencies toward ideological vacillation and "spontaneous capitalism," the CCP has always held the consolidation of this stratum to be of pivotal importance in determining the outcome of the "struggle between two roads." Within the middle peasant stratum, relatively firm socioeconomic and political distinctions have been drawn (since 1956) among "lower-middle peasants," "ordinary middle peasants," and "upper-middle peasants." Cross-cutting these three substrata, however, is the additional criterion of upward (or downward) mobility, measured in terms of the waxing or waning of the individual peasant's familial fortunes between the time of land reform (1949–52) and the subsequent collectivization of agriculture (1955–56). The resultant analytic configuration of middle peasant substrata is rather complex, and can best be presented schematically:

direction of socioeconomic mobility, 1952–1956

original class status, 1949–52	upward	static	downward
poor peasant	"new" middle peasant	"old" lower-middle peasant	"old" poor peasant
middle peasant	"new" upper-middle peasant	"old" middle peasant	"old" lower-middle peasant
upper-middle peasant	—	"old" upper-middle peasant	"old" middle peasant

For a detailed discussion of the specific criteria by which these various substrata have been defined, and of mobility patterns among the middle peasants since 1949, see *"T'u-ti Kai-ko I-hou, Wo-kuo Nung-ts'un She-hui Chu-i ho Tzu-pen Chu-i Liang-t'iao Tao-lu te Tou-cheng"* (Struggle Between the Two Roads of Socialism and Capitalism in China's Countryside Since Land Reform), *Ching-chi Yen-chiu* (*Economic Research*) nos. 7–9 (July-September, 1965).

29. Second Ten Points, Article V. 30. *Ibid.* 31. *Ibid.*

32. As indicated earlier, such intra-Party rectification was to be carried out primarily behind closed doors.

33. Second Ten Points, Article VIII. The call for Party rectification as a precondition for the successful resolution of political, economic, and organizational problems in the countryside had initially been raised by Mao Tse-tung in May 1963. At that time, the Chairman stated that "This kind of class struggle has not been waged for over ten years. This time, it is to be conducted from within the Party to outside the

Party, from top to bottom, and from the cadres to the masses." See "Miscellany of Mao Tse-tung Thought (1949–68)," in *JPRS* 61,269-2 (February 20, 1974), p. 314.

34. Second Ten Points, Article VIII.   35. *Ibid.*   36. *Ibid.*, Article IV.

37. *Ibid.*   38. *Ibid.*

39. *Ibid.* It is interesting to note that the provision for peasants' association representatives to "attend" management committee meetings did not include the right of these representatives to vote in such meetings. The relevant term in the September 1963 directive is *"lieh-hsi"* (to attend in a nonvoting capacity).

40. *Ibid.* Such regulations were, in fact, drafted and promulgated in June 1964. See below, chapter 3.

41. *Ibid.*, Article VI.   42. *Ibid.*   43. *Ibid.*   44. *Ibid.*

45. *Ibid.* It should be noted that this two percent limit was regarded as provisional; and a stipulation was added stating that "the percentages of cadres to be punished in different regions should be fixed by various provincial, municipal, and autonomous regional Party committees on the basis of actual [local] conditions."

46. *Ibid.*

47. Subsequently, during the Cultural Revolution, it was charged that the Second Ten Points had incorporated so many dilatory measures and procedural restraints that the net effect had been to "bind the masses hand and foot," thus rendering the prompt, effective punishment of unclean cadres all but impossible. While it is true that the September 1963 directive did come down clearly on the side of caution and circumspection in the handling of aberrant rural cadres, it is by no means clear that this represented either a conscious attempt to undermine the Four Cleanups campaign or a violation of Mao's own prescriptions for cadre rectification.

48. In support of the contention that the Second Ten Points was a "highly revisionist document," Charles Neuhauser ("Chinese Communist Party in the 1960's") has argued that under the terms of this directive, "private plots were to be encouraged . . . and the 'free market system' was to be left intact." Mr. Neuhauser is, of course, correct in this argument, as we have seen. His error lies in his apparent failure to note that the (Maoist) First Ten Points of May 1963, which had explicitly reaffirmed the correctness of the CCP's 1962 "60 Articles" on commune management, had thereby also actively encouraged the retention of private plots and free markets.

Secondly, Mr. Neuhauser has contended that a primary aim of the Second Ten Points was to ensure "continued growth in production and a further increase in material advantages for the peasantry." Correct again; but again somewhat misleading. To the best of my knowledge it has never been considered "revisionist" for a CCP member to be in favor of increased production or a higher standard of living for the peasantry.

Thirdly, Mr. Neuhauser has suggested that rural basic-level cadres were totally "circumscribed and denied initiative" in the Second Ten Points, since "all matters of importance [in the Socialist Education Movement] were to be referred to the *hsien* [county] Party committee for clarification and final decision." Obviously, much depends here on one's definition of what constitutes a matter of importance; in the eyes of the document's drafter(s), however, such "important matters" were expected to constitute no more than five percent of the total number of individual cases investigated and handled during the movement. Moreover, as we have seen, the work teams, which were dispatched from higher-level Party organs and assigned primary responsibility for guiding local Four Cleanups investigations, were specifically enjoined in the Second Ten Points from "shunting aside" basic-level cadres and Party organs; and the work teams were further required to serve as "staff advisors" to the basic-level cadres, and were specifically warned against "monopolizing" or "taking the place of" these local cadres. It is difficult to reconcile such injunctions with the allegation that basic-level cadres were totally "circumscribed and denied initiative."

Both Mr. Neuhauser and Professor Vogel (*Canton Under Communism*) have also erred in arguing that the Second Ten Points contained strong warnings for work teams and local Party organs to guard against the tendency of classifying more affluent peasants as "rich peasants." Actually, the September 1963 directive made no mention whatever of "rich peasants" (*fu-nung*) in this context. Rather, the relevant passages of the Second Ten Points refer to the need for exercising caution in the classification of *upper-middle peasants* (*shang-chung nung*)—a crucial distinction in light of the fact that while rich peasants by definition belonged to the "four category elements" (and were therefore to be considered as targets of "struggle"), upper-middle peasants belonged to the category of middle peasants (and were therefore to be the objects of "unity and consolidation").

Professor Vogel is similarly in error when he argues that the Second Ten Points placed the poor and lower-middle peasants' organizations squarely under the disciplinary thumb of local Party organs. As we have seen, questions as to the proper functional and political relationships between rural Party organs and local peasants' organizations were purposely left unanswered in the Second Ten Points; and it was not until some nine months later, in June 1964, that such questions were resolved in favor of strict Party supervision and control.

Both Vogel and Neuhauser are on somewhat firmer ground when they argue that the Second Ten Points set forth unusually lenient criteria for distinguishing between (antagonistic) "contradictions with the enemy" and (nonantagonistic) "contradictions among the people." For, as has been previously noted, the September 1963 directive did serve to narrowly restrict the category of rural class enemies to include only a small handful of the most "degenerate" and unrepentant thieves, speculators, and saboteurs. On the other hand, the document's operative slogan—"Unite and consolidate over 95 percent of the rural masses"—is clearly of Maoist origin. And in Mao's own words, "those who persist in taking the capitalist road [are] always a very small minority."

49. *JMJP*, November 23, 1967; also *Peking Review*, no. 49 (December 1, 1967), p. 17.

50. It may be hypothesized that the allegations concerning Teng's attempt to "protect the agents of the bourgeoisie within the Party" and "direct the spearhead of struggle against the poor and lower-middle peasants" were part of a conscious attempt to carry out a total political character assassination against Teng by linking him with the "bourgeois reactionary line" of Liu Shao-ch'i. For more on this point, see chapter 8, below.

51. Vogel, *Canton Under Communism*, pp. 315–16.

52. It is interesting to note that during the Cultural Revolution the radical critique of Teng Hsiao-p'ing was never very thoroughgoing or well-documented. This stands in marked contrast to the rather fully detailed and documented attacks that were concurrently being launched against Teng's alleged coconspirator, Liu Shao-ch'i. Moreover, the official campaign of vilification against Teng all but ceased after the winter of 1967–68, following the purge of a number of "ultra-leftists" in the CCP's propaganda department. Both of the above facts tend to reinforce the notion that Teng's political errors may have been less heretical than some of his more ardent detractors have been willing to admit. See note 48, above.

3. THE SMALL FOUR CLEANUPS

1. *NFJP*, December 14, 1963, also September 21, 1963.

2. See, for example, *NFJP*, December 28, 1963.   3. *JMJP*, October 8, 1963.

4. It is, of course, possible to argue (as the Maoists have done) that since the Party's propaganda machinery was largely in the hands of "bourgeois demons and monsters" in this period, it was impossible for the Maoists to propagate their orthodox ideas on the nature and requirements of class struggle in the mass media. This argument lacks a certain amount of credibility, however, since it appears to be largely a post-facto rationalization. Professor Vogel is probably closer to the truth in arguing that the liberalism of the Second Ten Points appealed to the vast majority of bureaucrats at all levels of the Party hierarchy (including the propaganda machinery), since these (presumably pragmatic) officials were probably "anxious to avoid a reckless campaign that might interfere with production." Ezra F. Vogel, *Canton Under Communism* [Cambridge: Harvard University Press, 1969], p. 316).

5. Mao Tse-tung, "Remarks at a Briefing" (March 1964), in "Miscellany of Mao Tse-tung Thought (1949–1968)," *JPRS* 61,269-2 (February 20, 1974), p. 340.

6. "Directive on Labor Reform" (April 28, 1964), in *ibid.*, p. 347.

7. Not until January 1965 did Chairman Mao indicate any displeasure with either Teng Hsiao-p'ing or the Second Ten Points. See chapter 5, n. 58, below.

8. See, for example, *JMJP*, November 29, 1963; and *NFJP*, December 14, 1963.

9. Significantly, throughout the autumn of 1963 virtually no media publicity was given to the work of mobilizing and organizing the poor and lower-middle peasants. For example, in a major address on the Socialist Education Movement presented to the Shensi provincial Party Congress in mid-November by Liu Lan-t'ao, head of the Central Committee's Northwest Party Bureau, there was not a single mention of the need to rely upon—let alone mobilize and organize—the poor and lower-middle peasants. See *Radio Sian*, Shensi, November 19, 1963. Moreover, to the limited extent that peasant mobilization was publicized in the mass media in this period, such publicity almost always included warnings (either tacit or explicit) against the twin "leftist" dangers of alienating the middle and upper-middle peasants and adopting an indiscriminate attitude of hostility toward the sons and daughters of landlord and rich peasant elements.

10. For a summary and analysis of these developments, see James R. Townsend, "Communist China: The New Protracted War," *Asian Survey*, 5, no. 1 (January

1965), 1–11; also Richard Baum, "Ideology Redivivus," *Problems of Communism*, 16, no. 3 (May–June 1967), 1–11.

11. For official explanations of the nature and purposes of this three-stage technique of campaign implementation, see *JMJP*, March 11, 1961, August 26, 1964, and July 3, 1965; *NFJP*, December 7, 1963; and Article II of the Second Ten Points, in Richard Baum and Frederick C. Teiwes, *Ssu-Ch'ing: The Socialist Education Movement of 1962–1966* (Berkeley: Center for Chinese Studies, 1968), Appendix C.

12. *JMJP*, January 1, 1964.

13. Western agricultural economists have variously estimated China's total grain output for 1963 at 175–185 million metric tons, representing a 10–15 percent increase over the lean years of 1959–61. See, for example, Steve Washenko, "Agriculture in Mainland China," *Current Scene* (Hong Kong), 7, no. 6 (March 31, 1969), 8.

14. Mao Tse-tung, "Remarks at a Briefing" (March 1964), in "Miscellany of Mao Tse-tung Thought (1949–1968)," *JPRS* 61,269-2 (February 20, 1974), p. 342.

15. Mao Tse-tung, "Talk at the Hantan Forum on Four Cleanups Work" (March 28, 1964), in *ibid.*, p. 337.

16. *Ibid.*, pp. 337–38.

17. T'ao Chu, *"Jen-min Kung-she tsai Ch'ien-chin"* (People's Communes on the March), *Hung-ch'i*, no. 4 (February 26, 1964), 1–12. An abridged translation of this article was serialized in *Peking Review*, nos. 13 and 15 (March 27 and April 10, 1964).

18. Second Ten Points, Article II.

19. *Ibid.* The distinction between "points" and "planes" is crucial in attempting to understand the development of the Socialist Education Movement in 1964. For it was only in those relatively few rural communes and production brigades which had been designated as keypoints (constituting perhaps five to ten percent of the total) that the movement was conducted on an intensive basis in that year.

Individual rural keypoint areas were selected by Party committees at each level, from the commune to the Central Committee. The criteria for such selection varied. According to the testimony of a former provincial-level cadre, it had been the intention of the Party center to select a cross-section of economically and politically "progressive" *(chin-pu te)*, "ordinary" *(p'u-t'ung te)*, and "backward" *(lo-hou te)* rural administrative units to serve as keypoints. In practice, however, Party committees at each level often selected only the more progressive units within their jurisdiction for such concentrated work. The reason for this was that the prestige of leading Party cadres depended to some extent upon the success of their work in organizing and guiding keypoint demonstrations. And since such success was most easily gauged in economic terms, there was a natural tendency to send work teams to those rural communes and production brigades where economic problems were fewer and where the local cadres were more cooperative and manipulable. An excellent illustration of this tendency is provided in the five criteria set down for the selection of basic-level keypoints by the Kwangtung provincial Party committee. At a meeting of the provincial Party Organization Department *(Tsu-chih Pu)* held in May 1965, leading cadres at the provincial, special district, and county levels were instructed to designate as keypoints only those basic-level units in which (1) the commune members had demonstrated "higher socialist consciousness"; (2) production had been increasing before the advent of the Socialist Education Movement; (3) the basic-level cadres were relatively "clean" at the outset of the movement; (4) no serious natural disasters had occurred in recent years; and (5) local transportation and communication facilities were relatively well-developed and convenient.

20. The criteria for "five good" commune members were (1) good in observing the laws and decrees of the government; (2) good in protecting the collective; (3) good in labor attendance; (4) good in protecting public property; and (5) good in uniting with and helping other people. The criteria for selection of "five good" basic-level cadres were (1) good in holding fast to the socialist road; (2) good in executing Party policies; (3) good in labor participation and production leadership; (4) good in observing the PLA's "three-eight" work style of diligence, thrift, honesty, and concern for the masses; and (5) good in political and ideological study. See *NFJP*, April 17, 1963.

For documentation on the "compare, learn, catch-up, and help" movement, see *Jen-min Shou-ts'e (People's Handbook)*, 1964 (Shanghai: *Ta-kung Pao She*, 1964), pp. 88–96. On the development of the "four histories" movement in this period, see *CNP*, June 18, 1964; and *JMJP*, December 28, 1964. And on the institutionalization of the "three fixes" for cadre participation in labor, see *JMJP*, October 29, 1963; and *NFJP*, November 26, 1963.

21. I spent several months in Hong Kong in 1967 and 1968 conducting intensive interviews with over fifty participants in the rural Socialist Education Movement. The following discussion draws largely upon these interview materials. In addition, the author is indebted to Professors Ezra Vogel, Frederick C. Teiwes, and Gordon A. Bennett for making available additional transcripts of refugee interviews, many of which proved invaluable in the preparation of the following section.

22. Party committees at every level, from the Central Committee to the county, each selected one or more rural administrative units under their jurisdiction to serve as keypoints. For example, the Central-South Party Bureau (with jurisdiction over the five provinces of Honan, Hupeh, Hunan, Kwangtung, and Kwangsi) initially selected two production brigades in Kwangtung—one in Hua County and the other in Polo County—to serve as its primary keypoints. Similarly, the Kwangtung provincial Party Committee selected as its initial keypoints three communes in the rural suburbs of Canton municipality. And at the subprovincial level in Kwangtung, the Party committees of Huiyang, Foshan, and Shant'ou special districts selected communal keypoints in Huiyang, Chungshan, and Ch'aoan counties, respectively.

Generally speaking, each keypoint commune was assigned from 100 to 500 work team personnel (depending on the size of the commune), with each keypoint production brigade receiving from 10 to 20 outside personnel, who were then dispersed in groups of one, two, or three to squat at points in individual production teams for the duration of the movement—generally about three to six months. Once the movement had been completed at a given keypoint, the work teams would be recalled for further study and training, and would then be reassigned to new keypoints. In this manner, the movement was to be systematically extended throughout the countryside "group-by-group and stage-by-stage."

23. Exceptions to this hierarchical command structure were made in those cases

where high-level Party officials—members of the Central Committee, regional Party bureaus, or provincial Party committees—personally participated in rural keypoint investigations at the basic levels. In such cases (e.g., the notorious squatting experience of Mme. Liu Shao-ch'i), the work team was responsible directly to the Party committee at the level from which it had been dispatched, thus bypassing the provincial and subprovincial organizational hierarchy.

24. The practice of striking roots with a preselected handful of reputedly reliable poor peasant informants in each village—a practice first popularized by Teng Hsiao-P'ing—was discontinued in the first half of 1965 on the grounds that this tended to interfere with the overall objectivity and detachment of the work team's investigations. See chapter 5.

25. Mao Tse-tung, "Talk on the Four Cleanups Movement" (January 3, 1965), in "Miscellany of Mao Tse-tung Thought," pp. 441–42.

26. Throughout 1964 the official voice of the Communist Youth League, *Chung-kuo Ch'ing-nien (China Youth)*, published numerous articles and letters encouraging young work team members in the countryside to conscientiously integrate themselves with the poor and lower-middle peasants. These articles were used as educational materials in the weekly or biweekly study session attended by work-team members. See, for example, *Chung-kuo Ch'ing-nien* (hereafter, *CKCN*), no. 22 (November 16, 1964), 2–4, and no. 23 (December 1, 1964), 2–3.

27. This policy was in full accord with the prescriptions for cadre rectification that had been set down in both the First and Second Ten Points.

28. It should be remembered that the work team members had already studied the dossiers of all local cadres before arriving at their squatting points, and thus had a fair idea in advance of which cadres were most likely guilty of the "four uncleans."

29. The latter were known as "controlled elements," since they had long been placed under official surveillance and varying degrees of "dictatorship" by the local authorities. These hapless "enemies of the people" (of whom there were usually at least two or three in each village) were always the first to be "dragged out" and subjected to public humiliation at the onset of every mass political campaign in the countryside. In effect, they served as sacrificial lambs; and their humiliation was designed to "set the masses in motion."

30. The exemption of rural Party members and leading cadres from investigation at this stage represented an implicit violation of Mao's May 1963 dictum that the movement should be conducted "from within the Party to outside the Party; from top to bottom."

31. Although the Second Ten Points had expressly called for work teams to rely upon local Party cadres, the possible danger of conspiratorial concealment of corruption that inhered in such reliance had been clearly implied in Article II of that document, which stated that "It would obviously be wrong for the work teams to circulate exclusively among the local cadres without taking root and linking up with . . . the poor and lower-middle peasant masses." The problem of conspiratorial collusion between higher- and lower-level cadres was first expressly revealed in the revised edition of the Second Ten Points, promulgated by Liu Shao-ch'i in September 1964. See Baum and Teiwes, *Ssu-Ch'ing*, Appendix E, Article VI.

32. Vogel, *Canton Under Communism*, p. 314.   33. *Ibid.*

34. The tendency for rural work teams to pass the buck to higher-level authorities in all but the most clear-cut and unambiguous cases of economic corruption was tacitly criticized by Mao in June of 1964 as a "right-opportunist" deviation, since it served the self-interest of the work team members, many of whom did not want to take the initiative in passing judgment on local cadres and peasants, and at the same time removed the most controversial cases from the immediate purview of the rural masses. See, e.g., Article IV of the "Twenty-Three Points" of January 1965, in Baum and Teiwes, *Ssu-Ch'ing*, Appendix F.

35. It will be recalled that the Second Ten Points of September 1963 had explicitly called for the issuance of such a directive in the first half of 1964.

36. Mao's personal authorship of the above six criteria, together with the date and occasion of their issuance, were confirmed in the Twenty-Three Points of January 1965. See Baum and Teiwes, *Ssu-Ch'ing*, Appendix F, Article IV.

37. The most important source concerning Mao's thought on the question of peasant mobilization is his famous 1926 essay, "Report on an Investigation into the Peasant Movement in Hunan." See *Selected Works of Mao Tse-tung*, vol. 1 (Peking: Foreign Language Press, 1964), pp. 23–59.

38. Franz Schurmann has rightly observed that "Mao's emphasis on the masses . . . reveals his deep belief that the forces of society control the state, and not the reverse. Concretely, this means that . . . in the villages it must be the poor peasants who control the communes." See Schurmann, *Ideology and Organization in Communist China* (enlarged edition) (Berkeley: University of California Press, 1968), p. 520. Schurmann has also argued that it was precisely in the area of Mao's dominant "populist" approach to social organization and control that he came into sharp conflict with Liu Shao-ch'i in the mid-1960s. See below, n. 42 and 50.

39. The phenomenon of work teams secretly "striking roots" was first explicitly criticized by Chairman Mao in January 1965. See "Miscellany of Mao Tse-tung Thought," pp. 443–44.

40. Article V of Mao's Twenty-Three Points thus states that ". . . from start to finish we must grasp production [and] pay attention to . . . the question of the peasants' livelihood. . . . Otherwise . . . we shall become divorced from the masses."

41. A full translation of this document appears in Baum and Teiwes, *Ssu-Ch'ing*, Appendix D.

42. The distinction between the "populism" of Mao and the "elitism" of Liu Shao-ch'i is highly important in attempting to understand the subsequent split between these two leaders. The best short account of this distinction appears in Schurmann, *Ideology and Organization*, pp. 513–519: "Though both Mao and Liu accept the notions of democracy and centralism as crucial to proper organizational function, Mao stresses the primacy of democracy and Liu the primacy of centralism. For Mao, democracy means a populist upsurge of the masses, a spiritual liberation that unleashes their creative energies. . . . For Liu, centralism means the rule of organization, specifically that of the Party."

43. Baum and Teiwes, *Ssu-Ch'ing*, Appendix D, Article XIII.

44. *Ibid.*, Article IV.   45. *Ibid.*, Article XV.   46. *Ibid.*, Article XIV.

47. *Ibid.*, Article XVI.   48. *Ibid.*, Preface (emphasis added).

49. *Ibid.*, Article II.

50. It has been suggested that Liu Shao-ch'i has long harbored a profound distrust of the "crude and backward" peasant masses, and that his stress upon the need for organizational (read: Party) discipline to be exercised over the rural masses stemmed directly from such distrust. Schurmann (*Ideology and Organization*) has been the most articulate spokesman for this interpretation. In support of his argument, Schurmann cites a fragment from a Red Guard publication which purports to describe the attitude of Mme. Liu (Wang Kuang-mei) toward the newly-established peasants' associations in a rural district in North China in 1964: Wang Kuang-mei "called the class organizations in the village 'blackguards' and 'ruffians.' Analyzing the poor and lower-middle peasants' organizations in Kaochen, she said: '. . . a lot of them used to be bandits with secret societies. Too many [of them] have defects in their personal history. No matter how much you teach the poor and lower-middle peasants, hardly any among them lacks defects. The only pure ones are a few young people. . . . There's hardly a one over 35 who is any good. . . .' " (from *Tung-fang Hung* [*The East is Red*, Peking], May 7, 1967, quoted in Schurmann, *Ideology and Organization*, pp. 538–39).

51. See Leonard Schapiro and John W. Lewis, "The Roles of the Monolithic Party under the Totalitarian Leader," *The China Quarterly*, no. 40 (October–December 1969), 50–57; also Schurmann, *Ideology and Organization*, p. 539.

4. THE "T'AOYÜAN EXPERIENCE"

1. The major sources used in the preparation of the following dicussion of Wang Kuang-mei's T'aoyüan Experience are of two main varieties: official (Party) media reports and unofficial (Red Guard) newspapers and "big character posters." Although all of these sources are extremely biased in their descriptions and analyses of particular events (for Wang, along with Liu, was regarded as a primary public enemy during the Cultural Revolution), I have attempted to distinguish between the facts of Wang's T'aoyüan Experience and the retrospective (and highly prejudicial) *interpretations* of these facts, which appeared during the campaign of vilification against Liu and Wang in 1967 and 1968. All published sources have been cross-checked for inconsistencies and logical contradictions, and have been compared with the personal recollections of a number of refugees who had first- or second-hand knowledge of the events of this period (including two former cadres who actually heard tape recordings of Wang's Shanghai address of July 1964). Through such cross-checking it has been possible to extract a certain amount of relatively hard data; and it is this data that forms the basis of the following discussion.

The most important official sources concerning Wang's T'aoyüan Experience are: "*Chia Ssu-ch'ing Chen Fu-pi*" ("False Four Cleanups, True Restoration"), *JMJP*, September 6, 1967; "*Chung-kuo Nung-ts'un Liang-t'iao Tao-lu te Tou-cheng*" ("Struggle Between the Two Roads in China's Countryside"), *JMJP*, November 23, 1967; "Exposing a Big Scheme for Restoring Capitalism," *Peking Review*, no. 38 (September 15, 1967), 23–24; "The Crimes of China's Khrushchev in the Socialist Education

Movement," *ibid.*, pp. 25–27; and *New China News Agency* (hereafter, *NCNA*) (Peking), April 3, 1968.

The most important unofficial sources used in the following discussion are: *"Chien-chüeh Ta-tao Chung-kuo te Ho-lu-shao-fu—Liu Shao-ch'i"* ("Resolutely Strike Down China's Khrushchev—Liu Shao-ch'i"), *Wei-tung (Eastern Guard)*, April 29, 1967; *"Wang Kuang-mei te 'T'ao-yüan Ching-yen' shih Fan-Mao Ssu-hsiang te Tu-ts'ao"* ("Wang Kuang-mei's T'aoyuan Experience is a Poisonous Weed in Opposition to Mao's Thought"), *Tsao-fan Yu-li Pao (Rebellion is Justified News)*, February 12, 1967; *"Liu Shao-ch'i, Wang Kuang-mei tsai 'Ssu-ch'ing' Yün-tung chung te Hsing 'Tso' Shih Yu Fan-tung Lu-hsien Pi-hsü Ch'e-ti P'i-p'an"* ("Liu Shao-ch'i and Wang Kuang-mei's 'Left' in Form but Right in Essence Reactionary Line in the Four Cleanups Movement Must be Thoroughly Repudiated"), *Tsao-fan Yu-li Pao*, March 10, 1967; *"Wang Kuang-Mei tsai T'ao-yüan Fan-hsia te T'ao-ta Tsui-hsing"* ("The Towering Crimes Committed by Wang Kuang-mei in T'aoyüan"), *Pei-ching Yüan-hsiao Hung-wei-ping (The Peking Institute Red Guard)*, March 4, 1967; *"Liu Shao-ch'i, Wang Kuang-mei tsai Pao-ting Ti-ch'ü Ssu-ch'ing Yün-tung chung te Tsui-hsing Tiao-ch'a Pao-kao"* ("Report on an Investigation into the Crimes of Liu Shao-ch'i and Wang Kuang-mei in the Four Cleanups Movement in Paoting District"), *Tung-fang Hung (The East is Red)*, May 7, 1967; and "A Factual Account of an Investigation Conducted at T'aoyüan," *Cheng-fa Kung-she (Commune of the College of Political Science and Law, Peking)*, no. 17 (April 7, 1967), in *Survey of the China Mainland Press* (hereafter, *SCMP*), no. 3958, pp. 10–23.

For a brief secondary account of Wang Kuang-mei's T'aoyuan Experience, based upon the above sources, see Richard Baum, "Peach Garden Pestilence," *Far Eastern Economic Review*, 58, no. 7 (November 16, 1967), 323–25. See also Rewi Alley, *Travels in China*, 1966–71 (Peking: New World Press, 1973), pp. 135–39.

2. Although Wang was at that time a leading cadre in the Hopei provincial Public Security Bureau, her work team was directly responsible to the Party Central Committee, rather than the provincial Party committee. It was later revealed that she had been sent to the T'aoyüan brigade at the behest of her husband, Liu Shao-ch'i.

3. The practice of having high-ranking Party officials conduct basic-level investigations without revealing their identity was a common one, designed to ensure the objectivity of the investigation by minimizing the likelihood of flattery and other forms of dissimulative behavior on the part of local cadres and peasants.

4. *JMJP*, September 6, 1967.

5. See *Tsao-fan Yu-li Pao*, March 10, 1967. It was also during the course of her T'aoyüan investigation that Wang Kuang-mei reportedly characterized a number of local peasants' association members as "ruffians" and "blackguards" (see chapter 3, n. 50, above).

6. It should be noted that such instructions were not necessarily in violation of either (Mao's) First Ten Points or (Teng Hsiao-p'ing's) Second Ten Points, both of which had authorized rural work teams, upon approval by higher-level authorities, to dismiss and replace local cadres in those communes and production brigades where leadership had been usurped by four category elements or other "degenerate" elements (First Ten Points, Article VIII; Second Ten Points, Article II).

7. *Peking Review*, no. 38 (September 12, 1967), 25.

8. For example, it was alleged that the principal target of Wang Kuang-mei's attack,

T'aoyüan Party branch secretary Wu Ch'en, after steadfastly refusing to "bow his head to the masses" and admit his guilt, was forced to assume the uncomfortable "flying sparrow" position—head down, knees bent, bent over at the waist, with arms fully extended to the rear—for several hours on end in the course of the prolonged public struggle against him. See *JMJP*, September 6, 1967; and *Wei-tung*, April 29, 1967. Also Alley, *Travels in China*, p. 138.

9. See "The Trials of Wang Kuang-mei," *Current Background* (hereafter *CB*), no. 848 (February 27, 1968), 7, 21.

10. These seven points represent the lowest common denominator of the personal recollections of two former cadres who heard tape recordings of Wang Kuang-mei's Shanghai speech in the latter part of 1964. In addition to the seven points raised above (each of which was mentioned independently by both informants), a number of other points relating to Wang's July 1964 speech were raised by one or the other informant; but since there was a lack of consensus between the two on these additional points, I have deleted them in the interest of accurate reportage.

It is of interest to note that no text—full or fragmentary, official or underground—of Wang's speech was ever publicized during the Cultural Revolution. This is noteworthy because the speech was repeatedly condemned as "bourgeois reactionary claptrap" during the Cultural Revolution. It is possible (although this is merely speculation) that the text of Wang's Shanghai address was deliberately suppressed in this latter period because the speech may have included a reference to Mao's personal approval of Wang's squatting-point investigation. One of the two informants claimed that this was in fact the case. This hypothesis would also accord with Wang Kuang-mei's own claim (made at the time of her first public trial in April 1967) that Chairman Mao had praised her for "eating together, living together, and working together with the masses . . . during the Four Cleanups." See n. 9, above. See also *JMJP*, November 15, 1964, which prominently displays a photo of the T'aoyüan brigade, with a caption praising the results of the Socialist Education Movement in the brigade.

11. The following discussion is based on Baum, "Peach Garden Pestilence," and Alley, *Travels in China*.

12. *CB*, No. 848.

13. In this connection, it should be noted that before Wang Kuang-mei's squatting experience, the T'aoyüan brigade had been widely publicized throughout Hopei province as an "advanced" unit. See, e.g., *JMJP*, November 15, 1964.

14. See *Tsao-fan Yu-li Pao*, February 12, 1967.

15. Such middle-level bureaucratic resistance to the radical cleansing of basic-level rural leadership was later explicitly criticized by Liu Shao-ch'i in his Revised Second Ten Points. See Richard Baum and Frederick C. Teiwes, *Ssu-Ch'ing: The Socialist Education Movement of 1962–1966* (Berkeley: Center for Chinese Studies, 1968), Appendix E, Article VI.

16. The principal sources used in the following discussion are "Drag Out Liu Shao-ch'i and Show Him to the Public," *Ching-kang-shan* (*Chingkang Mountains*, Peking), April 18, 1967, in *SCMP*, no. 3946, pp. 1–15; "Yet Another Crime of Opposing Chairman Mao's Revolutionary Line," *Pa-i-san Hung-wei-ping* (*August 13 Red Guard*, Tientsin), no. 68 (May 13, 1967), in *Selections From China Mainland Magazines* (hereaf-

ter, *SCMM*), no. 583, pp. 24–30; "Forty Instances of the Reactionary Statements of the Top Party Person in Authority Taking the Capitalist Road in Undermining the Socialist Revolution in the Countryside," *Nung-ts'un Ch'ing-nien (Rural Youth*, Shanghai), no. 9 (May 10, 1967), in *Union Research Service* (hereafter, *URS*), vol. 48, no. 6 (July 21, 1967), 74–89; *Tsao-fan Yu-li Pao*, March 10, 1967; *JMJP*, November 23, 1967; and *Tung-fang Hung*, May 7, 1967.

17. In distributing these tapes, Liu and Wang tacitly indicated their lack of approval of certain policy guidelines laid down in Teng Hsiao-p'ing's Second Ten Points. Before the late summer of 1964, the "Double Ten Points" had been the major policy documents used in the training of work team personnel. Moreover, Liu Shao-ch'i's acknowledged, in his first self-criticism of October 1966, that he had become dissatisfied with Teng's Second Ten Points in the late summer of 1964. This tends to controvert the Maoists' later claimed that Liu and Teng had been coconspirators in sabotaging the Socialist Education Movement.

18. Quoted in *Nung-ts'un Ch'ing-nien*, May 10, 1967; and *Ching-kang-shan*, April 18, 1967; see also *Tsao-fan Yu-li Pao*, March 10, 1967. In view of the Maoists' subsequent allegation that Liu Shao-ch'i had drastically overestimated both the extent and seriousness of the four uncleans in the countryside, it is rather curious that the Chairman himself personally concurred with Liu's diagnosis of disorder at the time the diagnosis was first made. Thus, in a "Talk on Problems of Philosophy" delivered on August 18, 1964, Mao explicitly endorsed Liu's grim assessment of the rural political situation: "In our nation now, about one third of the power is held by the enemy or those who sympathize with the enemy. . . . Today a Party branch secretary can be bribed with a few packs of cigarettes; and there's no telling what one could achieve by marrying off his daughter to such a person. . . . From the look of things, there are more than a few problems at the present time." (Quoted in "Miscellany of Mao Tse-tung Thought," p. 387.)

19. *Nung-ts'un Ch'ing-nien*, May 10, 1967.

20. Quoted in *Pa-i-san Hung-wei-ping*, May 13, 1967. Liu's derogation of the value of investigation reports was subsequently criticized by Mao as a manifestation of a "metaphysical" viewpoint, which opposed the Party's correct epistemological principle of seeking knowledge through practice. "Without investigating," the Chairman stated, "one has no right to speak."

21. *Ibid*.

22. *Ibid*. In this passage, Liu implicitly modified his earlier view that such investigation reports were totally useless.

23. Liu's role as principal architect of the Revised Second Ten Points was initially revealed in his own self-criticism of October 1966. Subsequently this was confirmed in official Party media sources. See, for example, *JMJP*, November 23, 1967. An abridged translation of the Revised Second Ten Points appears in Baum and Teiwes, *Ssu-Ch'ing*, Appendix E.

24. Revised Second Ten Points, Article I.   25. *Ibid*., Article II.

26. *Ibid*., Article VI (emphasis added).   27. *Ibid*.   28. *Ibid*., Article II.

29. *Ibid*., Article VI. Although the earlier two percent quota of unclean cadres targeted for organizational discipline was retained in the revised version, it was now

(somewhat contradictorily) argued that "the offender should be given whatever punishment he deserves"—including expulsion from the Party, dismissal from his job, or both.

30. *Ibid.*

31. *Ibid.*, Article II. The apparent anomaly of Liu Shao-ch'i (the "organization man" par excellence) stressing the Maoist technique of populistic mass peasant mobilization is explained by the fact that Liu was primarily concerned with rooting out decadent local Party members and cadres; and since local peasants were considered the best source of information concerning the attitudes and behavior of these rural officials, it was considered absolutely essential to "mobilize the masses"—i.e., to overcome, through "striking roots and linking up," the peasants' natural reluctance to inform on their leaders. However, by placing the work teams in absolute control of the mobilization process (including the preselection of local "roots" and the recruitment and screening of peasants' association leaders), it became certain that the local peasants would be subjected to organizational discipline and control, thereby preventing the mass movement from getting out of hand. It was this latter aspect— the firm control over the peasant masses exercised by the work teams—that led to the subsequent charge that the Revised Second Ten Points was " 'left' in form but right in essence." On this point, see Franz Schurmann, *Ideology and Organization in Communist China* (enlarged edition) (Berkeley: University of California Press, 1968), pp. 508, 519, and 539. In several of the Cultural Revolutionary documents cited in n. 1, above, the charge was made that Wang Kuang-mei, in her T'aoyüan Experience, had opposed giving the local peasant masses free rein in criticizing and rectifying local cadres, since "their sentiments are somewhat excessive . . . and they may have to be restrained." See, e.g., *Tsao-fan Yu-li Pao*, March 10, 1967.

32. *Ibid.* It will be recalled that a similar "insurance policy" had been incorporated into the Central Committee's peasants' association regulations of June 1964. The idea of consolidating the results of the Four Cleanups by having work team personnel periodically revisit their squatting points following the completion of the movement was derived from Wang Kuang-mei's T'aoyüan Experience.

33. *Ibid.*, Article V.   34. *Ibid.*, Article IV.   35. *Ibid.*, Article VI.

36. *Ibid.* (emphasis added) See also n. 31, above.

37. Such safeguards included: (1) the call for disciplinary action in all serious cases of cadre corruption to be approved by higher-level Party authorities before being carried out; (2) the call for all such disciplinary measures to be delayed until the later stages of the movement when the masses had had time to "cool off"; and (3) the call for all cadre errors that were not clearly ascertained to be (antagonistic) "contradictions with the enemy" to be treated in the first instance as (nonantagonistic) "contradictions among the people."

38. Revised Second Ten Points, Article III.

39 *Ibid.*, Article VI. Combined with the new mandate, mentioned earlier, which called for work teams to "lead the movement from beginning to end," this provision served to further tip the balance of power in favor of the work teams (vis-à-vis the rural Party establishment) by tacitly granting to the work teams the right to review (and contest) all verdicts handed down from higher levels.

40. *Ibid.* (emphasis added)

41. See, e.g., Article II of the Twenty-Three Points of January 1965, in Baum and Teiwes, *Ssu-Ch'ing*, Appendix F.

42. Revised Second Ten Points, Article V.

43. *Ibid.*, Articles III and IX. In each of the above respects, the Revised Second Ten Points was less permissive—and therefore ostensibly less "revisionist"—than the original version.

44. *Ibid.*, Article VIII. In this connection, it will be recalled that Liu Shao-ch'i had been quoted as saying that the dismissal of aberrant Party members was a necessary educational measure.

45. *Ibid.*

46. This difference in emphasis may be illustrated by means of rudimentary quantitative content analysis of the two documents. In the Second Ten Points of September 1963, which contained approximately 19,000 words (or characters), approximately 2,500 words (13%) were devoted to questions of educating and consolidating the peasantry, drawing correct distinctions between "acceptable" privatism and illegitimate speculations and profiteering, and prescribing methods for correctly treating such contradictions; in addition, approximately 1,750 words (9%) dealt with questions pertaining to the correct handling of "four category elements" and their families. By way of contrast, in the Revised Second Ten Points, which contained approximately 20,000 words, only about 1,500 words (7.5%) pertained to the class education and consolidation of the peasantry, with an additional 1,250 words (6%) devoted to questions concerning the "four category elements." On the other hand, whereas the September 1963 document devoted some 3,500 words (18%) to questions concerning cadre malpractices, the Four Cleanups, and the nature and functions of work teams, the revised document of September 1964 devoted more than 5,000 words (25%) to these same questions.

47. *Nung-ts'un Ch'ing-nien*, May 10, 1967.

48. Liu's emphasis on the contradiction between the four cleans and the four uncleans was explicitly repudiated in Mao's Twenty-Three Points of January 1965, on the grounds that it was devoid of specific class content and therefore "did not clarify the fundamental characteristics of the Socialist Education Movement." See Baum and Teiwes, *Ssu-Ch'ing*, Appendix F, Article II.

49. In support of their argument that Liu "bound the masses hand and foot" by placing work teams in absolute control of the Four Cleanups campaign, the Maoists later argued that in many rural areas the Four Cleanup work teams had not mobilized the masses at all and had failed to solicit the opinions of the masses, thus leading to the rendering of unjust verdicts and the imposition of excessively harsh penalties in the cases of many allegedly "good and relatively good" cadres—a phenomenon that became known in Cultural Revolutionary jargon as "attacking the many."

5. THE BIG FOUR CLEANUPS

1. Michel Oksenberg, "Local Leaders in Rural China, 1962–65: Individual Attributes, Bureaucratic Positions, and Political Recruitment," in A. Doak Barnett, ed., *Chinese Communist Politics in Action* (Seattle: University of Washington Press, 1969), p. 184.

2. Three former work team members interviewed by the author stated that as there were only a few keypoint communes and brigades in each county it was officially reckoned that the demotion or dismissal of 50 to 80 percent of the cadres in such keypoint units was fully compatible with the countywide five percent target figure. Thus, for example, in a county with 20 communes and 300 production brigades, ten percent of which had been designated as keypoint units, the absolute majority of cadres in each keypoint could be purged without substantially exceeding the overall five percent quota. In terms of provincewide statistics, the only credible report I have seen to date states that "over 23 percent of all basic-level cadres in [Honan] province were under attack [in the latter half of 1964]; some ten percent were either dismissed, expelled from the party, or similarly punished." (*Radio Chengchow*, Honan, December 12, 1967).

3. This calculation is based on the CCP's official 1963 estimate that there were currently more than 20 million cadres at the production brigade and team levels in the countryside (*JMJP*, July 4, 1963). In addition, there were an estimated two to three million cadres at the commune level, making a total of approximately 25 million rural cadres at the three levels of commune, brigade, and team.

4. The following discussion is based on Richard Baum and Frederick C. Teiwes, "Liu Shao-ch'i and the Cadre Question," *Asian Survey*, 8, no. 4 (April 1968), 331–33.

5. *JMJP*, October 29, 1964.   6. *NFJP*, October 11, 1964.

7. See, for example, *NFJP*, October 14, 1964.

8. *Ibid.* See also *JMJP*, December 11, 1964.

9. *NFJP*, December 26, 1964. Here we see a concrete manifestation of the difference in emphasis between the Small Four Cleanups and the Big Four Cleanups; prior to the late summer and autumn of 1964, cadre corruption in the area of workpoint allocation was regarded as a "common mistake" and a (nonantagonistic) "contradiction among the people." By now labeling such corruption as antisocialist and exploitative, however, four unclean cadres were implicitly regarded as "enemies of the people."

10. *Radio Tientsin*, Hopei, December 19, 1964.

11. *Radio Nanchang*, Kiangsi, December 18, 1964.

12. *JMJP*, December 4, 1964. Interestingly, the role of four cleanup work teams in launching the rural masses to criticize and supervise local cadres received virtually no mention—favorable or unfavorable—in the mass media in this period. Nevertheless, it is clear both from the context of these events, and from interviews conducted with numerous peasant and cadre refugees, that it was the work teams who had been responsible for precipitating the high tide of anticadre criticism in the latter part of 1964. Hence, the cadres' allegation that "we are relying too much on the poor and lower-middle peasants" may be interpreted as an indirect attack by the local rural establishment against the work teams, who had carried out the policy of "bodly mobilizing the masses."

13. *NFJP*, November 9, 1964.

14. *Radio Wuhan*, Hupeh, November 11, 1964.

15. This represented a significant turnabout from the prevalent practice during the previous Small Four Cleanups, when ordinary cadres had been required to face the masses while principal cadres had been allowed to conduct their self-criticism behind closed doors.

16. In theory, all such organizational discipline required the prior approval of Party committees at the county level. In practice, however, the recommendations of the work team were (at least in the latter part of 1964) routinely rubber-stamped by the county Party committee.

17. In Hua county, Kwangtung, for example, it was subsequently reported that more than 20 local cadres had died under "mysterious circumstances" during the keypoint stage of the Big Four Cleanups in the autumn of 1964. See *SCMM*, no. 578, p. 28; and *CB*, No. 824. Although Party regulations explicitly prohibited beating or other forms of corporal punishment for corrupt cadres, such prohibitions clearly did not extend to those cadres and four category elements guilty of major crimes. Chairman Mao himself on two occasions stated that where the crimes were serious and the situation warranted capital punishment, execution of offenders was permissible. In May 1963, he stated that "We shall not prohibit killing . . . if the masses demand nothing less than death and if it is reasonable. . . ." And again in December 1964 he gave the following response when asked about the wisdom of killing criminal elements: "It may be necessary to shock the people. . . . It is impossible for us not to kill, but we must not kill too many. Kill a few to shock them. Why should we be afraid of shocking them? We must shock them." (Quoted in "Miscellany of Mao Tse-tung Thought," pp. 322, 426.)

18. For an annotated bibliography of official media reports concerning events in the Shengshih brigade in this period, see Richard Baum, *Bibliographic Guide to Kwangtung Communes, 1959–1967* (Hong Kong: Union Research Institute, 1968), pp. 77–79.

19. *NFJP*, April 12, 1963.   20. *JMJP*, April 4, 1964.

21. *NFJP*, June 11 and 26, 1964.

22. See *Hsiang-kang Shih-pao* (*The Hong Kong Times*), March 7, 1965; and *Hsing-tao Jih-pao* (*The Star-Island Daily*, Hong Kong), November 6, 1965.

23. On this point one of my principal informants speculated that Ch'en's patrons at the provincial level (possibly including T'ao Chu and/or Chao Tzu-yang), who were the only ones who could have known the true nature of Wang Kuang-mei's mission to Shengshih, had tipped him off.

24. There is some conflict on this point in the reports of my two principal informants.

25. For partial corroboration of these events, see *Hsiang-kang Shih-pao*, March 7, 1965; and *Hsing-tao Jih-pao*, November 6, 1965.

26. During the Cultural Revolution, a few Red Guard journals made oblique references to the Shengshih affair in their criticisms of such high-ranking local Party leaders as T'ao Chu and Chao Tzu-yang. See, for example, *Ming Pao* (*Tomorrow's News*, Hong Kong), May 17, 1967. Similarly, when the Chungshan County Party committee First Secretary came under Red Guard criticism in the winter of 1966–67, his name was explicitly linked to the scandal at Shengshih. See *Kuan-yü*

Kwang-tung Sheng Fan-ko-ming Hei-pang Chi-t'uan Fen-tzu te Chuan-an Tiao-ch'a Ts'ai-liao (Special Investigatory Materials Concerning Counter-Revolutionary Black Gang Elements in Kwangtung Province) (Canton: Joint Publication of the Central Committee Investigatory Work Group and the Kwangtung Provincial Party Committee Cultural Revolution Small Group, January 1967), pp. 7–18.

27. In this connection it will be recalled that before Wang's arrival Ch'en had received merely a token censure from the commune Party committee for his "impure work style."

28. The Shengshih affair was by no means unique in the autumn of 1964. A number of other model brigades and cadres were similarly discovered to be fraudulent in the course of the Big Four Cleanups. To cite just one additional example, the Shach'iao brigade of Nienshan commune, Huiyang County, Kwangtung, was also the scene of an investigation led by Wang Kuang-mei in the autumn of 1964, following which the brigade's leading cadres were purged and the model status of the brigade officially rescinded. In this latter case, as in the Shengshih affair, Party officials throughout the province were castigated for having been unable—or unwilling—to see through the fraud perpetrated by local cadres. For documentation on this case, see *NFJP*, October 12, November 15, and December 25, 1964. See also Baum, *Bibliographic Guide*, pp. 113–14.

29. See *Tung-fang Hung*, May 7, 1967; and *Wei-tung*, April 29, 1967. It will be recalled that Wang had similarly come into direct conflict with Party authorities in T'angshan special district at the time of her T'aoyüan investigation.

30. See, for example, *Ta-kung Pao (Great Harmony News*, Peking), September 29, 1963; *China Reconstructs* (Peking), February 1964, pp. 37–39; *JMJP*, February 10, 1964; *Hung-ch'i*, no. 7–8 (April 20, 1964), pp. 12–15; and *China Reconstructs*, July 1964, pp. 2–6.

31. *Hung-ch'i*, no. 11 (October 1, 1965), p. 8. One *chin* equals approximately 1.1 lbs.; one *mou* equals approximately one-sixth of an acre.

32. The slogan "learn from Tachai" first appeared in the Chinese mass media in the spring of 1963.

33. *JMJP*, October 16, 1964.

34. The main sources used in the following discussion are: *Hung-ch'i*, no. 5 (March 10, 1967), pp. 48–51; *NCNA* (Peking), April 4 and 5, 1967; *Peking Review*, no. 49 (December 1, 1967), pp. 19–22; *China Pictorial* (Peking), no. 1 (January 1968), pp. 27–29; *Hung-ch'i*, no. 1 (January 1, 1969), pp. 21–23; *NCNA* (Peking), February 26, 1969; and *Peking Review* no. 50 (December 12, 1969), pp. 13–15. In addition to these primary sources, two important secondary sources are Gerald Tannenbaum, "The Real Spirit of Tachai," *Eastern Horizon*, 10, no. 2 (1971); and Neale and Deirdre Hunter, "Our Man in Tachai: Ch'en Yung-kuei and the Two-Line Struggle in Agriculture," *Monthly Review*, 24, no. 1 (May 1972).

35. *Hung-ch'i*, no. 5 (March 10, 1967), pp. 48–49.

36. As early as 1961, the Party secretary of Hsiyang County had reportedly sent an investigatory group to Tachai to look into the "boasts" and "exaggerations" of the brigade's cadres. According to Ch'en Yung-kuei's testimony, this early (pre-Four-Cleanups) work team "unjustly charged that in our reports we had underestimated

our acreage. They compelled us to reduce our yield figures." (*Peking Review*, no. 49 [December 1, 1967], p. 21.)

37. *Ibid.*, p. 22.   38. *China Pictorial*, no. 1 (January 1968), p. 27.

39. Cf. *JMJP*, February 10, 1964; and *Nung-ts'un Ch'ing-nien*, September 10, 1967.

40. Cf. *JMJP*, May 24, 1961; and *China Recontructs*, July 1964.

41. *Peking Review*, no. 49 (December 1, 1967), p. 22.

42. See *Hung-ch'i*, no. 5 (March 10, 1967), pp. 49–50. Although the precise date of this meeting was never revealed, the subsequent flow of events strongly indicates that it most likely took place on or about December 20.

43. *Ibid.* Although the contents of Mao's "important instructions" concerning Tachai were never revealed, Ch'en's account of this meeting strongly implies that the instructions in question concerned Mao's decision to repudiate both the T'aoyüan Experience and the Revised Second Ten Points—a decision which was made manifest in mid-January with the promulgation of the Twenty-Three Points.

44. *JMJP*, December 21, 1964. Gerald Tannenbaum, who interviewed Ch'en Yung-kuei after the Cultural Revolution, states that the Tachai work team went so far as to propose that Ch'en be barred from attending the National People's Congress. (Tannenbaum, "The Real Spirit of Tachai," p. 29.) Apparently, Mao's personal intervention prevented this from occurring.

45. *Peking Review*, no. 1 (January 1, 1965), pp. 9, 16.

46. *JMJP*, December 27, 1964.

47. *Ibid.*; see also *Hung-ch'i*, no. 1 (January 6, 1965), pp. 20–24.

48. *JMJP*, December 30, 1964.   49. *Hung-ch'i*, no. 5 (March 10, 1967), p. 50.

50. Mao's commentaries are translated in "Miscellany of Mao Tse-tung Thought (1949–1968)," *JPRS* 61,269-2 (February 20, 1974), pp. 408–44. I have checked these translations against the Chinese originals, and in some cases I have slightly altered the *JPRS* translations to better convey the precise meaning of the original texts.

51. Mao Tse-tung, "Talk on the Four Cleanups Movement" (January 3, 1965), in *ibid.*, p. 440 (emphasis added).

52. "Highlights of a Forum on Central Committee Work" (December 20, 1964), in *ibid.*, pp. 415–17 (emphasis added).

53. *Ibid.*, p. 414 (emphasis added). It is my impression that the "tide toward the left" mentioned by Mao in this passage was not a hypothetical one, but rather referred to a situation that had already developed in those rural units which had implemented the Big Four Cleanups in accordance with the T'aoyüan Experience and the Revised Second Ten Points—e.g., the Tachai brigade.

54. Mao Tse-tung, "Speech at the Central Working Conference" (December 28, 1964), in *ibid.*, p. 429. The reference in this passage to "intertwining contradictions" refers to Liu Shao-ch'i's assertion, first made in August 1964, that implementation of Mao's instructions on class struggle was rendered difficult by the fact that contradictions within the Party were closely intertwined with contradictions outside of the Party, and that contradictions among the people were closely intertwined with contradictions with the enemy—thus making the drawing of firm class lines in the

countryside difficult, if not impossible. On this point see Liu's "self-criticism" of October 1966, cited in n. 82, below.

55. Mao, "Speech at the Central Working Conference," p. 430.   56. *Ibid.*

57. Mao, "Talk on the Four Cleanups Movement," pp. 437–38, 441.

58. *Ibid.*, pp. 437–38, 443–44. Mao's opposition to the method of discretely "striking roots" was further indicated in his assertion that "Genuine leaders and good people stand out only in struggle; you can't find them merely by visiting and interviewing poor people. . . . I don't believe in visiting and interviewing them" (*ibid.*, p. 439).

In contrast to the method of discretely "striking roots and linking up" advocated by Teng Hsiao-p'ing and Liu Shao-ch'i, Mao repeatedly emphasized the need for work teams to convene mass meetings and public rallies soon after entering a village, to put the peasants at their ease and to openly discuss the purposes of the campaign: "I think that after entering a village and meeting the masses, we must first of all announce several things. First, we should announce to the commune members that we have not come to rectify them. . . . We should openly announce that the targets of rectification are inside the Party. . . . Secondly, we should also announce the purpose of our visit to the cadres. . . . After entering the village, a rally should be held within a month or so. The rally should be held with the county as the unit: each team being represented by its leader and two poor and lower-middle peasants; each brigade by the Party branch secretary and brigade leader; and each commune by the Party secretary and commune leader. Several such rallies should be held, each lasting one day. . . . [In addition] a rally must be held as soon as each village is entered, and it should be attended by all poor and lower-middle peasants, including those landlords and rich peasants who have escaped [class] determination. . . . What you have been doing seems so insipid. So many work teams have been set up; yet after several months of endeavor, the mass movement still has not developed. . . . I think if we make revolution in this way [i.e., by "striking roots and linking up"], the revolution will take 100 years. . . . In order to annihilate the enemy in a matter of months, I think you must change the method. If you don't rely on the masses, the movement cannot be launched in a few months." (*Ibid.*, pp. 438–39.) It is instructive to compare the Chairman's recommendations with the various mobilization techniques utilized by work teams during earlier stages of the movement. See pp. 69–74 and 107–11.

59. Mao, "Talk on the Four Cleanups Movement," p. 437. Throughout his speech of January 3, Mao derided the common practice of taking up to two months to study documents as a manifestation of "scholasticism," and he recommended that such study be limited to one week: "One should only study documents for a week, and then go down to the countryside to learn from the poor and lower-middle peasants" (*ibid*).

60. *Ibid.*, pp. 440–42.

61. "Highlights of a Forum on Central Committee Work," pp. 412, 418. In a subsequent passage, Mao stated: "We must catch the king before the thieves are caught. . . . The focal point is the Party" (*ibid.*, p. 419.).

62. *Ibid.*, p. 412. Mao went on to argue that the tactic of the "united front" was useful in striving to win over middle-of-the-roaders, since it enabled the Party to

"utilize contradictions, secure the majority, oppose the minority, and break up [hostile forces] one by one."

63. *Ibid.* It is interesting to note that of the four "rotten" provincial committees mentioned in this passage, only that of Kweichow was substantially reorganized prior to the Cultural Revolution.

64. The full text of the Twenty-Three Points is translated in Baum and Teiwes, *Ssu-Ch'ing*, Appendix F.

65. *Ibid.*, Preface.   66. *Ibid.*, Article II.   67. *Ibid.*

68. *Ibid* (emphasis added). This represents the earliest known usage of a slogan that was to gain widespread currency during the subsequent Cultural Revolution—a slogan that was most frequently used in connection with Maoist attacks against Liu Shao-ch'i, Teng Hsiao-p'ing, and a small number of their alleged "counterrevolutionary black gang" within the Party hierarchy.

69. *Ibid.*   70. See, for example, *Hung-ch'i*, no. 5 (March 10, 1967).

71. Twenty-Three Points, Article V.

72. *Ibid.* Article IX (emphasis added). Since Mao had previously acknowledged that petty graft and corruption were extremely prevalent among rural cadres, his second category of "relatively good" cadres clearly included those rural officials who, having committed minor offenses, voluntarily "dumped their burdens" and made financial restitution, thereby enabling them to escape being labeled as "corrupt elements" or "cadres with many problems."

73. *Ibid.*, Article V.   74. *Ibid.*, Article XIX.   75. *Ibid.*, Article X.

76. *Ibid.*, Article IX.

77. *Ibid.* Mao's demand for liberation of cadres with "many problems" (i.e., the third of Mao's four categories of cadres) constituted a clear reversal of policy from the Revised Second Ten Points.

78. *Ibid.*, Article VI.

79. *Ibid.*, Article V. It will be recalled that the "bound foot" analogy was raised repeatedly during the Cultural Revolution in connection with the Maoists' attack against Liu Shao-ch'i. The reference to "women with bound feet" in the Twenty-Three Points concerned the tendency for work teams to monopolize local leadership and establish strict authoritarian controls over the mobilization process.

80. *Ibid.*, Article I.

81. For a similar interpretation of the Twenty-Three Points, see Franz Schurmann, *Ideology and Organization in Communist China* (enlarged edition) (Berkeley and Los Angeles: University of California Press, 1968), pp. 538–43; also Charles Neuhauser, "The Chinese Communist Party in the 1960's: Prelude to the Cultural Revolution," *The China Quarterly*, no. 32 (October–December 1967).

82. *Yomiuri Shimbun* (Tokyo), December 27, 1966. For a translation of Liu's self-criticism, see *Atlas*, April 1967, pp. 13–17. Interestingly, in his self-criticism Liu also acknowledged that he had not actively opposed such revisionist economic measures of the early 1960s as "contracting production to individual households" and "distributing farmlands to individual households."

83. See, for example, *JMJP*, November 23, 1967.

84. *JMJP*, October 1, 1965. Liu's activities and speeches continued to receive undiminished favorable publicity in the Party media throughout 1965 and the first half of 1966. And as late as mid-July 1966 he was still regarded as Mao's heir-apparent.

85. For an elaboration of this point, see Baum and Teiwes, "Liu Shao-ch'i and the Cadre Question," pp. 336–345.

6. TRANSITION

1. *Radio Sian*, Shensi, February 24, 1965.   2. *JMJP*, May 22, 1965.

3. *Radio Sian*, Shensi, February 24, 1965.

4. In this connection it will be recalled that the goal of increasing production had been relegated to sixth (and last) place among Mao's "six criteria" for evaluating the results of the Socialist Education Movement, formulated in June 1964.

5. W. F. Dorrill, "Power, Policy and Ideology in the Making of China's Cultural Revolution," in Thomas W. Robinson, ed., *The Cultural Revolution in China* (Berkeley: University of California Press, 1971); also Philip Bridgham, "Mao's Cultural Revolution: Origin and Development," *The China Quarterly*, no. 29 (January–March 1967), pp. 14–15.

6. On the upgrading of the political role of the people's militia in this period, see *Peking Review*, no. 6 (February 5, 1965), pp. 17–20.

7. For a discussion of the PLA's entry into the field of civilian propaganda and political work in 1965, see Charles Neuhauser, "The Chinese Communist Party in the 1960's: Prelude to the Cultural Revolution," *The China Quarterly*, no. 32 (October–December 1967), pp. 25–26; see also Chalmers Johnson, "Lin Piao's Army and its Role in Chinese Society," *Current Scene*, 4, no. 14 (July 15, 1965), 5–7, and *passim*.

8. In a speech delivered to a Central Committee working conference in October 1966, Mao reportedly stated that "When the Twenty-Three Points were adopted I became aware of something funny going on. In Peking, . . . I couldn't get a needle in edgewise. . . . There was nothing I could do. . . ." (quoted in *Yomiuri Shimbun*, January 7, 1967. For a translation, see *CB*, no. 891, pp. 75–77).

9. Franz Schurmann, *Ideology and Organization in Communist China* (Enlarged Edition) (Berkeley and Los Angeles: University of California Press, 1968), pp. 549–50.

10. Only at the provincial level and above does sufficient personnel data exist to make it possible to determine, in the absence of firsthand information, whether or not extensive purging has occurred in a given period. In 1965, apart from the initiation of a purge in the Ministry of Culture, there was evidence of an extensive personnel shakeup only in Kweichow province. During the Cultural Revolution this latter shakeup was explicitly linked to the Four Cleanups movement. See, for example, *Radio Kweiyang*, Kweichow, June 3, 1967. There have been, in addition, some unconfirmed reports by refugees and foreign residents in China that a certain amount of purging took place at the commune and county levels in 1965, although the extent of this purging cannot be determined with any precision. See, for example, Ray Wylie, "Struggle at Horse Bridge," *Far Eastern Economic Review*, August 31, 1967.

11. See, for example, Honan Provincial Party First Secretary Liu Chien-hsün's speech to the Provincial Congress of Poor and Lower-Middle Peasants and Advanced Producers, in *Radio Chengchow*, Honan, May 4, 1965. In this speech, Liu Chien-hsün declared that the poor and lower-middle peasants must be made "master of the house" [*chia-tso chu*] in the countryside and must uninterruptedly exercise supervision over rural cadres to ensure that the latter would not fall victim to the "sugar-coated bullets" of class enemies and thus "change color."

12. A good example of this is the previously noted case of Shensi province, where Maoist imperatives of class struggle and "politics takes command" were clearly subordinated to productive goals in provincial propaganda broadcasts throughout 1965.

13. Cf. *Radio Canton*, Kwangtung, June 14, 1965; and *Radio Changsha*, Hunan, June 16, 1965.

14. *JMJP*, May 21, 1965.

15. Cf. *NFJP*, March 22, 1965; and *JMJP*, May 10, 1965.

16. See Amitai Etzioni, *A Comparative Analysis of Complex Organizations* (New York: Free Press of Glencoe, 1961), Part I.

17. For a somewhat different application of Etzioni's typology of power and compliance to rural mass movements in China, see G. William Skinner, "Compliance and Leadership in Rural Communist China: A Cyclical Theory," (unpublished paper delivered at the 1965 Annual Meeting of the American Political Science Association, Washington, D.C., September 3–11, 1965). According to Skinner, rural campaigns in China typically demonstrate a succession of "power-mix phases" in their natural life cycle, beginning with the preponderance of normative power, shifting steadily to coercion as apathy and passive resistance are encountered among the peasants and cadres, and finally moving toward a preponderance of remunerative power in order to reduce the amount of popular alienation generated in the first two phases of the cycle. This "compliance cycle" hypothesis is valid as far as it goes, but it clearly does not go far enough, since it neglects the possible ramifications of intra-elite conflict on the course of a given mass campaign and fails to take account of the perturbational effects of exogenous influences—influences such as the existence of an "external threat" or the exigencies of seasonal fluctuations in the agricultural cycle.

18. For official policy statements concerning these various developments, see, *inter alia, JMJP*, May 10, 12, and 22, June 21, and August 10, 1965; *Radio Kunming*, Yunnan, April 28, 1965; *Chung-kuo Ch'ing-nien*, August 14, 1965; and *Ta-kung Pao*, November 10, 1965.

19. The criticisms by P'eng and Lu were contained in secret Party documents seen by a former Chinese trade official who defected to the United States in the summer of 1966. See *The Washington Star*, August 31, 1966. See also Bridgham, "Mao's Cultural Revolution," pp. 16–19; and Dorrill, "Power, Policy, and Ideology." Both P'eng Chen and Lu Ting-yi were purged as bourgeois powerholders in the early stages of the Cultural Revolution.

20. "Counterrevolutionary Revisionist P'eng Chen's Towering Crimes of Opposing the Party, Socialism, and Mao Tse-tung's Thought" (June 10, 1967), in *SCMM* 639, pp. 18–22.

21. For an excellent secondary account of the events leading up to Mao's 1965 cam-

paign against oppositionist elements within the Party establishment, see Bridgham, "Mao's Cultural Revolution;" also Dorrill, "Power, Policy, and Ideology."

22. The following discussion is drawn from Richard Baum, "Revolution and Reaction in the Chinese Countryside: The Socialist Education Movement in Cultural Revolutionary Perspective," *The China Quarterly* no. 38 (April–June, 1969), pp. 198–219.

23. *JMJP*, October 12, 1966.

24. For extensive documentation concerning the above allegations, see *CB*, no. 779.

25. In one county of Chekiang province, for example, it was reported that poor peasant activists and basic-level cadres advanced over 5,000 concrete "opinions" and criticisms directly to the county Party committee in October 1965. These criticisms dealt mainly with the types of problems discussed in the preceding paragraph. See *JMJP*, November 8, 1965; also *Yang-ch'eng Wan-pao* (Canton), May 9, 1966.

26. This conclusion is fully consistent with our earlier observations concerning Mao's apparent failure to gain widespread top-level support within the Party for his radical thesis on class struggle at the time of the Central Committee Work Conference of September 1965.

27. See *Yang-ch'eng Wan-pao*, September 8, 1965, in *SCMP*, no. 3540, pp. 1–12.

28. *Radio Changsha*, Hunan, February 1, 1966. The *Shansi Jih-pao* had claimed, a few days earlier, that 3 million people in that province's rural areas were currently studying Mao's works. *Radio Taiyuan*, Shansi, January 27, 1966.

29. Further evidence that Mao-study in effect supplanted the Four Cleanups as the central activity of the Socialist Education Movement was provided in several public media reports in the late winter and spring of 1966. See, for example, *Radio Nanchang*, Kiangsi, March 4, 1966; also *Yang-ch'eng Wan-pao*, June 14, 1966.

30. Note, for example, the following authoritative statement which was contained in the above-cited Central-South Regional Party Bureau directive of mid-January 1966: "The movement for the study of the works of Mao Tse-tung constitutes the most basic guarantee for the success of the Socialist Education Movement."

31. *Radio Nanking*, Kiangsu, March 10, 1966; see also *Radio Changsha*, Hunan, April 4, 1966. During the Cultural Revolution a great deal of criticism was leveled at those bourgeois powerholders who allegedly opposed giving prominence to politics and studying Mao's works during the Socialist Education Movement. For example, Li Ching-ch'üan, erstwhile First Secretary of the Southwest Regional Party Bureau, was quoted as having said: "What! Give Prominence to Politics? Better we should give prominence to fertilizer. Fertilizer can solve problems." (*Radio Kweiyang*, Kweichow, June 28, 1967.) While this incident is perhaps apocryphal, nevertheless there is good reason to credit the argument that opposition to Mao-study was indeed relatively widespread among high-level Party leaders at the Central Committee, Regional Bureau, and Provincial levels. See Bridgham, "Mao's Cultural Revolution."

32. A common anecdote among peasants in Kwangtung province in the spring of 1966 concerned a newly prosperous peasant who, when asked the secret of his success in raising vegetables on his private plot, claimed that the answer lay in giving

prominence to politics. Instead of giving over his family's quota of night soil to the production team for use on collective fields, he used a "superior" natural fertilizer—quotations from Chairman Mao—on the collective fields while reserving the "inferior" night soil for his private plot.

33. *NFJP*, February 18, 1966; also *Radio Canton*, Kwangtung, February 17, 1966.

34. *Radio Canton*, February 17, 1966. During the Cultural Revolution, many high-level Party officials were criticized for "economism," "extravagance," and "vainglory" in connection with their activities in leading Four Cleanup work teams in the countryside. See, for example, the critiques of Wang Kuang-mei, T'ao Chu, and Li Ching-ch'üan in *JMJP*, September 6, 1967; *CB* 824, pp. 10–17; and *Radio Chengtu*, Szechuan, March 10, 1968, respectively.

35. Note, for example, the allegation that ". . . the class struggle between socialism and capitalism is being rekindled *even in those areas which have gone through systematic socialist education*. In these areas, after their frantic assaults were initially repulsed, . . . class enemies turned to 'softening up' tactics to corrupt our cadres. . . ." (*Radio Lanchow*, Kansu, December 21, 1965; emphasis added).

36. *Hung-wei Pao* (Canton), October 23, 1966. Among the "old, great, and difficult problems" cited in this connection were: inability of peasants and cadres to clearly distinguish the boundary between the "people" and the class enemies; inability to destroy the concept of "self-interest"; inability to refute the viewpoint that "being a cadre means suffering a loss"; and inability to persuade certain poor and lower-middle peasants (the so-called *p'o chu-kan*, or "spineless poles") to take the socialist road. In a rare display of candor, the *Hung-wei Pao* article cited above acknowledged that the Socialist Education Movement had been relatively ineffective in resolving these problems. The basic reason for this failure was held to be that "the broad masses of cadres and peasants were not yet armed with the thought of Mao Tse-tung." See also *Radio Wuhan*, Hupeh, February 20, 1966.

37. Over 3,000 new members were reportedly recruited into the Party in a single county in Shensi Province in 1965. The majority of these new Party members were former servicemen, Youth League members, and peasants' association activists who had distinguished themselves during the Socialist Education Movement. See *Radio Sian*, Shensi, January 29, 1966. In a predominantly rural county in Kiangsi Province, it was similarly reported that over 200 basic-level rural cadres had received promotion to leadership positions during the movement. See *Radio Nanchang*, Kiangsi, January 26, 1966. One young refugee interviewed by the author was elected to be the work-point recorder in his production team in February 1966 solely because he had led his peer group in attendance at Mao-study sessions during the previous winter. His father had been a local landlord and the youth himself had previously been arrested by the security police for attempting to escape to Hong Kong. However, these facts were not raised at the election meeting, where only his "virtues" in Mao-study were discussed.

38. See Stephen Uhalley Jr., "The Cultural Revolution and the Attack on the 'Three Family Village,' " *The China Quarterly*, no. 27 (July–September 1966), pp. 149–61. P'eng Chen did not come under criticism for his role in undermining Mao's leadership of the Socialist Education Movement until 1967. See n. 20, above.

39. *Radio Wuhan*, Hupeh, June 29, 1966 (emphasis added).

40. This discussion is based in part on information supplied to the author by refugees from 14 widely separated rural communes in Kwangtung Province. Wherever possible, interview data have been compared and correlated with official documentary sources or unofficial Red Guard materials.

41. In some rural areas, the launching of the Cultural Revolution apparently served to freeze local administrative organs in both the Party and the government in the spring of 1966, with the result that political movements in these areas ground to a temporary halt. See Ray Wylie, "Red Guards Rebound," *Far Eastern Economic Review*, 57, no. 10 (September 7, 1967), 462–66.

42. The first wall poster reportedly appeared on the campus of Peking University on May 25. On June 2, *JMJP* editorially approved the use of this technique, and on June 20 Mao's personal approval was reported, also in *JMJP*.

43. *Hung-ch'i* 9 (July 1966) editorial, "Trust the Masses, Rely on the Masses."

44. It should be emphasized that throughout the period of the Cultural Revolution, only a relatively small percentage of China's rural villages were directly affected by revolutionary struggles of any kind. In general, the more remote the village, the smaller the impact of the Cultural Revolution. See Richard Baum, "The Cultural Revolution in the Countryside: Anatomy of a Limited Rebellion," in Thomas W. Robinson, ed., *The Cultural Revolution in China* (Berkeley and Los Angeles: University of California Press, 1971).

45. A *Hung-ch'i* editorial of early June had indicated only that the Socialist Education Movement and the Cultural Revolution were to be treated as two distinct—though complementary—movements, with the central objective of each being "to ensure that Mao Tse-tung's thought is placed in the forefront." *Hung-ch'i* no. 8 (June 8, 1966), p. 2. Somewhat contradictorily, a provincial radio broadcast of late May had explicitly stated that the Cultural Revolution was an "important, integral part of the Socialist Education Movement." (*Radio Sian*, Shensi, May 23, 1966).

46. The text of this important document is translated in *Peking Review*, no. 33 (August 12, 1966), pp. 6–12.

47. *Ibid.*, Article XIII.   48. *Ibid.*   49. *Ibid.*

50. Chou's speech is translated in *SCMP*, no. 3785, pp. 3–5.

51. See *JMJP*, December 26, 1966, and January 1, 1967.

52. "Draft Directive of the Central Committee of the Chinese Communist Party on the Great Proletarian Cultural Revolution in Rural Districts" (December 15, 1966), in *CB* 852, pp. 31–32.

7. THE JANUARY REVOLUTION

1. See, for example, *SCMP* 4151, pp. 8–9; also *SCMP* 3910, p. 14. The first official indication that the activities of work teams were a major source of intra-Party controversy was contained in the Central Committee's Sixteen-Point Decision of August 1966, which alleged that "certain work teams" had committed errors of orientation and had wrongly criticized and struggled against some "really revolutionary activists." (*Peking Review*, no. 33, August 12, 1966, p. 9).

2. "Notification on Safeguarding the Achievements of the Four Cleanups Movement" (January 25, 1967), in *CB* 852, p. 52.

3. *Ibid.*

4. *Ibid.* Significantly, this was the first official public reference to Liu Shao-ch'i's "erroneous line" with respect to the Socialist Education Movement.

5. *Ibid.*   6. *Hung-ch'i*, no. 4 (March 1, 1967), pp. 49–50.   7. *Ibid.*

8. Throughout the month of February the Party media consistently hedged on this question by stating that in those areas where the Four Cleanups had been completed, "most" of the surviving cadres were "good or comparatively good." See, e.g., *NFJP*, February 24, 1967, in *SCMP* 3904, pp. 12–13.

9. Official media reports in the summer and autumn of 1966 confirmed that the Four Cleanups had been completed in only about one-third of China's rural villages before the initiation of the Cultural Revolution.

10. In some areas it was alleged that as many as 70–85 percent of the basic-level cadres had been purged erroneously during the Four Cleanups. See, for example, *NCNA* (Peking), April 18, 1967, in *SCMP* 3924, pp. 11–12; also *Peking Review*, no. 38 (September 15, 1967), p. 26; and *China Pictorial*, no. 1 (January 1968), pp. 27–28.

11. For a cogent illustration of the type of normative confusion engendered by the attempt to evaluate local power struggles solely in terms of proletarians vs. bourgeoisie, see Richard Baum, "A Parting of Paupers," *Far Eastern Economic Review*, 59, no. 1 (January 4, 1968), 17–19.

12. "Decision of the Central Committee . . . on Resolute Support for the Revolutionary Masses of the Left" (January 23, 1967), in *CB* 852, pp. 49–50.

13. "Order of the Central Military Commission of the Central Committee" (January 28, 1967), in *CB* 852, pp. 54–55.

14. "Notice of the CCP Central Committee on the Question of Dealing with Work Teams in the Great Proletarian Cultural Revolution" (February 17, 1967), in *CB* 852, p. 80.

15. The last significant official reference to the "great achievements" of the Four Cleanups came on November 23, 1967, in a joint editorial published by *People's Daily* and *Red Flag*. This editorial also contained the first (and only) official attack against Teng Hsiao-p'ing for his role in drafting the Second Ten Points in 1963. Significantly, this editorial marked the demise of the *Red Flag* editorial staff. The journal was not published again until July 1, 1968, following the purge of top staff members Chi Pen-yü, Wang Li, and Kuan Feng as "ultra-leftists."

16. See, e.g., *SCMP* 4151, pp. 8–9; *NCNA* (Peking), February 28, 1968; and *Peking Review*, no. 27 (July 5, 1968), p. 15.

17. See the collection of documents concerning the questions of "reversal of verdicts" and "rehabilitation of cadres" in *SCMM* 617, pp. 8–50. Note particularly the following report of a conversation held between members of the joint Cultural Revolution Reception Center of the General Office of the CCP Central Committee and representatives of a Kwangtung mass organization in November 1967: "*Question:* Is it right or wrong for us to brand as counterrevolutionaries or 'bad elements' those

who have survived the Four Cleanups campaign. . . ? *Answer:* It is wrong. . . ." (*ibid.*, p. 19).

18. *Ibid.*, pp. 46–50; also *SCMP* 4151, pp. 8–9.

19. For a comprehensive analysis of the impact of the Cultural Revolution on the Chinese countryside, see Richard Baum, "The Cultural Revolution in the Countryside: Anatomy of a Limited Rebellion," in Thomas W. Robinson, ed., *The Cultural Revolution in China* (Berkeley and Los Angeles: University of California Press, 1971).

20. Stuart Schram correctly observes in this connection that Mao's Twenty-Three Points did in fact provide a rough blueprint for the subsequent Cultural Revolution. Yet it was precisely because the Twenty-Three Points failed to bring about a substantial reorientation of the Socialist Education Movement that Mao was ultimately compelled to terminate the movement prematurely. See Schram, "The Cultural Revolution in Historical Perspective," in Stuart R. Schram, ed., *Authority, Participation and Cultural Change in China* (Cambridge: Cambridge University Press, 1973), p. 85.

21. See notes 35 and 36, chapter 6.

22. It is hypothesized that since the Four Cleanups was directly implemented by work teams dispatched by Party organs at the provincial, municipal, and county levels, the work teams themselves were conservatively oriented with respect to the question of defending Party establishments in the period after May 16, when students launched the first massive assaults against Party powerholders. We shall explore this question in greater depth in chapter 8.

23. In the light of the above developments, it is likely that in the period after May 16, work teams acting under the protective mantle of higher-level Party organs tacitly conspired in the initiation of a counteroffensive against those radical insurgents who were demanding the overthrow of the rural establishment—as represented by local Party committees and the work team themselves. The Maoist charge of "attacking the many to protect the few" undoubtedly refers to this type of self-protective action. See, e.g., *Peking Review*, no. 27 (July 5, 1968), pp. 14–16.

24. See, e.g., *NFJP*, February 24, 1967, in *SCMP* 3904, pp. 12–13; also, *NCNA*, February 22, 1967.

25. For extensive documentation and analysis of the various strategies for survival and self-defense utilized by Party powerholders during the Cultural Revolution, see Richard Baum, "Elite Behavior Under Conditions of Stress: The Lesson of the *'Tang-ch'üan P'ai'* in the Cultural Revolution," in Robert A. Scalapino, ed., *Elites in the People's Republic of China* (Seattle: University of Washington Press, 1972), pp. 540–74; also Parris Chang, "Provincial Leaders' Strategies for Survival during the Cultural Revolution," in *ibid.*, pp. 501–39.

8. CONCLUSION

1. " 'Bombard the Headquarters': My First Wall Poster," in *SCMP* 3997; see also K. Fan, *Mao Tse-tung and Lin Piao: Post-Revolutionary Writings* (Garden City, New York: Anchor Books, 1972), pp. 279–80.

2. See note 82, chapter 5.

3. See "Struggle Between Two Roads in China's Countryside," *Peking Review*, December 1, 1967; also *JMJP*, November 23, 1967.

4. Note, for example, Mao's January 1965 injunction that "where basic-level organizations [of the Party] have become paralyzed . . . we may implement [the policy of] all power to the poor and lower-middle peasants' associations" (Twenty-Three Points, Article X).

5. At the time of the Tenth Party Congress in August 1973, Premier Chou En-lai alluded to the idea that "Liu Shao-ch'i-type swindlers" frequently covered their deviations in one direction with excessive attacks against deviations in the opposite direction. See *Peking Review*, no. 35–36 (September 7, 1973), p. 21.

6. See, e.g., Liu's self-examination of October 1966, and the Central Committee's Sixteen Point Directive of August, 1966.

7. See Parris Chang, "Struggle Between the Two Roads in China's Countryside," *Current Scene*, 6, no. 3 (February 15, 1968); also, Parris Chang, "Patterns and Processes of Policy Making in Communist China, 1955–1962: Three Case Studies" (Ph.D. dissertation, Columbia University, Department of Political Science, 1969), chapter 5.

8. Quoted in Stuart R. Schram, ed., *Authority, Participation, and Cultural Change in China* (Cambridge: Cambridge University Press, 1973), p. 70.

9. For two stimulating analyses of basic stylistic and attitudinal differences between Mao and Liu, see Lowell Dittmer, "Power and Personality in China: Mao Tse-tung, Liu Shao-ch'i and the Politics of Charismatic Succession," *Studies in Comparative Communism*, vol. 7, nos. 1–2 (Spring–Summer 1974), pp. 21–49; and Harry Harding, "Maoist Theories of Policy-Making and Organization," in Robinson, *The Cultural Revolution in China*, pp. 113–64.

10. A similar conclusion is reached by Jack Gray, who states that "it would appear that at this time [i.e., 1964] and in this context, Liu Shao-ch'i was prepared to be less tolerant than Mao." See Gray, "The Two Roads: Alternative Strategies of Social Change and Economic Growth in China," in Schram, *Authority, Participation and Cultural Change*, p. 151. It will be recalled that one of the charges leveled against Wang Kuang-mei was that she had forced the peasants of T'aoyüan to "dump" over 500 "burdens" (i.e., self-criticisms) stemming from such petty capitalist tendencies as selling too many chickens on the local market.

11. Gray, "The Two Roads," p. 156.

12. Note Liu's complaint in the Revised Second Ten Points that "our enemies . . . utilize certain articles of our documents to carry out legalistic struggles against us." (Article II).

13. Earlier it was noted that public attacks on Teng Hsiao-p'ing ceased shortly after the purging of *Red Flag*'s ultra-radical editorial board in the winter of 1967–68. Teng was quietly rehabilitated in 1973, and at the Party's Tenth Congress in August 1973, Teng was elected to the Central Committee, while concurrently holding the post of Vice Premier of the State Council. Subsequently, he regained a seat on the Central Committee Politburo. Unlike Teng, P'eng was never rehabilitated, and remains in disgrace as of this writing.

14. Revised Second Ten Points, Article VI (emphasis added).

15. "Decision of the Central Committee," Article VII. One of the worst of the alleged offenders, a work team sent by Liu Shao-ch'i to Peking's Tsinghua University, was led by Wang Kuang-mei. See Chiang Ch'ing's allegations, in *SCMP* 3836. Wang's interesting self-examination appears in *CB* 848. See also, *Hung-ch'i* no. 5 (April 1967), pp. 26–30.

16. Note, for example, the allegation made by pro-Maoist Politburo member K'ang Sheng in late July 1966: "A major characteristic of [the work teams] was their fear of chaos. . . . Fear of chaos meant fear of the masses, fear of revolution. . . ." (quoted in *CB* 819).

17. See, e.g., *SCMP* 3874 and 3878; also *Radio Nanchang*, Kiangsi, February 15, 1967.

18. See *Radio Nanchang*, February 20 and 28, 1967; *Hung-ch'i* no. 4 (March 1967); and *SCMP* 3880, 3893, and 3899.

19. The disingenuousness of this accusation is apparent from the fact that Liu Shao-ch'i simply could not have been personally responsible for the anarchistic tendencies of the January Revolution—he had already been demoted in rank and virtually stripped of all authority within the Party.

20. For further elaboration and analysis of these developments, see Baum and Teiwes, "Liu Shao-ch'i and the Cadre Question," pp. 338–45.

21. The Snow interview was published in *The New Republic*, February 27, 1965. See also A. Doak Barnett, *China After Mao* (Princeton: Princeton University Press, 1967), pp. 35–68.

22. In this regard it is interesting to note the Cultural Revolutionary attacks on officials who had apparently sought to balance such pressures. For example, several leading officials were accused of supplementing Mao's Twenty-Three Points with additional articles of their own in order to subvert Mao's directive. What probably happened was that the leaders in question simply added material dealing more specifically with local conditions and problems. See, e.g., *Radio Kweiyang*, Kweichow, July 8, 1967; also *JMJP*, October 18, 1965.

BIBLIOGRAPHY

I. Bibliographical Note on Primary Sources

PRIMARY SOURCES CONSULTED in the preparation of this study fall into three main categories. First are official Party and governmental documents, serial publications (newspapers and magazines), and radio broadcasts of the People's Republic of China. Second are unofficial newspapers and journals published by Red Guards and other political groups within China during the Cultural Revolution. Third are such ancillary sources as Taiwanese and Hong Kong periodicals, and various refugee interview materials.

A. *Official Party and governmental sources.* The five primary CCP documents on the Socialist Education Movement used in this study were collected by the author in Taiwan in 1966–67. Full (or partially abridged) translations of each of these documents, prepared by the author and edited by John S. Service, appear in Baum and Teiwes, *Ssu-Ch'ing: The Socialist Education Movement of 1962–1966*, Appendices B–F. The Lienchiang documents cited in chapter 1 are available in translation in C.S. Chen, ed., *Rural People's Communes in Lien-chiang*. A number of Cultural Revolution documents pertaining to the Four Cleanups are translated in *CCP Documents of the Great Proletarian Cultural Revolution, 1966–1967* (Hong Kong: Union Research Institute, 1968). In addition to these official documents, much valuable information was gleaned from mainland Chinese periodical publications, including: *Jen-min Jih-pao* (*People's Daily*, Peking), *Nan-fang Jih-pao* (*Southern Daily*, Canton), *Hung-ch'i* (*Red Flag*, Peking), *Yang-ch'eng Wan-pao* (*Canton Evening News*), *Chung-kuo Ch'ing-nien* (*China Youth*, Peking), *Nung-ts'un Ch'ing-nien* (*Rural Youth*, Shanghai), and *Chung-kuo Ch'ing-nien Pao* (*China Youth News*, Peking). These and other official Chinese newspaper and magazine sources cited throughout this study (with the exception of *Jen-min Jih-pao* and *Hung-ch'i*, which are readily available worldwide) were obtained by the author—in some cases on microfilm—from the Union Research Institute, Hong Kong. Official Chinese publications in English (all of which are readily available worldwide) include *Peking Review* (weekly), *New China News Agency* (Peking, daily), *China Reconstructs* (Peking, monthly), and *China Pictorial* (Peking, monthly). Translations of Chinese government radio broadcasts used in this study were obtained from *News from China's Provincial Radio Stations*, a publication of the British Information Service, Hong Kong. Comparable daily translations are available in the United States from the U.S. Government *Foreign Broadcast Information Service*, Washington, D.C. Translations of a number of Chinese newspaper and journal articles were additionally drawn from *Survey of the China Mainland Press*, *Current Background*, and *Selections from China Mainland Magazines* (serial publications of the United States Consulate, Hong Kong). Other important periodical articles appear in English translation (with commentary) in *Union Research Service*, a semi-monthly publication of the Union Research Institute, Hong Kong.

B. *Unofficial sources*. The most important nongovernmental primary Chinese source used in this study was a collection of Mao Tse-tung's previously unpublished writings and commentaries compiled by Mao's supporters within China during the Cultural Revolution. This collection, known in the West under the title "Long Live the Thought of Mao Tse-tung," was first published in 1969 as *Mao Tse-tung T'ung-chih shih Tang-tai Tsui Wei-ta te Ma-K'o-Ssu Lieh-ning Chu-i-che* (*Comrade Mao Tse-tung is the Greatest Marxist-Leninist of the Contemporary Era*). Subsequently, a copy of the collection was obtained and reissued by the Taiwanese government. A translation of this valuable collection appears in two volumes under the title "Miscellany of Mao Tse-tung Thought (1949–1968)," in *Joint Publications Research Service* (Washington, D.C.) no. 61,269 (February 20, 1974). A second major unofficial primary source consisted of various publications (newspapers and wall posters) issued by Red Guards and other participants in China's Cultural Revolution. Throughout this book an effort has been made to distinguish these unofficial sources (which must be used with great caution because of their questionable reliability) from the official media sources mentioned in the preceding paragraph. The most important Red Guard and "irregular" Chinese sources dealing with the Socialist Education Movement are listed in chapter 4, notes 1 and 16, of the present volume. All Red Guard materials cited are available, *inter alia*, in the microfilm collections of the Association of Research Libraries, Washington, D.C.; The Hoover Institution, Stanford, California; and the Union Research Institute, Hong Kong. Some valuable compilations of these materials have been published (in Chinese), including Ting Wang, ed., *Chung-kuo Wen-hua-ta-ko-ming Tzu-liao Hui-pien* (*Compilation of Materials on China's Great Cultural Revolution*) (Hong Kong: *Ming Pao* Press, 1967); and Chiao I, ed., *Hung-wei-ping Hsüan-chi: P'ao-ta Liu Shao-ch'i, Chi-ch'in Wang Kuang-mei* (*Red Guard Selected Works: Shoot Down Liu Shao-ch'i, Seize Wang Kuang-mei*), vol. 1 (Hong Kong: *Ta Lu* Press, 1967).

C. *Ancillary sources*. A number of Taiwanese and Hong Kong journals have published data pertaining to the Socialist Education Movement. The most helpful sources are Chin Shui, *"Tang-ch'ien Fu-chien Nung-ts'un She-hui Chu-i Chiao-yü Yün-tung"* ("Fukien's Current Socialist Education Movement"), *Ch'ang-ch'eng Nei-wai* (*Both Sides of the Great Wall*, Hong Kong), February 16, 1965; *"Kung-fei She-hui Chu-i Chiao-yü Yün-tung tsai Nung-ts'un te Shih-pai"* ("The Failure of the Communists' Socialist Education Movement in the Countryside"), *Chin-jih Ta-lu* (*Mainland China Today*, Taipei), July 16, 1964; *"Ta-lu Nung-ts'un te She-hui Chu-i Chiao-yü Yün-tung"* ("Mainland China's Rural Socialist Education Movement"), *Chin-jih Ta-lu*, June 10, 1963; and Wang Hsiao-t'ang, *"Chung-kung te 'Ssu-Ch'ing' yü 'Wen-hua-ta-ko-ming'"* ("Communist China's 'Four Cleanups' and 'Great Cultural Revolution'"), *Fei-ch'ing Yen-chiu* (*Studies on Chinese Communism*, Taipei), January 1967. Hong Kong newspapers publishing occasional materials pertaining to the Socialist Education Movement include the *Hsing-tao Jih-pao* (*Star Island Daily News*), *Hsiang-kang Shih-pao* (*Hong Kong Times*), and *Ming Pao* (*Tomorrow's News*). In addition to these periodical sources, the Union Research Institute holds several bound volumes of classified refugee interview files which proved helpful in preparing this study. My own intensive interviews with 56 expatriot Chinese peasants and cadres (mainly from Kwangtung Province) were a final primary source of data on the Socialist Education Movement. Further information concerning these interview materials is available upon request.

II. Selected Bibliography of Secondary English Language Sources

Alley, Rewi. *Travels in China*, 1966–71. Peking: New World Press, 1973.

Baum, Richard. *Bibliographic Guide to Kwangtung Communes, 1959–1967*. Hong Kong: Union Research Institute, 1968.

——. "The Cultural Revolution in the Countryside: Anatomy of a Limited Rebellion." In Thomas W. Robinson, ed., *The Cultural Revolution in China*. Berkeley and Los Angeles: University of California Press, 1971.

——. "Ideology Redivivus." *Problems of Communism*, 16, no. 3 (May–June 1967).

——. "Peach Garden Pestilence." *Far Eastern Economic Review*, 58, no. 7 (November 16, 1967).

——. "Revolution and Reaction in the Chinese Countryside: The Socialist Education Movement in Cultural Revolutionary Perspective." *The China Quarterly* no. 38 (April–June 1969).

Baum, Richard, and Frederick C. Teiwes. "Liu Shao-ch'i and the Cadre Question." *Asian Survey* 8, no. 4 (April 1968).

——. *Ssu-Ch'ing: The Socialist Education Movement of 1962–1966*. Berkeley: University of California, Center for Chinese Studies Research Monographs, 1968.

Bridgham, Philip. "Mao's 'Cultural Revolution': Origin and Development." *The China Quarterly*, no. 29 (January–March 1967).

Chang, Parris. "Struggle between the Two Roads in China's Countryside." *Current Scene*, 6, no. 3 (February 15, 1968).

Chen, C. S., ed. *Rural People's Communes in Lien-Chiang*. Stanford: Hoover Institution Press, 1969.

Dittmer, Lowell. "Power and Personality in China: Mao Tse-tung, Liu Shao-ch'i, and the Politics of Charismatic Succession." *Studies in Comparative Communism*, 7, no. 1–2 (Spring–Summer 1974).

Dorrill, William. "Power, Policy, and Ideology in the Making of the Chinese Cultural Revolution." In Thomas W. Robinson, ed., *The Cultural Revolution in China*. Berkeley and Los Angeles: University of California Press, 1971.

Grey, Jack. "The Two Roads: Alternative Strategies of Social Change and Economic Growth in China." In Stuart R. Schram, ed., *Authority, Participation, and Cultural Change in China*. Cambridge: Cambridge University Press, 1973.

Harding, Harry Jr. "Maoist Theories of Policy-Making and Organization." In Thomas W. Robinson, ed., *The Cultural Revolution in China*. Berkeley and Los Angeles: University of California Press, 1971.

Hunter, Neale, and Deirdre Hunter. "Our Man in Tachai: Ch'en Yung-kuei and the Two-Line Struggle in Agriculture." *Monthly Review*, 24, no. 1 (May 1972).

Lewis, John W., and Leonard Schapiro. "The Roles of the Monolithic Party under the Totalitarian Leader." *The China Quarterly*, no. 40 (October–December 1969).

Neuhauser, Charles. "The Chinese Communist Party in the 1960's: Prelude to the Cultural Revolution." *The China Quarterly*, no. 32 (October–December 1967).

Oksenberg, Michel. "The Institutionalization of the Chinese Communist Revolution: The Ladder of Success on the Eve of the Cultural Revolution." *The China Quarterly*, no. 36 (October–December 1968).

——. "Local Leaders in Rural China, 1962–65: Individual Attributes, Bureaucratic Positions, and Political Recruitment." In A. Doak Barnett, ed., *Chinese Communist Politics in Action*. Seattle: University of Washington Press, 1969.

Schram, Stuart R. "The Cultural Revolution in Historical Perspective." In Stuart R. Schram, ed., *Authority, Participation, and Cultural Change in China*. Cambridge: Cambridge University Press, 1973.

Schurmann, Franz. *Ideology and Organization in Communist China* (Enlarged Edition). Berkeley and Los Angeles: University of California Press, 1968.

Skinner, G. William, and Edwin A. Winckler, "Compliance Succession in Communist China." In Amitai Etzioni, ed., *Complex Organizations: A Sociological Reader*. New York: Holt, Rinehart, and Winston, 1969.

Tannenbaum, Gerald. "The Real Spirit of Tachai." *Eastern Horizon*, 10, no. 2 (1971).

Vogel, Ezra F. *Canton Under Communism*. Cambridge: Harvard University Press, 1969.

——. "From Revolutionary to Semi-Bureaucrat: The 'Regularization' of Cadres." *The China Quarterly*, no. 29 (January–March 1967).

INDEX

"Abandoning agriculture to go into business," 15, 80; *see also* spontaneous capitalist tendencies

Activists, in peasants' associations, 31, 54; recruited into CCP, 203*n*; role of, 5

Anhwei, 126

"Attacking the many to protect the few," 7, 89, 135, 161, 166–67, 168–69, 193*n*, 206*n*, *see also* Liu Shao-ch'i

"Bad elements"; *see* four category elements

Barnett, A. Doak, 178*n*, 193*n*, 208*n*

Baum, Richard, 174*n*, 178*n*, 184*n*, 187*n*, 190*n*, 191*n*, 193*n*, 195*n*, 202*n*, 204*n*, 205*n*, 206*n*, 208*n*

Bennett, Gordon A., 185*n*

Big character posters, 107, 118, 168, 204*n*

Big Four Cleanups, 81, 82, 83, 103–12, 113, 116, 138, 141, 149, 194*n*, 195*n*, 196*n*; *see also* Four Cleanups; four uncleans

"Black cats, white cats . . . ," 3, 165, 173*n*

Black market, 50

Bourgeois powerholders, 139, 169; in Central Committee, 128; criticism of, 143, 148; in Cultural Revolution, 6–8; in Four Cleanups, 131; identification of, 153–54; obstruct Four Cleanups, 126–27; oppose politics in command, 202*n*; rectification of, 7–8, 139, 149, 156

Bourgeois reactionary line, 6–8; *see also* struggle between two roads

Bridgham, Philip, 200*n*, 201*n*, 202*n*

Bureaucracy, 170, 172; buckpassing by, 97; conservatism of, 206*n*; inertia of, 139; places "production in command," 142; reform of, 143–45; and Teng Hsiao-p'ing, 165; vested interests of, 116; *see also* bureaucratism, Chinese Communist Party

Bureaucratism, 3–4, 5; in CCP, 31–35; and Mao Tse-tung, 20, 22, 78; and Socialist Education Movement, 40–42; *see also* bureaucracy

Cadres, bureaucratization of, 3–4, 31–33; capitalist tendencies of, 17–18; corruption of, 13–14, 21–22, 72–75, 122–23, 177*n*; criticism of, 44–45, 107–12; demoralization of, 13–14, 136, 163, 168; demotion and dismissal of, 109–11,